Windows®

Internet Explorer® 7

Introductory Concepts and Techniques

Gary B. Shelly
Thomas J. Cashman
Steven M. Freund

THOMSON COURSE TECHNOLOGY   25 THOMSON PLACE   BOSTON MA 02210

Australia • Canada • Denmark • Japan • Mexico • New Zealand • Philippines • Puerto Rico • Singapore • South Africa • Spain • United Kingdom • United States

COURSE TECHNOLOGY

Windows Internet Explorer 7
Introductory Concepts and Techniques

Gary B. Shelly

Thomas J. Cashman

Steven M. Freund

Executive Editor
Alexandra Arnold

Product Manager
Heather Hawkins

Associate Product Manager
Klenda Martinez

Editorial Assistant
Jon Farnham

Senior Marketing Manager
Joy Stark-Vancs

Marketing Coordinator
Julie Schuster

Print Buyer
Denise Powers

Director of Production
Patty Stephan

Production Editor
Erin Dowler

Developmental Editor
Karen Stevens

Proofreader
Harry Johnson

Indexer
Liz Cunningham

QA Manuscript Reviewers
Serge Palladino, Chris Scriver, Teresa Storch

Art Director
Bruce Bond

Cover and Text Design
Joel Sadagursky

Cover Photo
Jon Chomitz

Compositor
GEX Publishing Services

Printer
Banta Menasha

Web site Developer
Kyle Dencker

COPYRIGHT © 2008 Thomson Course Technology, a division of Thomson Learning, Inc. Thomson Learning™ is a trademark used herein under license.

Printed in the United States of America

1 2 3 4 5 6 7 8 9 10 BM 09 08 07

For more information, contact:
Thomson Course Technology
25 Thomson Place
Boston, Massachusetts 02210

Or find us on the World Wide Web at:
www.course.com

ALL RIGHTS RESERVED. No part of this work covered by the copyright hereon may be reproduced or used in any form or by any means — graphic, electronic, or mechanical, including photocopying, recording, taping, Web distribution, or information storage and retrieval systems — without the written permission of the publisher.

For permission to use material from this text or product, submit a request online at http://www.thomsonrights.com.

Any additional questions about permissions can be submitted by e-mail to thomsonrights@thomson.com.

Thomson Course Technology, the Thomson Course Technology logo, the Shelly Cashman Series® are registered trademarks used under license. All other names used herein are for identification purposes only and are trademarks of their respective owners. Thomson Course Technology reserves the right to revise this publication and make changes from time to time in its content without notice.

ISBN-13: 978-0-619-20216-3
ISBN-10: 0-619-20216-5

Windows® Internet Explorer® 7
Introductory Concepts and Techniques

Contents

Appendices

Preface

The Shelly Cashman Series® offers the finest textbooks in computer education. We are proud of the fact that the previous editions of this textbook have been so well received by computer educators. With each new edition, we have made significant improvements based on the software and comments made by instructors and students. Windows Internet Explorer 7 continues with the innovation, quality, and reliability that you have come to expect from the Shelly Cashman Series.

In the few short years since its birth, the World Wide Web has grown beyond all expectations. During this time, Web usage has increased from a limited number of users to more than 600 million users worldwide, accessing Web pages on any topic you can imagine. Individuals, schools, businesses, and government agencies are all taking advantage of this innovative way of accessing the Internet to provide information, products, services, and education electronically. Windows Internet Explorer 7 provides the novice as well as the experienced user a window with which to look into the Web and tap an abundance of resources.

Objectives of This Textbook

Windows Internet Explorer 7: Introductory Concepts and Techniques is intended for use in a one-credit, three- to five-week course, or in combination with other books in an introductory computer concepts or applications course. The objectives of this book are:

- To teach students how to use Internet Explorer 7, including new features like tabbed browsing, RSS feeds, and the Instant Search box.

- To expose students to various World Wide Web resources

- To acquaint students with the more popular search engines

- To show students how to evaluate Web pages and do research using the World Wide Web

- To teach students how to communicate with other Internet users

The Shelly Cashman Approach

Features of Windows Internet Explorer 7 include:

- **Plan Ahead Boxes** The project orientation is enhanced by the inclusion of Plan Ahead boxes. These new features prepare students to create successful projects by encouraging them to think strategically about what they are trying to accomplish before they begin working.

- **Step-by-Step, Screen-by-Screen Instructions** Each of the tasks required to complete a project is clearly identified throughout the chapter. Now, the step-by-step instructions provide a context beyond point-and-click. Each step explains why students are performing a task, or the result of performing a certain action. Found on the screens accompanying each step, call-outs give students the information they need to know when they need to know it. Now, we've used color to distinguish the content in the call-outs. The Explanatory call-outs (in black) summarize what is happening on the screen and the Navigational call-outs (in red) show students where to click.

Can I change the home page in the Internet Explorer window?

Yes. You can change the home page by clicking Tools on the menu bar, clicking Internet Options on the Tools menu, and under the Home Page section clicking the Use current, Use default, or Use blank button.

Other Ways

1. Click Start button on Windows taskbar, click Internet Explorer icon on Start menu
2. Double-click Internet Explorer icon on desktop
3. Press CTRL+ESC, press I, press ENTER

The Internet
The Internet started as a government experiment for the military. The military wanted the ability to connect to and communicate via different computers running different operating systems. From this experiment, a communication technique originated called Transmission Control Protocol/Internet Protocol, or TCP/IP.

- **Q&A** Found within many of the step-by-step sequences, Q&As raise the kinds of questions students may ask when working through a step sequence and provide answers about what they are doing, why they are doing it, and how that task might be approached differently.

- **Experimental Steps** These new steps, within our step-by-step instructions, encourage students to explore, experiment, and take advantage of the new features of the Windows Internet Explorer 7 interface. These steps are not necessary to complete the projects, but are designed to increase the confidence with the software and build problem-solving skills.

- **Thoroughly Tested Projects** Unparalleled quality is ensured because every screen in the book is produced by the author only after performing a step, and then each project must pass Thomson Course Technology's Quality Assurance program.

- **Other Ways Boxes and Quick Reference Summary** The Other Ways boxes displayed at the end of most of the step-by-step sequences specify the other ways to do the task completed in the steps. Thus, the steps and the Other Ways box make a comprehensive reference unit. A Quick Reference Summary at the end of the book contains all of the tasks presented in the chapters, and all ways identified of accomplishing the tasks.

- **BTW** These marginal annotations provide background information, tips, and answers to common questions that complement the topics covered, adding depth and perspective to the learning process.

- **End-of-Chapter Student Activities** Extensive student activities at the end of each chapter provide the student with plenty of opportunities to reinforce the materials learned in the chapter through hands-on assignments. Several new types of activities have been added that challenge the student in new ways to expand their knowledge, and to apply their new skills to a project with personal relevance.

Organization of This Textbook

Windows Internet Explorer 7: Introductory Concepts and Techniques consists of three chapters, two appendices, and a Quick Reference Summary.

End-of-Chapter Student Activities

A notable strength of the Shelly Cashman Series books is the extensive student activities at the end of each chapter. Well-structured student activities can make the difference between students merely participating in a class and students retaining the information they learn. The activities in Windows Internet Explorer 7 include the following.

CHAPTER SUMMARY A concluding paragraph, followed by a listing of the tasks completed within a chapter together with the pages on which the step-by-step, screen-by-screen explanations appear.

LEARN IT ONLINE Every chapter features a Learn It Online section that is comprised of six exercises. These exercises include True/False, Multiple Choice, Short Answer, Flash Cards, Practice Test, and Learning Games.

APPLY YOUR KNOWLEDGE This exercise usually requires students to utilize skills that parallel those learned in the chapter.

EXTEND YOUR KNOWLEDGE This exercise allows students to extend and expand on the skills learned within the chapter.

IN THE LAB Three all new in-depth assignments per chapter require students to utilize the chapter concepts and techniques to solve problems on a computer.

CASES AND PLACES Five unique real-world case-study situations, including Make It Personal, an open-ended project that relates to students' personal lives, and one small-group activity.

Instructor Resources CD-ROM

The Shelly Cashman Series is dedicated to providing you with all of the tools you need to make your class a success. Information about all supplementary materials is available through your Thomson Course Technology representative or by calling one of the following telephone numbers: Colleges, Universities, and Continuing Ed departments, 1-800-648-7450; High Schools, 1-800-824-5179; and Career Colleges, Business, Government, Library and Resellers, 1-800-477-3692.

The Instructor Resources CD-ROM for this textbook include both teaching and testing aids. The contents of each item on the Instructor Resources CD-ROM (ISBN 1-4188-5943-5) are described on the following pages.

INSTRUCTOR'S MANUAL The Instructor's Manual consists of Microsoft Word files, which include chapter objectives, lecture notes, teaching tips, classroom activities, lab activities, quick quizzes, figures and boxed elements summarized in the chapters, and a glossary page. The new format of the Instructor's Manual will allow you to map through every chapter easily.

SYLLABUS Sample syllabi, which can be customized easily to a course, are included. The syllabi cover policies, class and lab assignments and exams, and procedural information.

FIGURE FILES Illustrations for every figure in the textbook are available in electronic form. Use this ancillary to present a slide show in lecture or to print transparencies for use in lecture with an overhead projector. If you have a personal computer and LCD device, this ancillary can be an effective tool for presenting lectures.

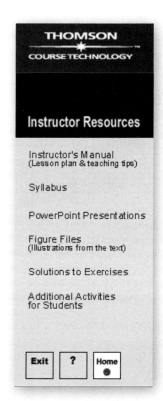

POWERPOINT PRESENTATIONS PowerPoint Presentations is a multimedia lecture presentation system that provides slides for each chapter. Presentations are based on chapter objectives. Use this presentation system to present well-organized lectures that are both interesting and knowledge based. PowerPoint Presentations provides consistent coverage at schools that use multiple lecturers.

SOLUTIONS TO EXERCISES Solutions are included for the Chapter Reinforcement exercises.

TEST BANK & TEST ENGINE In the ExamView test bank, you will find our standard question types (40 multiple-choice, 25 true/false, 20 completion) and new objective-based question types (5 modified multiple-choice, 5 modified true/false and 10 matching). Critical Thinking questions are also included (3 essays and 2 cases with 2 questions each) totaling the test bank to 112 questions for every chapter with page number references, and when appropriate, figure references. A version of the test bank you can print also is included. The test bank comes with a copy of the test engine, ExamView, the ultimate tool for your objective-based testing needs. ExamView is a state-of-the-art test builder that is easy to use. ExamView enables you to create paper-, LAN-, or Web-based tests from test banks designed specifically for your Thomson Course Technology textbook. Utilize the ultra-efficient QuickTest Wizard to create tests in less than five minutes by taking advantage of Thomson Course Technology's question banks, or customize your own exams from scratch.

ADDITIONAL ACTIVITIES FOR STUDENTS These additional activities consist of Chapter Reinforcement Exercises, which are true/false, multiple-choice, and short answer questions that help students gain confidence in the material learned.

Assessment & Training Solutions
SAM 2007

SAM 2007 helps bridge the gap between the classroom and the real world by allowing students to train and test on important computer skills in an active, hands-on environment.

SAM 2007's easy-to-use system includes powerful interactive exams, training or projects on critical applications such as Word, Excel, Access, PowerPoint, Outlook, Windows, the Internet, and much more. SAM simulates the application environment, allowing students to demonstrate their knowledge and think through the skills by performing real-world tasks.

Designed to be used with the Shelly Cashman series, SAM 2007 includes built-in page references so students can print helpful study guides that match the Shelly Cashman series textbooks used in class. Powerful administrative options allow instructors to schedule exams and assignments, secure tests, and run reports with almost limitless flexibility.

Student Edition Labs

Our Web-based interactive labs help students master hundreds of computer concepts, including input and output devices, file management and desktop applications, computer ethics, virus protection, and much more. Featuring up-to-the-minute content, eye-popping graphics, and rich animation, the highly interactive Student Edition Labs offer students an alternative way to learn through dynamic observation, step-by-step practice, and challenging review questions.

Online Content

Blackboard is the leading distance learning solution provider and class-management platform today. Thomson Course Technology has partnered with Blackboard to bring you premium online content. Content may include topic reviews, case projects, review questions, test banks, practice tests, custom syllabi, and more.

Thomson Course Technology also has solutions for several other learning management systems. Please visit http://www.course.com today to see what's available for this title.

CourseCasts Learning on the Go. Always Available...Always Relevant.

Want to keep up with the latest technology trends relevant to you? Visit our site to find a library of podcasts, CourseCasts, featuring a "CourseCast of the Week," and download them to your portable media player at http://coursecasts.course.com.

Our fast-paced world is driven by technology. You know because you are an active participant — always on the go, always keeping up with technological trends, and always learning new ways to embrace technology to power your life.

Ken Baldauf, a faculty member of the Florida State University (FSU) Computer Science Department, is responsible for teaching technology classes to thousands of FSU students each year. He knows what you know; he knows what you want to learn. He is also an expert in the latest technology and will sort through and aggregate the most pertinent news and information so you can spend your time enjoying technology, rather than trying to figure it out.

Visit us at http://coursecasts.course.com to learn on the go!

CourseNotes

Course Technology's CourseNotes are six-panel quick reference cards that reinforce the most important and widely used features of a software application in a visual and user-friendly format. CourseNotes will serve as a great reference tool during and after the student completes the course. CourseNotes for Microsoft Office 2007, Word 2007, Excel 2007, Access 2007, PowerPoint 2007, Windows Vista, Internet Explorer 7, and more are available now!

1

Introduction to Windows Internet Explorer

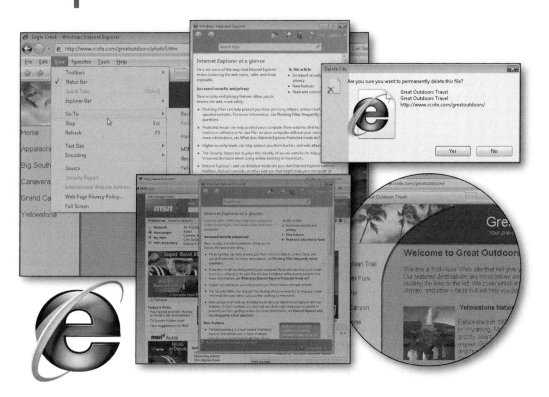

Objectives

You will have mastered the material in this chapter when you can:

- Define the Internet and the World Wide Web

- Discuss threats on the Internet

- Explain a link, Uniform Resource Locator (URL), and Hypertext Mark-up Language (HTML)

- Describe Internet Explorer features

- Enter a URL

- Use the History List and the Favorites Center

- Use buttons on the toolbar

- Add and remove a Favorite

- Save a picture or text from a Web page or an entire Web page

- Copy and paste text or pictures from a Web page into WordPad

- Print a WordPad document and Web page

- Use Internet Explorer Help

1 | Introduction to Windows Internet Explorer

Introduction

The Internet is the most popular and fastest growing area in computing today. Using the Internet, you can do research, send and receive files, get a loan, shop for services and merchandise, job hunt, buy and sell stocks, display weather maps, obtain medical advice, watch movies, listen to high-quality music, and converse with people worldwide.

Although a complex system of hardware and software comprises the Internet, it is accessible to the general public because personal computers with user-friendly tools have reduced its complexity. The Internet, with its millions of connected computers, continues to grow with thousands of new users coming online each day. Schools, businesses, newspapers, television stations, and government agencies all can be found on the Internet. Service providers are popping up all around the country providing inexpensive access to the Internet.

Overview

As you read this chapter, you will learn how to browse the Web and use Internet Explorer by performing these general tasks:

- Start Internet Explorer
- Enter a URL in the Address bar
- Browse a Web page by clicking links and using the Back and Forward buttons
- Navigate to previously viewed Web pages by using the History List and the Favorites Center
- Save a Web page
- Print a Web page

Plan Ahead

Internet Usage Guidelines

Internet usage involves navigating to, viewing, and interacting with the various resources on the Internet. Preparations you make before using the Internet will determine the effectiveness of your experience. Before using the Internet, you should follow these general guidelines:

1. **Determine whether your computer has the proper hardware and software necessary to connect to the Internet.** Connecting to the Internet requires your computer to communicate with other computers. Special hardware and software, discussed later in this chapter, are designed to facilitate this communication. If you are unsure of whether your computer is capable of connecting to the Internet, a technician from a company that provides Internet access will be able to help.

(continued)

Plan
Ahead

(continued)

2. **Choose an appropriate method to connect to the Internet.** The quality and speed of your Internet connection plays an important role in your overall experience. Various Internet connection options are available, and it is important to choose one that not only allows you to quickly and easily access the information that you desire, but also falls within your price range.

3. **Determine whether your computer is properly protected from threats on the Internet.** The Internet can be a breeding ground for software that can do harm to your computer. You should not connect to the Internet unless you have the proper software installed on your computer that will protect you from these various threats.

4. **Determine why you are connecting to the Internet.** Individuals connect to the Internet for personal or business-related reasons. If you are connecting to the Internet to accomplish a specific task, you first should identify the task and compile a list of locations on the Internet where you might look to complete your task.

5. **Determine how much time you wish to spend on the Internet.** For some individuals, the Internet can be an extremely addictive environment. In fact, many companies that provide Internet access to its employees have strict policies in place that outline what they consider to be acceptable Internet usage while on the job. The Internet has the potential to significantly lower an employee's productivity, therefore costing the employer money. Similarly, parents often monitor their children's time on the Internet to ensure they have a safe experience. Many dangers to children exist on it Internet, and it is important to monitor their activity.

   Using the Internet not only can be addicting, it also can be costly. Depending upon the method you use to connect to the Internet, the amount that you are charged to connect may directly relate to the number of minutes or hours that you spend connected. Some Internet connection plans allow unlimited connections, while others may only allow you to connect for a certain number of hours before charging you an additional fee.

   When necessary, more specific details concerning the above guidelines are presented at appropriate points in the chapter.

The Internet

The **Internet** is a worldwide collection of networks (Figure 1–1 on the next page), each of which is composed of a collection of smaller networks. A **network** is composed of several computers connected together to share resources and data. For example, on a college campus, the network in the student lab can connect to the faculty computer network, which is connected to the administration network, and they all can connect to the Internet.

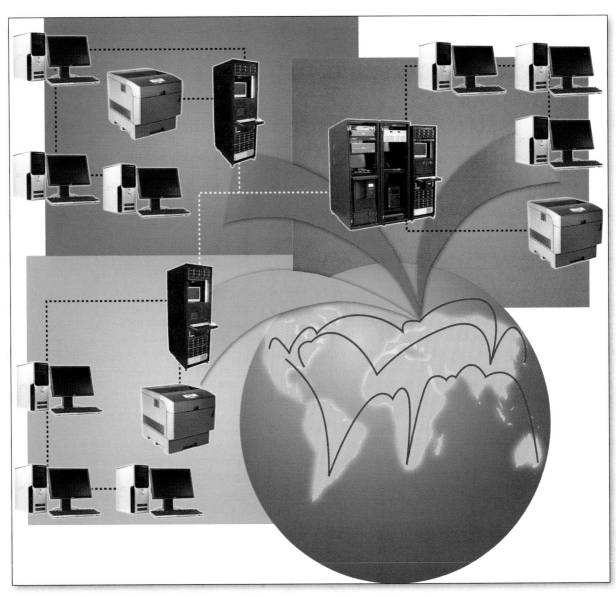

Figure 1–1

BTW

The Internet
The Internet started as a government experiment for the military. The military wanted the ability to connect to and communicate via different computers running different operating systems. From this experiment, a communication technique originated called Transmission Control Protocol/Internet Protocol, or TCP/IP.

Networks are connected with high-, medium-, and low-speed data lines that allow data to move from one computer to another (Figure 1–2). The Internet has high-speed data lines that connect major computers located around the world, which form the **Internet backbone**. Other, less powerful computers, such as those used by local ISPs (Internet service providers) often attach to the Internet backbone using medium-speed data lines. Finally, the connection between your computer at home and your local ISP, often called **the last mile**, employs low-speed data lines such as telephone lines and fiber optic cable. In some cases today, fixed wireless access is replacing wires over the last mile, which significantly improves access to information on the Internet.

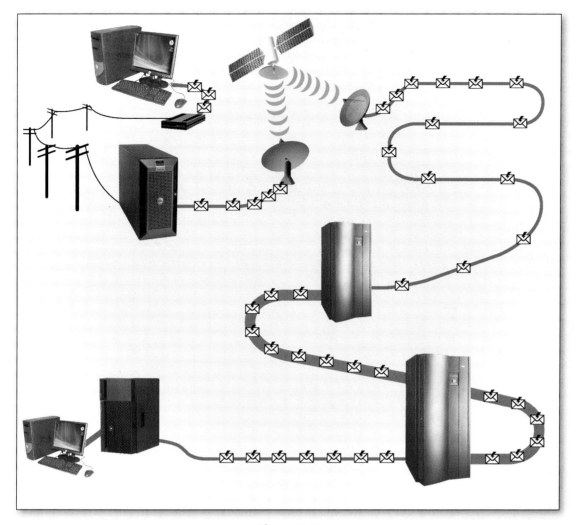

Figure 1–2

The World Wide Web

Modern computers have the capability of delivering information in a variety of ways, such as graphics, sound, video clips, animation, virtual reality, and, of course, regular text. On the Internet, this multimedia capability is available in a form called **hypermedia**, which is any variety of computer media, including text, graphics, audio, video, and virtual reality.

You access hypermedia clicking a **hyperlink**, or simply **link**, which points to the location of the computer on which the hypermedia is stored and to the hypermedia itself. A link, which can be in the form of text, a photo, or a graphic, can point to hypermedia on any computer connected to the Internet that is configured as a Web server. A **Web server**, which runs Web server software, provides resources such as text, graphics, and other files to other computers on the Internet. Thus, clicking a link on a computer in Miami could display hypermedia located in Seattle. The collection of links throughout the Internet creates an interconnected network called the **World Wide Web**, which also is referred to as the **Web**, or **WWW**.

Graphics, text, and other hypermedia available at a Web site are stored in a file called a **Web page**, and a collection of related Web pages make up a **Web site**. Therefore, a Web site is made up of a collection of related Web pages. When you are viewing hypermedia such as text, graphics, and video on the World Wide Web, you actually are viewing a Web page.

BTW

Web Sites
An organization can have more than one Web site. Separate departments may have their own Web servers, allowing faster response to requests for Web pages and local control over the Web pages stored at that Web site.

Figure 1–3 illustrates a Web page at the National Geographic Kids Web site. This Web page contains numerous links. For example, the seven graphics on the top of the Web page are links. Clicking a link, such as Videos, could display a Web page located on the other side of the world.

Figure 1–3

Security Concerns on the Internet

While many advantages can be realized from accessing the Internet, some disadvantages to Internet access are important to consider. When your computer connects to the Internet, other computers may be able to see your computer and possibly connect to it. Computer-savvy individuals with malicious intentions sometimes take advantage of Internet users who do not take the proper security precautions—deleting, modifying, or even stealing their data, sometimes without their knowledge. It also may be possible for an individual or Web site to install **spyware** on your computer. Spyware is a program that tracks the actions you take on your computer, such as what Web sites you visit, what products you purchase online, and your credit card information, and sends them to a third party. Spyware can decrease your computer's performance, as well as compromise any secure information you have stored on your computer. Another type of malicious software that may be installed on your computer without your knowledge is **adware**. Adware randomly displays advertisements and other messages while you use your computer. Adware and spyware may be installed by someone who connects to an unsecure computer, or by downloading and running a program or file from the Internet. To avoid downloading harmful files and programs, it is important to learn how to tell the difference between legitimate and fraudulent files and programs on the Internet.

In addition to adware and spyware, your computer also may be infected by a **computer virus** if you download an infected file from a Web page or open an infected e-mail attachment. E-mail and e-mail attachments are discussed further in Chapter 3. Your computer also can be infected by a virus if someone exploits a security vulnerability, or bug, in a program that is installed on your computer.

Adware, spyware, and viruses are not the only problems that exist on the Internet. **Phishing scams**, or attempts by individuals to obtain confidential information from you, often via the Internet, are growing in popularity. A phishing scam works by falsifying one's identity in an attempt to convince an unsuspecting victim into disclosing information such as credit card numbers, bank account information, and social security numbers. A phisher may falsify his or her identity by sending an e-mail that appears to come from someone else, or by creating a Web site that appears to be that of a legitimate company. The worst part about a phishing scam is that the victim often does not know that someone else took advantage of them until it is too late. Victims of phishing scams also can be exposed to identity theft and great financial loss.

Because these security threats exist, it is important for everyone to practice safe browsing techniques while connected to the Internet. Before connecting your computer to the Internet, you should make sure that you have **antivirus software** installed. Antivirus software will immediately inform you if it detects a virus on your computer. Antivirus software manufacturers also release virus **definition updates** that "teach" the software how to detect newly-created viruses. In addition to installing antivirus software, you also should install a **software firewall** on your computer. A software firewall blocks unauthorized connections to and from your computer. When using your computer on the Internet, it is important to regularly scan your computer for adware and spyware. Some adware and spyware scanners are available online free or for a fee, and some are available in retail stores that sell computer software.

To lower the risk of being victimized by a phishing scam, Internet Explorer 7 includes a **Phishing Filter**. The Phishing Filter is configured to help identify fraudulent Web sites, and will inform you of a fraudulent site by displaying an appropriate message in the display area and providing an indication in the Address bar. While the Phishing Filter may not detect all phishing Web sites, it greatly reduces your chances of becoming a victim of a phishing scam.

To combat security vulnerabilities that are present in programs installed on your computer, software manufactures may release updates, also known as **patches** or **service packs**, which correct these vulnerabilities. It is good practice to install these updates as soon as they become available. Windows Vista's **Automatic Update feature**, for example, can be configured to automatically download and install security updates as they become available. Finally, be selective with the Web sites you visit. Millions of Web sites exist on the Internet today, and it is easy to inadvertently arrive at a site other than the one you intended to visit. In addition, you should take extra precaution while visiting Web sites that are hosted by unknown individuals or obscure companies. Avoid downloading any-thing from these sites or entering any personal information. If you are unsure of whether a Web site is legitimate, it is better to be cautious and simply navigate to another site.

Uniform Resource Locator (URL)

Each Web page has a unique address, called a **Uniform Resource Locator** (**URL**), which distinguishes it from all other pages on the Internet. The URL in Figure 1–3 is http://kids.nationalgeographic.com.

A URL often is composed of multiple parts (Figure 1–4). The first part is the protocol. A **protocol** is a set of rules. Most Web pages use the Hypertext Transfer Protocol. **Hypertext Transfer Protocol (HTTP)** describes the rules used to transmit Web pages electronically over the Internet. You enter the protocol in lowercase as http followed by a colon and two forward slashes (http://). If you do not begin a URL with a protocol, Internet Explorer will assume it is http, and automatically will append http:// to the front of the URL.

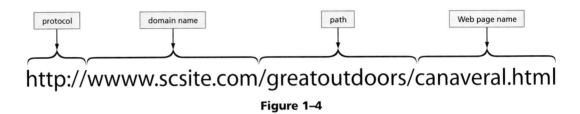

Figure 1–4

The second part of a URL is the domain name. The **domain name** is the Internet address of the computer where the Web page is located. Each computer on the Internet has a unique address, called an **Internet Protocol address**, or **IP address**. The domain name identifies where to forward a request for the Web page referenced by the URL. The domain name in the URL in Figure 1–4 is www.scsite.com. The last part of the domain name (com in Figure 1–4) is called an **extension** and indicates the type of organization that owns the Web site. For example, the extension .com indicates a commercial organization, usually a business or corporation. Educational institutions have the extension .edu at the end of their domain names. Government entities use the .gov extension. Countries throughout the world also have their own domain name extensions. For example, Germany's domain name extension is .de, and China's domain name extension is .cn. Table 1–1 shows some types of organizations and their extensions.

Table 1–1 Organizations and their Domain Name Extensions	
Types of Organizations	**Original Domain Name Extensions**
Commercial organizations, businesses, and companies	.com
Educational institutions	.edu
Government agencies	.gov
Military organizations	.mil
Network providers	.net
Nonprofit organizations	.org
Types of Organizations	**Newer Domain Name Extensions**
Accredited museums	.museum
Aviation community members	.aero
Business cooperatives such as credit unions and rural electric co-ops	.coop
Businesses of all sizes	.biz
Businesses, organizations, or individuals providing general information	.info
Certified professionals such as doctors, lawyers, and accountants	.pro
Individuals or families	.name

The optional third part of a URL is the file specification of the Web page. The **file specification** includes the file name and possibly a directory or folder name. This information is called the **path**. If no file specification of a Web page is specified in the URL, a default Web page appears. This means you can display a Web page even though you do not know its file specification.

You can find URLs that identify Web sites in magazines or newspapers, on television, from friends, or even from just browsing the Web. URLs of well-known companies and organizations usually contain the company's name and institution's name. For example, ibm.com is IBM Corporation, and ucf.edu is the University of Central Florida.

Hypertext Markup Language

Web page authors use a special language called **Hypertext Markup Language** (**HTML**) to create Web pages. Behind all the formatted text and eye-catching graphics is plain text. Special HTML formatting codes and functions that control attributes of a page, such as font size, colors, and text alignment, surround the text and picture references. Figure 1–5 shows part of the hypertext markup language used to create the Web page shown in Figure 1–3 on page IE 6.

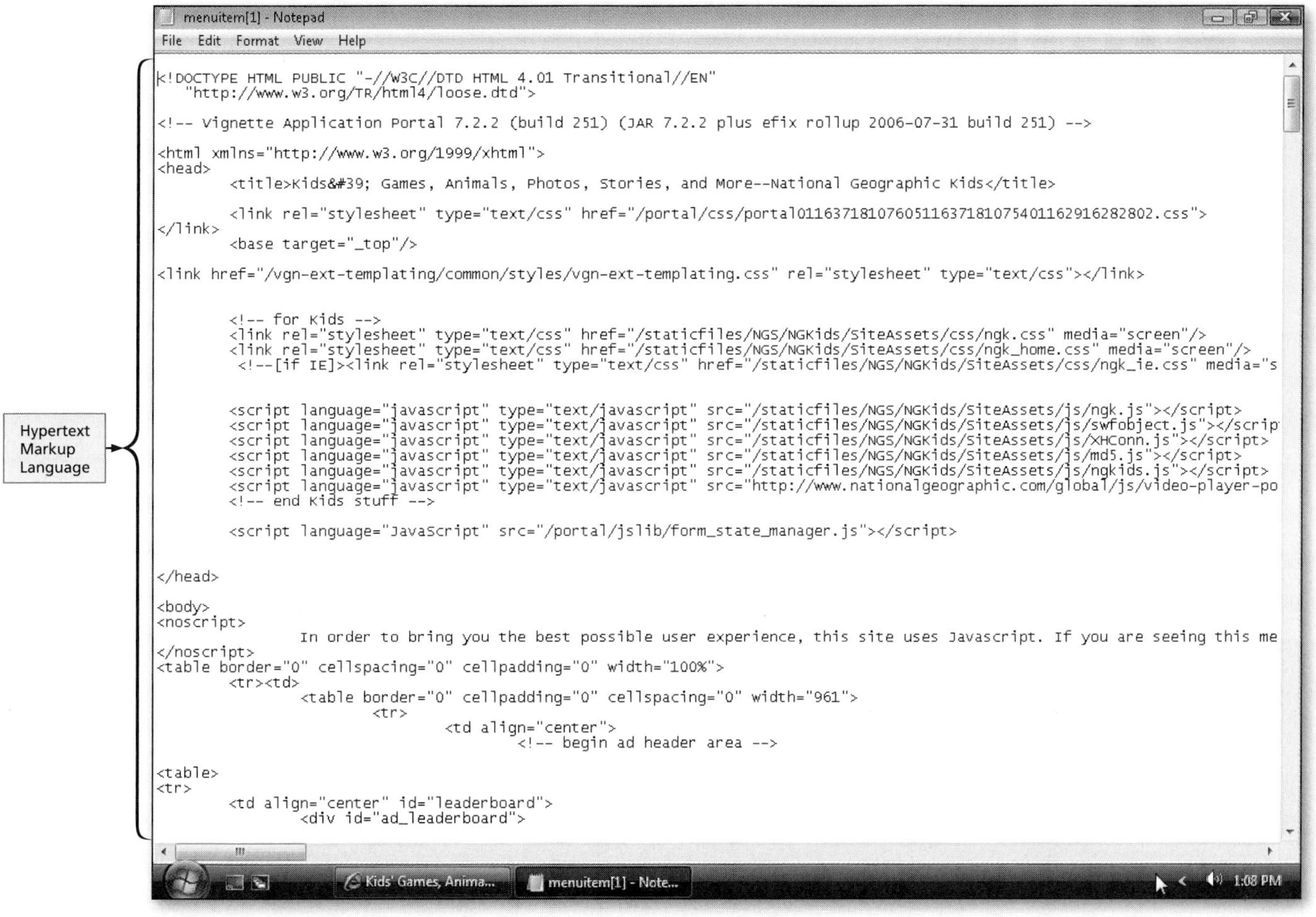


```
<!DOCTYPE HTML PUBLIC "-//W3C//DTD HTML 4.01 Transitional//EN"
   "http://www.w3.org/TR/html4/loose.dtd">

<!-- Vignette Application Portal 7.2.2 (build 251) (JAR 7.2.2 plus efix rollup 2006-07-31 build 251) -->

<html xmlns="http://www.w3.org/1999/xhtml">
<head>
        <title>Kids&#39; Games, Animals, Photos, Stories, and More--National Geographic Kids</title>

        <link rel="stylesheet" type="text/css" href="/portal/css/portal0116371810760511637181075401162916282802.css">
</link>
        <base target="_top"/>

<link href="/vgn-ext-templating/common/styles/vgn-ext-templating.css" rel="stylesheet" type="text/css"></link>


        <!-- for Kids -->
        <link rel="stylesheet" type="text/css" href="/staticfiles/NGS/NGKids/SiteAssets/css/ngk.css" media="screen"/>
        <link rel="stylesheet" type="text/css" href="/staticfiles/NGS/NGKids/SiteAssets/css/ngk_home.css" media="screen"/>
         <!--[if IE]><link rel="stylesheet" type="text/css" href="/staticfiles/NGS/NGKids/SiteAssets/css/ngk_ie.css" media="s

        <script language="javascript" type="text/javascript" src="/staticfiles/NGS/NGKids/SiteAssets/js/ngk.js"></script>
        <script language="javascript" type="text/javascript" src="/staticfiles/NGS/NGKids/SiteAssets/js/swfobject.js"></scrip
        <script language="javascript" type="text/javascript" src="/staticfiles/NGS/NGKids/SiteAssets/js/XHConn.js"></script>
        <script language="javascript" type="text/javascript" src="/staticfiles/NGS/NGKids/SiteAssets/js/md5.js"></script>
        <script language="javascript" type="text/javascript" src="/staticfiles/NGS/NGKids/SiteAssets/js/ngkids.js"></script>
        <script language="javascript" type="text/javascript" src="http://www.nationalgeographic.com/global/js/video-player-po
        <!-- end Kids stuff -->

        <script language="JavaScript" src="/portal/jslib/form_state_manager.js"></script>

</head>

<body>
<noscript>
                In order to bring you the best possible user experience, this site uses Javascript. If you are seeing this me
</noscript>
<table border="0" cellspacing="0" cellpadding="0" width="100%">
        <tr><td>
                <table border="0" cellpadding="0" cellspacing="0" width="961">
                        <tr>
                                <td align="center">
                                        <!-- begin ad header area -->

<table>
<tr>
        <td align="center" id="leaderboard">
                <div id="ad_leaderboard">
```

Figure 1–5

BTW

HTML
Many HTML editing programs make it easy to create Web pages without learning HTML syntax. Editing programs include SharePoint Designer, Microsoft Expression Web, Web-O-Rama, HomeSite, Coffee Cup, Power Web, Web Express, Cool Page, Sothink, and Dreamweaver.

HTML is considered a markup language. A **markup language** contains text, as well as information about the text. This information may include how the text is formatted and positioned on a page. Using HTML, you can create your own Web pages and place them on the Web for others to see. Easy-to-use Web page development software, such as Microsoft SharePoint Designer and Adobe Dreamweaver, are two of the many HTML authoring tools available. New versions of HTML are released periodically to allow Web developers to take advantage of new and exciting technologies that can be delivered over the World Wide Web. As new versions of HTML are released, software on your computer must be updated to support new and updated features.

Home Pages

No main menus or particular starting points exist in the World Wide Web, but most people start a visit to the Web via specially designated Web pages called home pages. A **home page** is the introductory page for a Web site. All other Web pages for that site usually are accessible from the home page via links. When you enter a domain name with no file specification, such as disneyland.com or nbc.com, the home page is the page that is displayed.

Because it is the starting point for most Web sites, Web designers try to make a good first impression and display attractive, eye-catching graphics, specially formatted text, and a variety of links to other pages at the Web site as well as to other related Web sites.

A home page also may refer to the first Web page or Web pages that appear when you start your Web browser. For example, if you normally read the news online when you connect to the Internet, you may set your browser's home page to your favorite news Web site.

Web Browsers

Graphical user interfaces (GUIs) such as Microsoft Windows Vista simplify working with a computer by using a point-and-click method. Similarly, a browser such as Internet Explorer makes using the World Wide Web easier by removing the complexity of having to remember the syntax, or rules, of commands used to reference Web pages at Web sites. A **browser** takes the URL associated with a link or the URL entered by a user, locates the computer containing the associated Web page, and then reads the HTML returned to display a Web page.

BTW

The Internet Explorer Icon
When you install the Windows Vista operating system or Internet Explorer 7, the Internet Explorer icon and name are displayed on the All Programs list and also may be displayed as the first entry on the Start menu. If the Quick Launch Toolbar appears on the Windows taskbar, the Internet Explorer icon also may appear on the toolbar.

What Is Internet Explorer 7?

Internet Explorer 7 is Web browsing software that allows you to search for and view Web pages, save links for future use, maintain a list of the pages you visit, obtain information from various sources, listen to radio stations, and watch videos. The Internet Explorer 7 application program is included with the Microsoft Windows Vista operating system and is available free-of-charge to individuals who have previous versions of Microsoft Windows, such as Windows XP and Windows 2000. The chapters in this book illustrate the use of the Internet Explorer 7 browser.

Starting Internet Explorer

If you are stepping through this chapter on a computer and want your screen to match the figures in this book, you should change your computer's resolution to 1024 × 768. For more information on how to change the resolution on your computer, see your instructor.

To Start Internet Explorer

The following steps, which assume Windows Vista is running, start Internet Explorer based on a typical installation. You may need to ask your instructor how to start Internet Explorer for your computer.

- Click the Start button on the Windows taskbar to display the Start menu.

- Point to All Programs on the Start menu to display the All Programs list, and then point to Internet Explorer on the All Programs list (Figure 1–6).

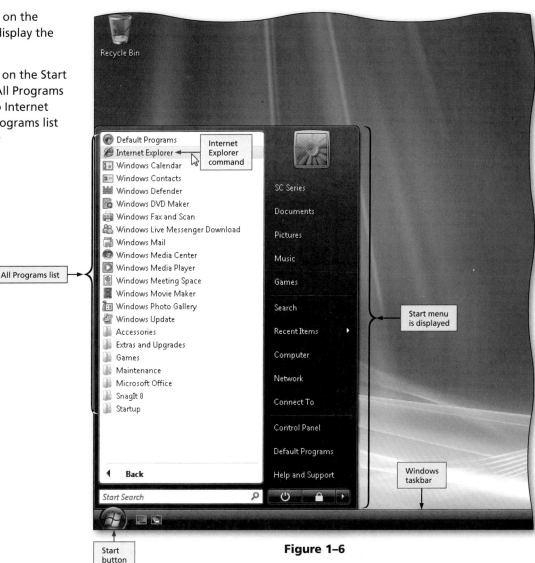

Figure 1–6

2

- Click Internet Explorer to start Internet Explorer and display the MSN.com - Windows Internet Explorer window (Figure 1–7). Depending on your computer's configuration, the home page may display differently.

- If the Internet Explorer window is not maximized, double-click its title bar to maximize it.

Q&A

Can I change the home page in the Internet Explorer window?

Yes. You can change the home page by clicking Tools on the menu bar, clicking Internet Options on the Tools menu, and under the Home Page section clicking the Use current, Use default, or Use blank button.

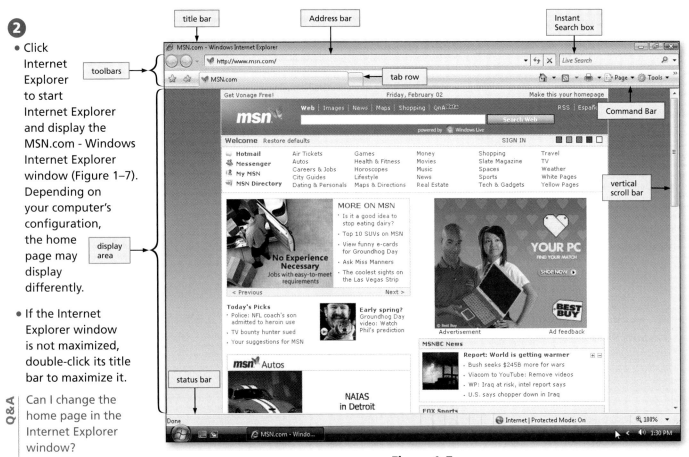

Figure 1–7

Other Ways

1. Click Start button on Windows taskbar, click Internet Explorer icon on Start menu
2. Double-click Internet Explorer icon on desktop
3. Press CTRL+ESC, press I, press ENTER

When Internet Explorer first starts, MSN.com is displayed as the default home page. Because it is possible to change the page that initially is displayed through the Internet Options command on the Tools menu, the home page shown in Figure 1–7 may be different on your computer. For example, some schools and businesses have their own Web site home page display when starting Internet Explorer.

The Internet Explorer Window

The **Internet Explorer window** (Figure 1–7) consists of a range of features that make browsing the Internet easy. It contains a title bar, a menu bar, toolbars, the Instant Search box, an Address bar, a tab row, the Command Bar, scroll bars, the status bar, and a display area where pages from the World Wide Web appear. The menu bar, toolbar, Address bar, Instant Search box, Command Bar, and tab row appear at the top of the screen just below the title bar. By default, the menu bar only appears when you press the ALT key. The status bar appears at the bottom of the screen.

Display Area   Only a portion of most pages will be visible on the screen. You view the portion of the page displayed on the screen in the **display area** (Figure 1–7). To the right of the display area is a scroll bar, scroll arrows, and a scroll box, which you can use to move the text in the display area up and down and reveal other parts of the page.

Notice the links on the Internet Explorer home page shown in Figure 1–7. When you position the mouse pointer on one of these links, the mouse pointer changes to a pointing hand. This change in the shape of the mouse pointer identifies these elements as links. Clicking a link retrieves the Web page associated with the link and displays it in the display area.

Title Bar   The title bar appears at the top of the Windows Internet Explorer window. As shown at the top of Figure 1–7, the **title bar** includes the System menu icon on the left, the title of the active Web page, and the Minimize, Restore (or Maximize), and Close buttons on the right. Clicking the **System menu icon** on the title bar will display the System menu, which contains commands to carry out the actions associated with the Windows Internet Explorer window. Double-click the System menu icon or click the Close button to close the Windows Internet Explorer window and quit Internet Explorer.

Click the **Minimize button** to minimize the Windows Internet Explorer window. When you minimize the window, it no longer appears on the desktop and the Windows Internet Explorer taskbar button becomes inactive (a lighter color). The minimized window is still open but it does not appear on the desktop. After minimizing, clicking the taskbar button on the Windows taskbar displays the Windows Internet Explorer window in the previous position it occupied on the desktop and changes the button to an active state (a darker color).

Click the **Maximize button** to maximize the Internet Explorer window so it expands to fill the entire desktop. When the window is maximized, the Restore button replaces the Maximize button on the title bar. Click the **Restore button** to return the window to the size and position it occupied before being maximized. The Restore button changes to the Maximize button when the Windows Internet Explorer window is in a restored state.

You also can double-click the title bar to restore and maximize the Internet Explorer window. If the window is in a restored state, you can drag the title bar to move the window on the desktop.

Menu Bar   The **menu bar** is located below the title bar. Because the most common Internet Explorer commands are accessible via the toolbar and the Command Bar, Internet Explorer hides the menu bar when it is not in use. You may display the menu bar by pressing the ALT key. When displayed, the menu bar displays menu names. Each **menu name** represents a menu of commands you can use to perform actions such as saving Web pages, copying and pasting, customizing toolbars, sending and receiving e-mail, setting Internet Explorer options, quitting Internet Explorer, and so on. To display a menu when the menu bar is displayed, click the menu name on the menu bar. To select a command on a menu, click the command name or press the **keyboard shortcut** shown to the right of some commands on the menu.

Toolbars The **toolbars** (Figure 1–7 on page IE 12) in Internet Explorer contain buttons that allow you to perform frequently-used tasks more quickly than using the menu bar. For example, to go back to the most recent page you have visited, click the Back button on the toolbar. Table 1–2 illustrates the buttons on the toolbar.

Table 1–2 Toolbar Buttons and Functions	
Button	**Function**
⬅	Retrieves the previous page (provided it was previously just viewed); to go more than one page back, click the Recent Pages arrow, and then click a Web page title in the list
➡	Retrieves the next page; to go more than one page forward, click the Forward button arrow, and then click a Web page URL in the list. This button only is available after you have clicked the Back button one or more times to return to a previous page
▾	Displays a list of Web pages you recently have visited since you started Internet Explorer
↻	Requests the Web page in the display area to be retrieved from the Web site again
✕	Stops the transfer of a Web page
☆	Displays the Favorites Center
⭐	Displays a menu that allows you to add the current Web site to your Favorites, add the current tab group to your Favorites, import and export Favorites, and organize your Favorites

BTW

The Address Bar
To move the insertion point to the Address bar when the box is empty, or to highlight the URL in the Address bar, press ALT+D.

Address Bar The **Address bar** (Figure 1–7) holds the URL for the page currently shown in the display area. The Address bar also can be used to search for information on the World Wide Web. Chapter 2 discusses Internet searching techniques.

The URL updates automatically as you browse from page to page. If you know the URL of a Web page you want to visit, click the URL in the Address bar to highlight it, type the new URL, and then press the ENTER key to display the corresponding page. In addition, you can click the **Address bar arrow** at the right end of the Address bar to display a list of previously displayed Web pages. Clicking a URL in the Address list displays the corresponding Web page.

You also can access information on your computer by typing an application name in the Address bar and pressing the ENTER key to start the corresponding application, typing a folder name and pressing the ENTER key to open a folder window, typing a document name and pressing the ENTER key to start an application and display the document in the application window, or typing a keyword or phrase (search inquiry) and pressing the ENTER key to display Web pages containing the keyword or phrase.

Command Bar

The **Command Bar**, new to Internet Explorer 7, provides quick and easy access to most Internet Explorer functions. The buttons on the Command Bar allow you to change your home page options, access RSS feeds (discussed further in Chapter 3), print the current Web page and access printing options, access Web page options, access Internet Explorer tools, and more. You can customize the tools that appear on the Command Bar by right-clicking the Command Bar, pointing to Customize Command Bar on the shortcut menu, and then clicking Add or Remove Commands. Depending on the size of the Command Bar in your Internet Explorer window, not all commands may display. If a right-arrow button displays on the right side of the Command Bar, you can click the button to access additional options. The options on your Command Bar may be different, depending on the software installed on your computer and your computer's configuration. Table 1–3 identifies the default commands on the Command Bar and briefly describes the function of each command.

Table 1–3 Commands on the Command Bar	
Commands	**Function**
🏠	Displays the home page
🔊	When active, this button allows you to view the RSS feeds on the current Web page
🖨	Prints the current Web page
Page ▼	Displays a menu containing selected popular commands from the menu bar's File, Edit, and View menus
Tools ▼	Displays commonly used commands that are also accessible on the View and Tools menus on the menu bar
❓▼	Displays the Help menu, which is also accessible via the menu bar
📖	Displays the Research bar, containing access to multiple reference sites on the Internet

The Home, Feeds, and Print buttons on the Command Bar also have a drop-down arrow displayed on the right-hand side. Clicking the button itself will perform the tasks described in Table 1–3; clicking the drop-down arrow will display a menu containing more options related to that button. For example, clicking the Print drop-down arrow will display a menu that allows you to not only print the current Web page, but also to view a Print Preview and access the Page Setup dialog box.

Instant Search Box   The **Instant Search box**, a new feature to Internet Explorer 7, is located to the right of the Address bar and allows you to perform a search on the World Wide Web by entering your search criteria and pressing the ENTER key. By default, the Instant Search box will perform your search using Windows Live search, but other searching options are available by customizing the Instant Search box. Chapter 2 discusses the Instant Search box in detail.

Tab Row   The **tab row**, another new feature to Internet Explorer 7, is located adjacent to the Command Bar. The tab row enables you to simultaneously keep multiple Web pages open in one browser window. After clicking the New Tab button in the tab row, you can type in the Address bar the URL of the Web page you want to display in the new tab. The tab row also allows you to switch between tabs, reorder tabs, close single tabs, and view the Web pages you currently have open in tabs. Previous versions of Internet Explorer did not support tabbed browsing, and it was necessary to open a new browser window each time you wanted to display additional Web pages. Opening multiple browser windows consumes additional system resources, which can decrease your computer's performance. Even though you are able to open multiple Internet Explorer windows simultaneously, it is recommended that you open new Web pages in tabs. While a Web page loads in the display area, the

BTW

The Command Bar
If the text label is not displayed on the buttons on the Command Bar, right-click the Command Bar, point to Customize Command Bar on the shortcut menu, and then click Show All Text Labels. You also can change the size of the icons on the Command Bar by using the Use Large Icons command on the shortcut menu. When a check mark appears next to the Use Large Icons command, the icons on the Command Bar are displayed in their largest size. When a check mark does not appear, small icons are displayed on the Command Bar.

BTW

The Great Outdoors Travel Web Site
Notice that the URL you enter for The Great Outdoors page contains a domain name (scsite.com) that belongs to the publishing company. The Great Outdoors Travel Web site has been developed exclusively for use with this textbook.

Internet Explorer icon in the corresponding tab changes to an animated circle. When the Web page finishes loading, the Internet Explorer icon displays in the tab.

Browsing the World Wide Web

The most common way to browse the World Wide Web is to obtain the URL of a Web page you want to visit and then enter it into the Address bar. By visiting various Web sites, you can begin to understand the enormous appeal of the Web. The following steps show how to visit the Web page titled Great Outdoors Travel, which contains information and photographs of five popular outdoor destinations in the United States. The URL for The Great Outdoors Web site is: www.scsite.com/greatoutdoors.

To Browse the Web by Entering a URL

To navigate to the home page for the Great Outdoors Travel Web site, you will need to enter the URL in the Address bar. You are not required to provide the leading http:// protocol when initially typing the URL in the Address bar. Internet Explorer will insert http:// and assume the www automatically, if you do not supply it.

1

• Click the Address bar to highlight the URL (Figure 1–8).

Figure 1–8

2

• Type scsite.com/ greatoutdoors in the Address bar to display the new URL. (Figure 1–9)

 Why don't I have to type www. at the beginning of each URL?

Depending on how the Web server is configured, it may not require you to type www. at the beginning of the URL. In the case of this Web site, you can type scsite.com/ greatoutdoors or www.scsite. com/greatoutdoors.

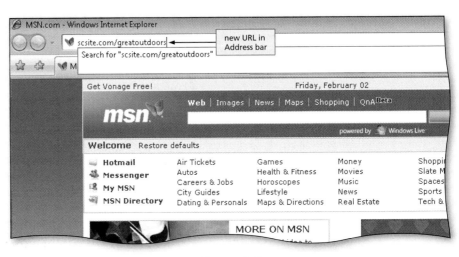

Figure 1–9

3

• Press the ENTER key to load the Great Outdoors Travel Web page (Figure 1–10).

Figure 1–10

4

• Click the Yellowstone link to display the Yellowstone National Park Web page (Figure 1–11).

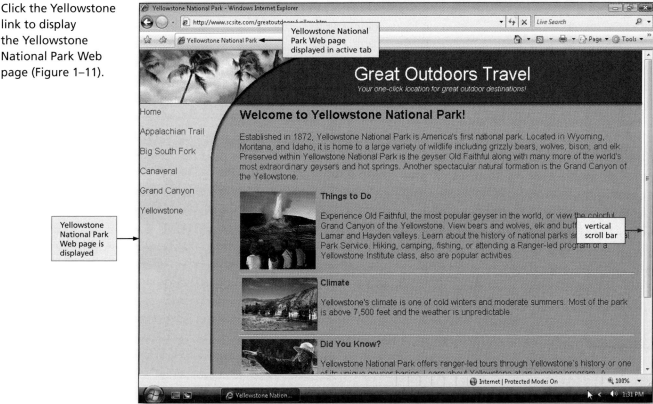

Figure 1–11

5

- Scroll through the display area using the vertical scroll bar to display the photo gallery link (Figure 1–12).

Why is the text, photo gallery, underlined?

Links to other Web pages and Web sites usually are underlined. Individuals who create Web pages typically do not underline text unless the text will act as a hyperlink.

Figure 1–12

6

- Click the photo gallery link to display the Yellowstone National Park Photo Gallery Web page (Figure 1–13).

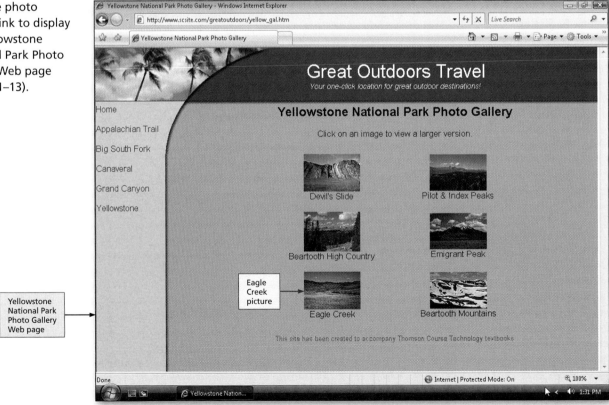

Figure 1–13

- If necessary, scroll through the display area to view the six pictures.

- Click the Eagle Creek picture to display the Eagle Creek Web page, which contains a larger version of the Eagle Creek picture (Figure 1–14).

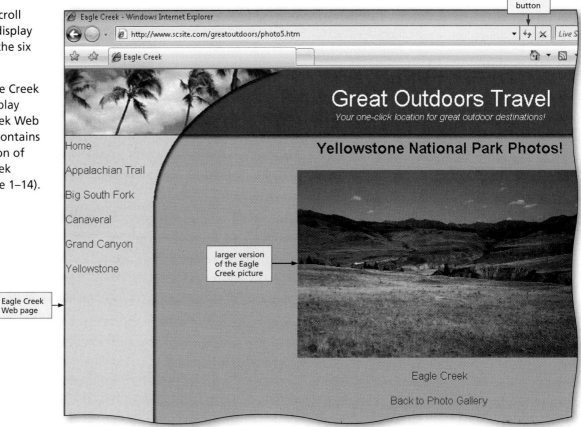

Figure 1–14

The preceding steps illustrate how simple it is to browse the World Wide Web. Displaying a Web page associated with a link is as easy as clicking a text or picture link.

Step 2 on page IE 16 involved typing a URL. If you type the wrong letter and notice the error before pressing the ENTER key, use the BACKSPACE key to erase all the characters back to and including the one that is wrong. If the error is easier to retype than correct, click the URL in the Address bar and retype it.

Pointing to an image on a Web page may display **alternate text** in a small pop-up box (Figure 1–15 on the next page). Alternate text is text that displays in place of the image if a user configures his or her Web browser not to display images. In addition, visually impaired users typically have special software installed on their computer that reads the contents of their screen through the computer's speakers. Because this software cannot read an image, it reads the alternate text instead. Web page authors typically write alternate text that briefly describes the image it represents. Poorly-written alternate text can make it difficult for visually impaired users to understand what is on the Web page.

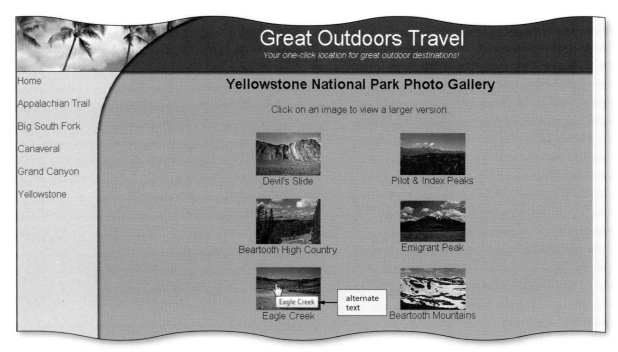

Figure 1–15

BTW

Stopping the Transfer of a Web Page
In addition to clicking the Stop button on the toolbar to stop the transfer of a Web page, you also can click the Stop command on the View menu, press the ESC key, or press ALT+V and then press the P key.

Stopping the Transfer of a Page

If a Web page you are trying to view is taking too long to transfer or if you have clicked the wrong link, you may decide not to wait for the page to finish transferring. The Stop button on the toolbar (Figure 1–16) allows you to stop the transfer of a page while the transfer is in progress. You will know that the transfer still is in progress if the icon on the current tab is moving. Stopping the transfer of a Web page will leave a partially trans-ferred Web page in the display area. Pictures or text displaying before the Stop button is clicked remain visible in the display area and any links can be clicked to display the associ-ated Web pages. Because the speed at which individuals are connecting to the Internet has been increasing, Web pages load quickly and the need for the Stop button is decreasing. However, individuals who connect to the Internet with a slower Internet connection, such as dial-up access, may have a greater need to use the Stop button.

Refreshing a Web Page

The content of some Web pages frequently may change. As you display different Web pages, Internet Explorer keeps track of the pages you visit, so you can quickly find those pages in the future. Internet Explorer stores the Web pages you visit in the **Temporary Internet Files folder** on the hard disk. When you display a previously viewed Web page, the page is displayed quickly because Internet Explorer is able to retrieve the page from the Temporary Internet Files folder on the hard disk instead of from a Web server on the Internet. For this reason, the Web page you are viewing may not be the most up-to-date version. Web pages containing stock quotes, weather, and news are updated frequently to reflect the most current information. If you are unsure of whether the content you are view-ing on a Web page is current, you should refresh the Web page. You also should refresh a Web page if you think the Web page has loaded incorrectly. You can refresh the Web page by using the **Refresh button** on the toolbar (Figure 1–16).

To Refresh a Web Page

The following steps refresh the contents of the Web page you currently are viewing, to ensure that you are viewing the most recent version of the page.

- Click the Refresh button on the tool-bar to cause Internet Explorer to initiate a new transfer of the Web page from the source computer to your computer (Figure 1–16).

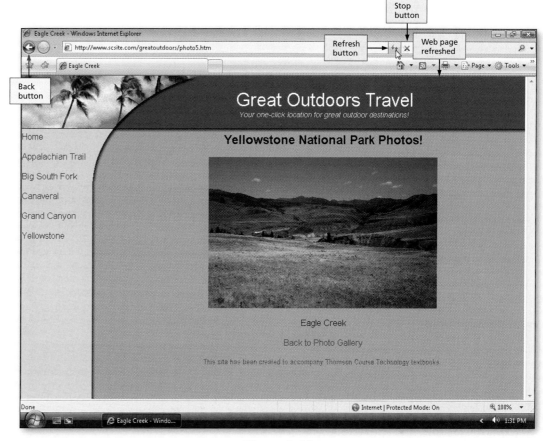

Figure 1–16

Other Ways

1. Click URL in Address bar, press ENTER key

2. On View menu click Refresh

3. Press ALT+V, press R

4. Press F5

Finding a Previously Displayed Web Page

One method to find a previously displayed Web page is to use the Back button and the Recent Pages list on the toolbar (Figure 1–17a on the next page). Each time a Web page appears in the display area, the title of the previously displayed page is added to the Recent Pages list. Clicking the **Recent Pages arrow** displays the **Recent Pages list**, which allows you to display a previously viewed page from the list (Figure 1–17a). The Forward button activates only after you click the Back button to return to a recent page. Each time you end an Internet session by quitting Internet Explorer, the entries on the Recent Pages list are cleared.

A second method allows you to display the **Go To list** containing the names of all Web pages in the order they were displayed during the current session (Figure 1–17b). A check mark preceding a name in the list identifies the page currently displayed. To view the Go To list, press the ALT key to display the menu bar, click View on the menu bar, and then point to Go To on the View menu. Clicking a name in the Go To list displays the associated Web page in the display area.

A third method uses the Address bar arrow to display previously viewed Web pages. Clicking the **Address bar arrow** displays the **Address bar list** containing a list of previously visited Web pages (Figure 1–17c).

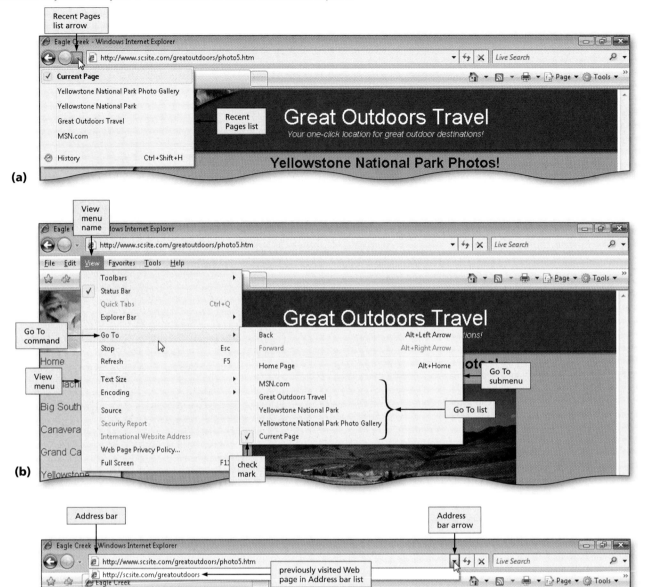

Figure 1–17

Finding a Recently Displayed Web Page Using the Back and Forward Buttons

When you start Internet Explorer, the Back and Forward buttons and the Recent Pages arrow appear dimmed and are unavailable (see Figure 1–7 on page IE 12). When you visit the first Web page after starting Internet Explorer, the Back button is no longer dimmed and is available for use. Pointing to the button changes the color of the button, indicating the button is active.

To Use the Back and Forward Buttons to Find Recently Displayed Web Pages

The Back and Forward buttons are often used when you wish to revisit a Web page you recently have visited since you last opened Internet Explorer. The following steps use the Back and Forward buttons.

1
- Click the Back button on the toolbar to display the Yellowstone National Park Photo Gallery Web page (Figure 1–18).

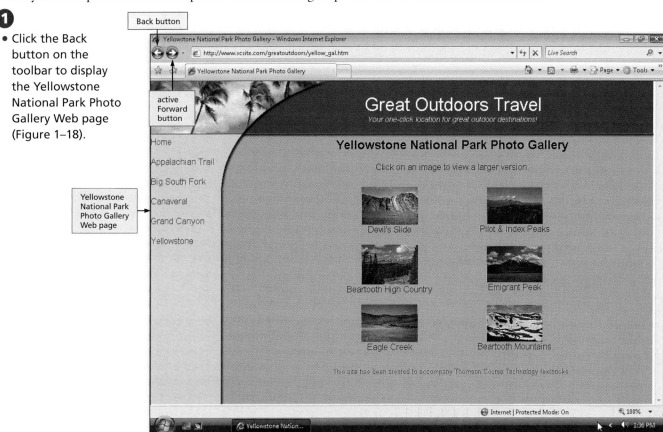

Figure 1–18

2
- Click the Back button again to display the Yellowstone National Park Web page (Figure 1–19).

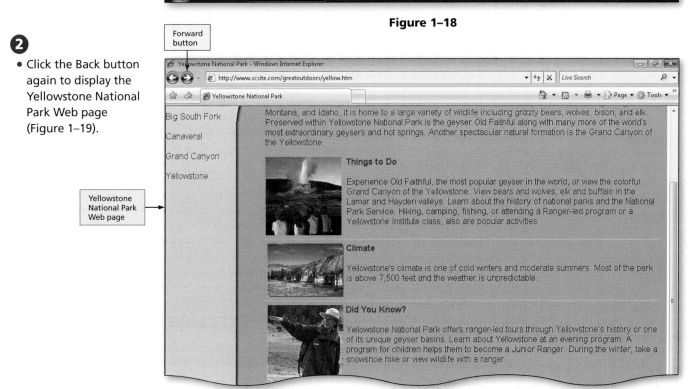

Figure 1–19

3

• Click the Forward button on the toolbar to display the Yellowstone National Park Photo Gallery Web page (Figure 1–20).

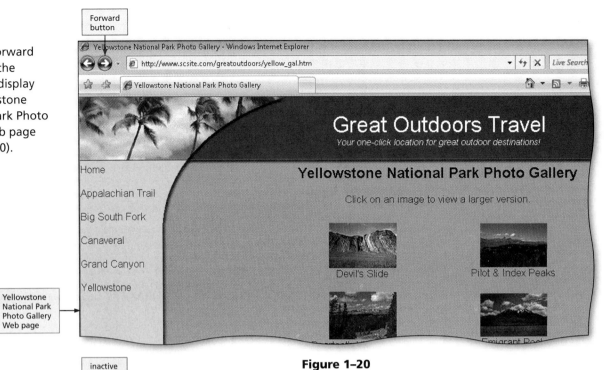

Figure 1–20

4

• Click the Forward button again to display the Eagle Creek Web page (Figure 1–21).

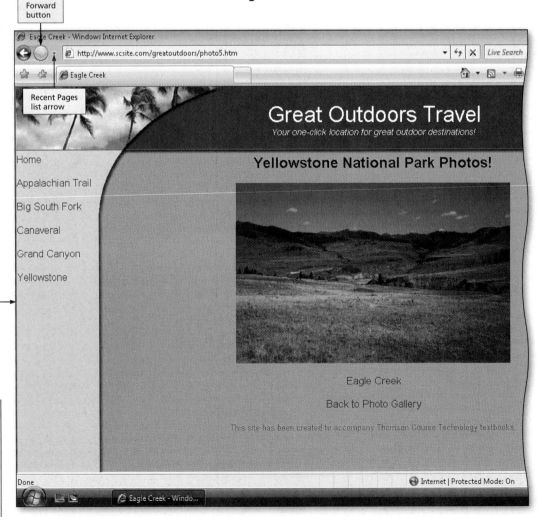

Other Ways

1. Click Recent Pages arrow, click Web page title
2. On View menu, point to Go To, click Web page title on Go To submenu (or Back or Forward)
3. Back: press ALT+LEFT ARROW; forward: press ALT+RIGHT ARROW

Figure 1–21

You can continue to page backward until you reach the beginning of the Recent Pages list. At that time, the Back button becomes inactive, which indicates that the list contains no additional pages to which you can move back. You can, however, move forward by clicking the Forward button.

You can see that traversing the list of pages is easy using the Back and Forward buttons. However, this method can be time consuming if many pages must be displayed before the one you want to view.

To Display a Web Page Using the Recent Pages List

It is possible to jump to any previously visited page by clicking its title in the Recent Pages list. In this way, you can find a recently visited page without displaying an intermediate page. The following steps illustrate how to quickly and easily navigate to a recently visited page without having to click the Back button multiple times to reach the page.

- Click the Recent Pages list arrow on the toolbar to display the Recent Pages list (Figure 1–22).

Q&A

Why does my Recent Pages list look different?

If Internet Explorer was open before beginning this chapter, there may be additional pages in your Recent Pages list.

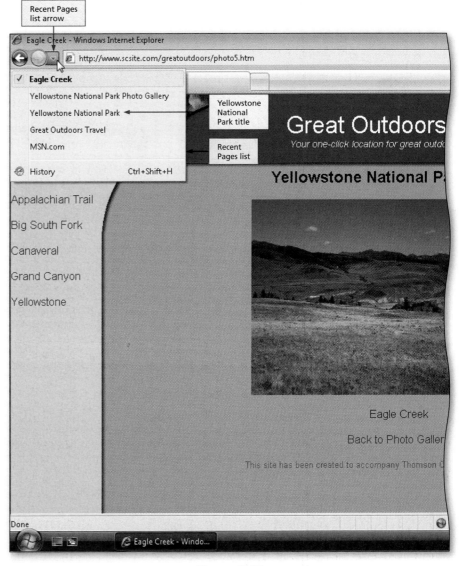

Figure 1–22

2

- Click Yellowstone National Park on the Recent Pages list to display the Yellowstone National Park Web page (Figure 1–23).

Q&A

Why do some Web page names only partially display in the Recent Pages list?

Some Web page names are too long to fully display in the Recent Pages list. For this reason, the end of the Web page names might be cut off.

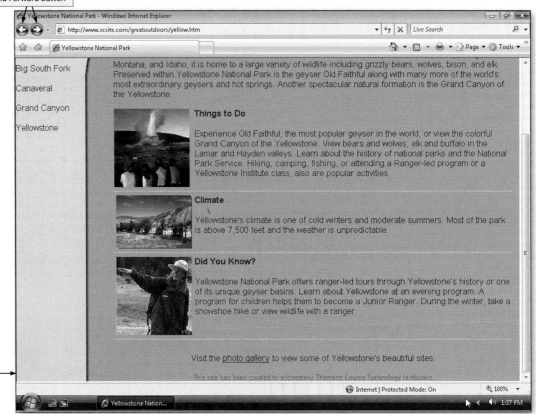

Figure 1–23

Other Ways

1. On View menu point to Go To, click Back on Go To submenu
2. Press ALT+LEFT ARROW

BTW

Clearing the History List

If the list of Web sites you have visited has become too large to be meaningful, you may want to clear the History List. You can clear the History List by clicking Tools on the Command Bar, clicking Internet Options, clicking the Delete button in the Internet Options dialog box, clicking the Delete history in the Delete Browsing History dialog box, clicking the Yes button, clicking the Close button, and then clicking the OK button. Clearing the History List also clears the Address bar list.

If you have a small list of pages you have visited, or the Web page you wish to view is only one or two pages away, using the Back and Forward buttons to traverse the lists will likely be faster than displaying the Recent Pages list and selecting the correct title. If you have visited a large number of pages, however, you will need to step forward or back through many pages, and it may be easier to use the Recent Pages list to select the exact page.

Using the History List to Display Web Pages

Internet Explorer maintains another list of previously visited Web pages in the History List. The **History List** is an alphabetical list of Web pages visited over a period of days or weeks (over many sessions). You can use this list to display Web pages you may have accessed during that time. Pressing the ALT key to display the menu bar, clicking View on the menu bar, pointing to Explorer Bar, and then clicking History displays the Explorer Bar containing the History List.

When the Explorer Bar is visible, the display area contains two panes. The left pane contains the Explorer Bar and the right pane contains the current Web page. The Explorer Bar will remain on the screen until you close it. To find a recently visited Web page using the History List, first display the entire History List, and then click the desired Web page title. The Web page titles are categorized by the Web site's URL.

To Display a Web Page Using the History List

To display a recently visited Web page without having to click the Back button multiple times, perform the following steps to display the Web page using the History List.

1

• Press the ALT key to display the menu bar (Figure 1–24).

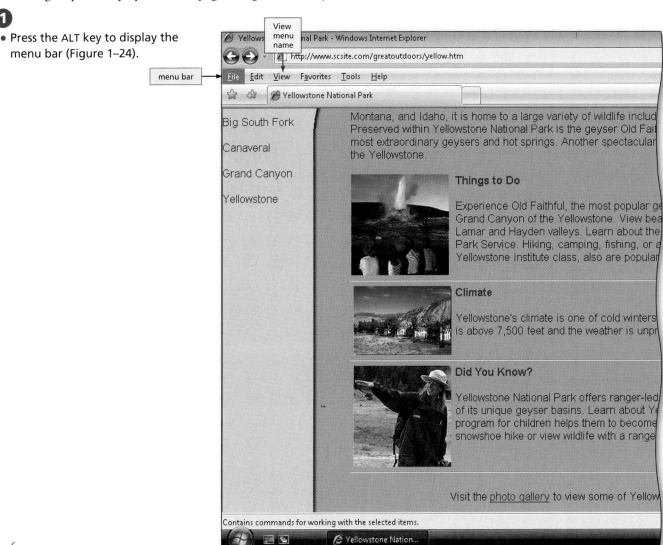

Figure 1–24

2

- Click View on the menu bar to display the View menu, point to Explorer Bar on the View menu to display the Explorer Bar submenu, and then click History to display the History List on the Explorer Bar in the left pane of the Internet Explorer display area (Figure 1–25).

Q&A

Why is the Explorer Bar often hidden from the Internet Explorer window?

When browsing the Web, it is important to reserve as much space as possible to display the Web pages in the display area. Continuously displaying the Explorer Bar will take precious screen real estate away from the Web page, possibly resulting in visitors needing to scroll the page horizontally to view all content.

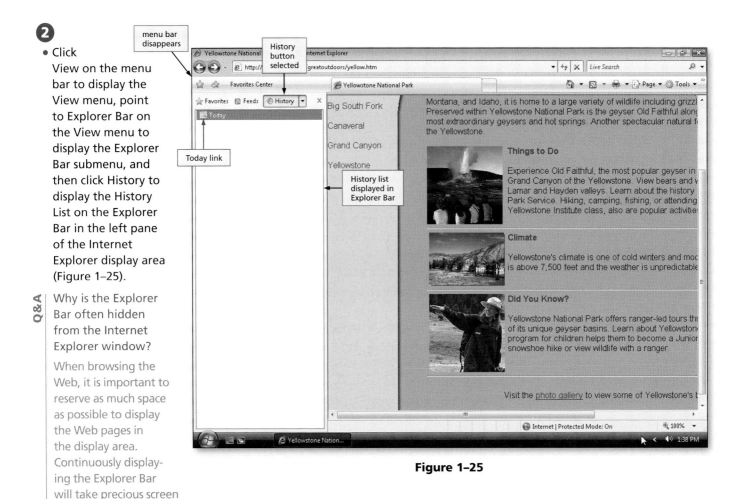

Figure 1–25

3

- Click Today in the History List to display a list of Web sites that have been accessed today (Figure 1–26).

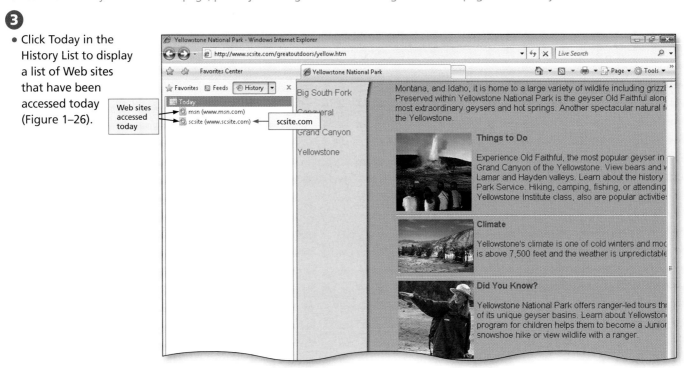

Figure 1–26

- Click scsite.com to display the list of Web pages that were accessed from scsite.com.

- Click Great Outdoors Travel to display the Great Outdoors Travel Web page (Figure 1–27).

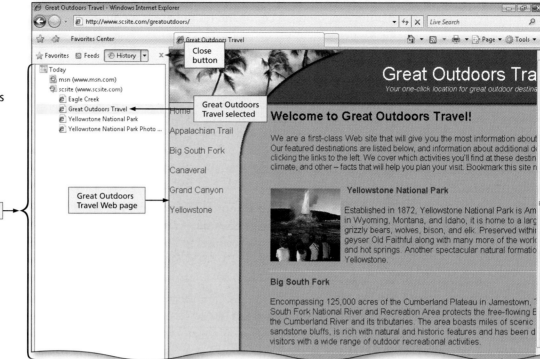

Figure 1–27

- Click the Close button on the Explorer Bar to close the Explorer Bar (Figure 1–28).

Figure 1–28

Other Ways

1. Click Tools on the Command Bar, point to Toolbars, click History
2. Press CTRL+SHIFT+H

If you do not have many pages on your History List or the page you want is only one or two pages away, you can display a Web page more quickly by using the Back and Forward buttons than by displaying the Explorer Bar and then selecting individual pages. If you have visited a large number of Web pages, however, you may find it easier to use the History List to find the precise page to display.

History Lists are useful for returning to a Web page you have visited recently. You can set the number of days Internet Explorer keeps the URLs in the History List by using the Internet Options command on the Tools menu. Because the History List does not keep a permanent list of Web pages you have visited, you should not use the History List to store the URLs of favorite or frequently visited pages.

You can see from the previous figures that URLs can be long and cryptic. It is easy to make a mistake while entering such URLs. Fortunately, Internet Explorer can keep track of favorite Web pages. You can store the URLs of favorite Web pages permanently in an area appropriately called the Favorites list.

Keeping Track of Favorite Web Pages

The Favorites feature of Internet Explorer allows you to save the URLs of Web pages you visit frequently. A **favorite** consists of the title of the Web page and the URL of that page. The title of the Web page is added to the Favorites Center. Your favorites appear in both the Favorites menu and the Explorer Bar.

To Add a Web Page to the Favorites Center

The following steps add a Web page to the Favorites Center, so that you easily can access the Web page in the future.

- Click the Add to Favorites button on the toolbar to display the Add to Favorites menu (Figure 1–29).

Figure 1–29

2

• Click the Add to Favorites command on the Add to Favorites menu to display the Add a Favorite dialog box (Figure 1–30).

3

• Click the Add button in the Add a Favorite dialog box to add the Great Outdoors Travel Web page to the Favorites Center.

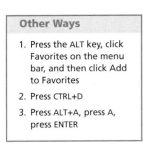 **Experiment**

• After you add the favorite, check the Favorites menu to verify that your new favorite appears in the list. Press the ALT key to display the menu bar, click the Favorites menu, verify that the favorite appears, and then press the ESC key twice to close the Favorites menu and hide the menu bar.

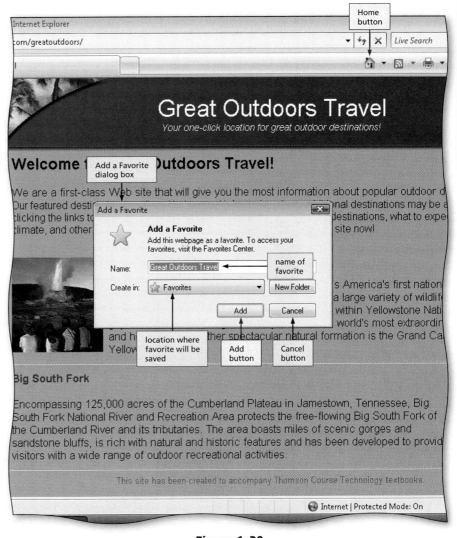

Figure 1–30

Other Ways

1. Press the ALT key, click Favorites on the menu bar, and then click Add to Favorites
2. Press CTRL+D
3. Press ALT+A, press A, press ENTER

In Figure 1–29, clicking the Organize Favorites command displays the Organize Favorites dialog box, which allows you to move, rename, organize, and delete your favorites.

If you plan to store many favorites on your computer, you might choose to give your favorites meaningful names by renaming them and store them in folders. In Figure 1–30, clicking the New Folder button adds a new folder to the Favorites list. Immediately after adding a new folder to the Favorites list, you can name the folder by typing an appropriate name and then pressing the ENTER key. After renaming the folder, you can drag an existing favorite to the folder to store the favorite in that folder. You also can change the name of a folder or favorite by clicking a folder or favorite, clicking the Rename button, typing the new name, and then pressing the ENTER key. For example, if you frequently visit many Web sites to read the news, you might choose to store the URLs of these sites as favorites in a News folder. A student, for example, may store school-related Web sites in an Academics folder.

BTW

Importing and Exporting Favorites
If you already have favorite Web sites set up on another computer, or wish to transfer your favorite Web sites to another computer, you can use Internet Explorer's Import/Export Wizard to preserve your favorites. Click the Add to Favorites button on the toolbar, click Import and Export on the Add to Favorites menu to start the Import/Export wizard. Click the Next button, and then follow the remaining steps in the wizard to import or export your favorites.

To Display the Home Page Using the Home Button

In many cases, individuals designate their home page as the Web page they most frequently visit. The Home button on the Command Bar provides a quick way to navigate to your home page. If you want to navigate back to your home page quickly and easily, perform the following steps to display the home page in Internet Explorer's display area.

- Click the Home button on the toolbar to display the MSN.com home page in the Windows Internet Explorer window (Figure 1–31). Your computer may display a different home page.

Figure 1–31

Q&A

Can I have more than one home page?

Yes. If you designate more than one Web page as your home page, Internet Explorer will open each home page in a separate tab when you open Internet Explorer, or when you click the Home button on the Command Bar. To create multiple home pages, click the Tools menu, click the Internet Options command, type the URL for each Web page on its own line in the Home page box, and then click the OK button.

Other Ways

1. Click drop-down arrow to the right of the Home button on Command Bar, click Home Page

2. On View menu point to Go To, click Home Page on Go To submenu

3. Press ALT+V, press G, press H

4. Press ALT+HOME

To Display a Web Page Using the Favorites Center

The Favorites Center is used to display favorite Web pages quickly, without having to navigate through several unwanted pages. Using a favorite to display a Web page is similar to using the History List to display a Web page. While you are browsing the Internet, you may want to access one of your favorites. The following steps display the Great Outdoors Travel home page by using the Favorites Center.

- Click the Favorites Center button on the toolbar to display the Explorer Bar.

- If necessary, click the Favorites button on the Explorer Bar to display the Favorites Center (Figure 1–32).

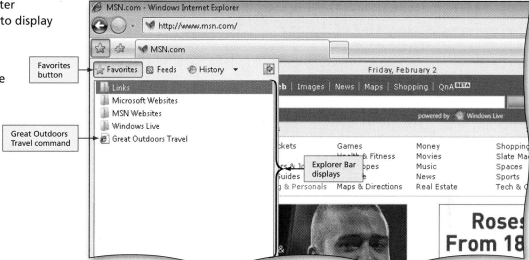

Figure 1–32

- Click the Great Outdoors Travel command in the Explorer Bar to display the Great Outdoors Travel Web page in the display area (Figure 1–33).

Figure 1–33

Other Ways
1. On Favorites menu click favorite
2. Press ALT+A, click favorite
3. Press CTRL+I, click favorite

Additional favorites are displayed in the Favorites Center shown in Figure 1–32. Folders included in the favorites list include the Links folder, the Microsoft Websites folder, the MSN Websites folder, and the Windows Live folder. Other folders and favorites may display in the Favorites Center on your computer.

To Remove a Web Page from the Favorites Center

You may have a variety of reasons for wanting to remove a favorite. With the World Wide Web changing every day, the URL that worked today may not work tomorrow. Perhaps you just do not want a particular Web site on your favorites list anymore, or maybe the list is getting too big to be meaningful. Once you decide that you no longer need a favorite, perform the following steps to delete the favorite.

- Click the Favorites Center button on the toolbar to display a list of your favorites on the Explorer Bar.

- Right-click the Great Outdoors Travel entry in the Favorites Center to display a shortcut menu containing the Delete command (Figure 1–34).

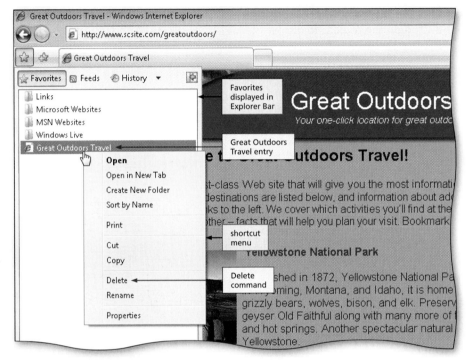

Figure 1–34

❷

- Click Delete on the shortcut menu to display the Delete File dialog box (Figure 1–35).

Q&A

Why does the dialog box tell me that I am deleting a file?

Internet Explorer and Windows Vista store your favorites as small text files in a special folder on your computer. When you add a favorite, you are creating a file. When you delete a favorite, you are deleting a file.

Figure 1–35

3

- Click the Yes button in the Delete File dialog box to remove the Great Outdoors Travel Web page from the Favorites Center.

- Click the Favorites Center button to display the Explorer Bar (Figure 1–36).

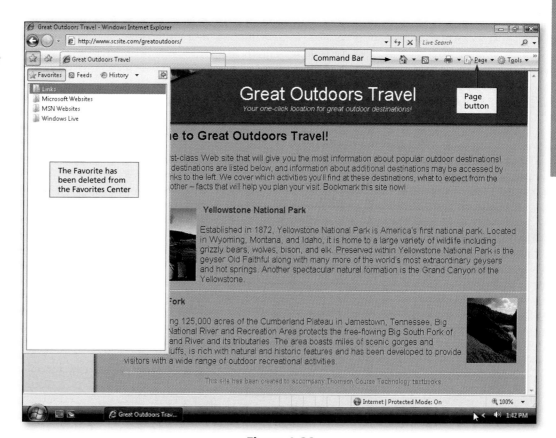

Figure 1–36

The steps required to delete a folder in the favorites list are the same as those required to delete a favorite. If you delete a folder, however, Internet Explorer also will delete all favorites stored in that folder. Because favorites are stored as files on your computer, deleting a folder or favorite will move it to Windows Vista's Recycle Bin. The Recycle Bin stores files marked for deletion before they are permanently deleted. While a file or folder is in the Recycle Bin, it can be restored by double-clicking the Recycle Bin icon on the desktop, clicking the item you wish to restore, and then clicking the Restore this item button. Because not all operating systems are configured to handle deleted items in the same manner, you should not delete a favorite or a folder unless you are sure that you no longer want it.

You have learned to create, use, manage, and remove favorites. Saving favorites is not the only way to save information you obtain using Internet Explorer. Some of the more important text and pictures you locate while displaying Web pages also can be worth saving.

Saving Information Obtained with Internet Explorer

Many different types of Web pages are accessible on the World Wide Web. Because these pages can help you gather information about areas of interest, you may wish to save the information you discover for future reference. The different types of Web pages and the various uses you have for the information require different methods of saving. Internet Explorer allows you to save an entire Web page, individual pictures, or selected pieces of text. Before saving a Web page or information from a Web page, you first should determine whether the information is free for you to use. If content on a Web page is protected by a copyright, or if it displays a copyright symbol, you should contact the Web page author to obtain permission before copying or using the content. Copying an image that is protected by a copyright could carry legal consequences. If you are not sure whether content is protected by a copyright, you should seek permission before duplicating it. The following pages illustrate how to save an entire Web page, how to save a single picture, and how to save text.

To Save a Web Page

One method of saving information on a Web page is to save the entire page. The following steps save the Great Outdoors Travel Home Page to your computer so you can access it even when you are not connected to the Internet.

- Click the Page button on the Command Bar to display the Page menu (Figure 1–37).

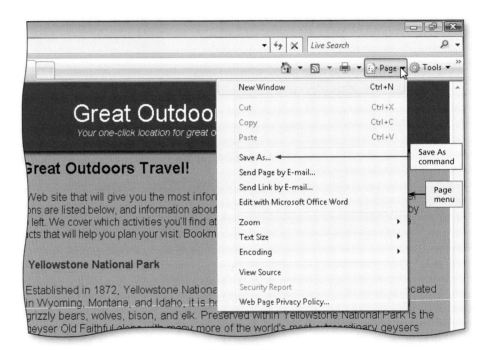

Figure 1–37

- Click Save As on the Page menu to display the Save Webpage dialog box. If necessary click the Browse Folders button, click the Documents button under the Favorite Links heading, and then click the Hide Folders button (Figure 1–38).

- Click the Save button in the Save Webpage dialog box to save the Web page to the Documents folder on your computer.

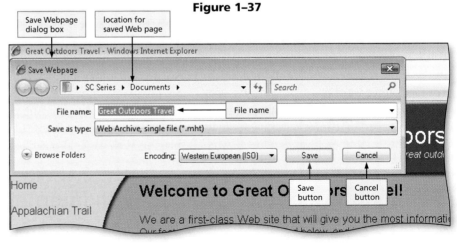

Figure 1–38

Other Ways

1. Press ALT+F, press A

Internet Explorer saves the instructions to display the saved Web page in the Great Outdoors Travel.mht file in the Documents folder on your computer. You can view the saved Web page in the Internet Explorer window by double-clicking the Great Outdoors Travel.mht file in your Documents folder. An .mht file is a Web archive file, capable of storing the text and graphics for a Web page in a single file.

Saving a Picture on a Web Page

You may want to save only an image located on a Web page. In the following steps, the Yellowstone National Park picture located on the Great Outdoors Travel Web page is saved in the Documents folder on your hard drive using the **Joint Photographic Experts Group (JPEG)** format. The JPEG file format is a method of encoding pictures on a computer. When you save a picture as a JPEG file, Internet Explorer can display it.

To Save a Picture on a Web Page

The following steps show how to save the Yellowstone National Park picture in the Pictures folder on your computer in the JPEG format using the file name yellowstone.jpg.

- Right-click the Yellowstone National Park picture on the Great Outdoors Travel Web page to display a shortcut menu containing the Save Picture As command (Figure 1–39).

Figure 1–39

2

• Click Save Picture As on the shortcut menu to display the Save Picture dialog box (Figure 1–40).

Figure 1–40

3

• If necessary, click the Browse Folders button to expand the Save Picture dialog box.

• If necessary, click the Pictures button in the Save Picture dialog box (Figure 1–41).

4

• Click the Save button in the Save Picture dialog box to save the picture in the Pictures folder on your computer and to close the Save Picture dialog box.

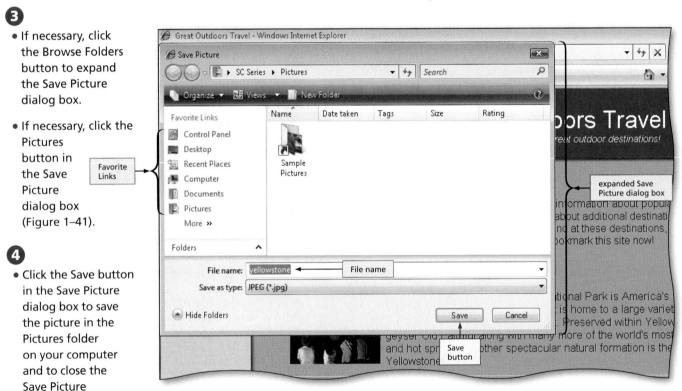

Figure 1–41

Q&A

Should I store all my pictures in the Pictures folder?

Yes. You can use folders to organize your pictures and you easily can back up the folders in the Pictures folder to another storage device for safekeeping. Three other folders (Documents, Music, and Videos) are available to store document, music, and video files.

Copying and Pasting Using the Clipboard

A third method of saving information, called the **copy and paste method**, allows you to copy an entire Web page, or portions of a page, and insert the information into any Windows document. The **Clipboard** is a storage area in main memory that temporarily holds the information being copied. The portion of the Web page you select is **copied** from the page to the Clipboard and then **pasted** from the Clipboard into the document. Information you copy to the Clipboard remains there until you add more information or clear it.

The following pages demonstrate how to copy text and pictures from the Yellowstone National Park Web page into a WordPad document using the Clipboard. **WordPad** is a word processing program that is supplied with Microsoft Windows Vista.

BTW

Setting a Picture as a Background
In addition to saving a picture, you also can set a picture as a background on your desktop by right-clicking the image and clicking Set as Background.

To Start WordPad

Before copying information from the Web page in Internet Explorer to the Clipboard, you first should start WordPad. The following steps start WordPad.

1

- Click the Start button on the Windows taskbar to display the Start menu.

- Click All Programs on the Start menu to display the All Programs list.

- Click Accessories on the All Programs list to display the Accessories list (Figure 1–42).

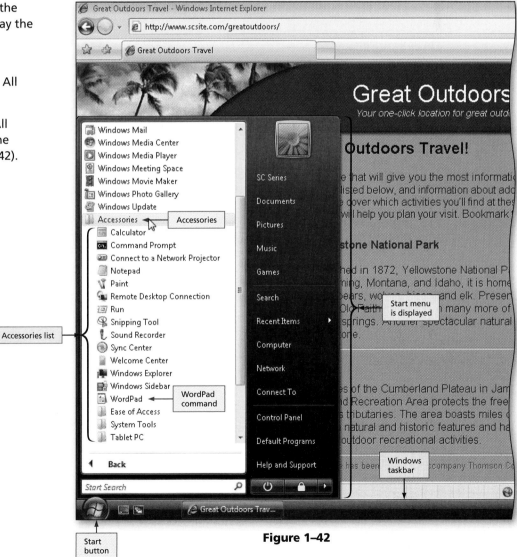

Figure 1–42

• Click WordPad to start WordPad (Figure 1–43).

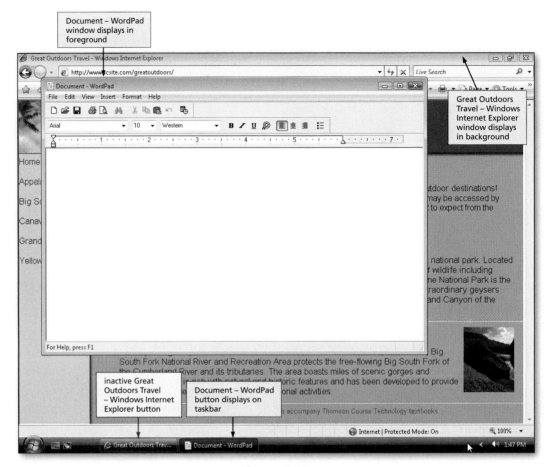

Figure 1–43

The Document - WordPad window appears on top of the Great Outdoors Travel - Windows Internet Explorer window. The Document - WordPad window is the active window. The **active window** is the window currently being used. A dark title bar identifies the active window. The Great Outdoors Travel - Windows Internet Explorer window is the inactive window. A light title bar identifies the **inactive window**.

To Display the Yellowstone National Park Web Page

Currently, the active Document - WordPad window displays on top of the inactive Great Outdoors Travel - Windows Internet Explorer window. After starting WordPad and before copying text from a Web page to the Clipboard, make the Great Outdoors Travel - Windows Internet Explorer window active and then display the Yellowstone National Park Web page. The following steps display the Yellowstone National Park Web page.

1

- Click the Great Outdoors Travel - Windows Internet Explorer button on the taskbar to activate the Great Outdoors Travel - Windows Internet Explorer window (Figure 1–44).

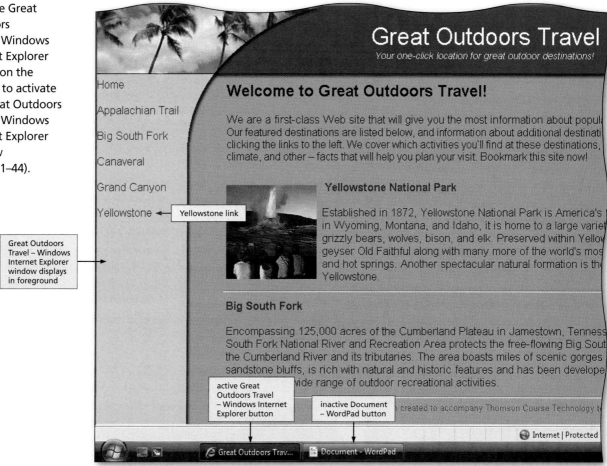

Figure 1–44

2

- Click the Yellowstone link on the Great Outdoors Travel Web page to display the Yellowstone National Park Web page (Figure 1–45).

Figure 1–45

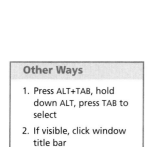

Other Ways

1. Press ALT+TAB, hold down ALT, press TAB to select

2. If visible, click window title bar

To Copy and Paste Text from a Web Page into a WordPad Document

With the Document - WordPad window open and the text you wish to copy contained on the Yellowstone National Park Web page, the next steps are to copy the text from the Yellowstone National Park Web page to the Clipboard, and then paste the text into the WordPad document. The following steps copy the text about Yellowstone National Park into the WordPad document.

- Position the mouse pointer (I-beam) to the left of the "E" in "Established" to prepare to select the text to be copied (Figure 1–46).

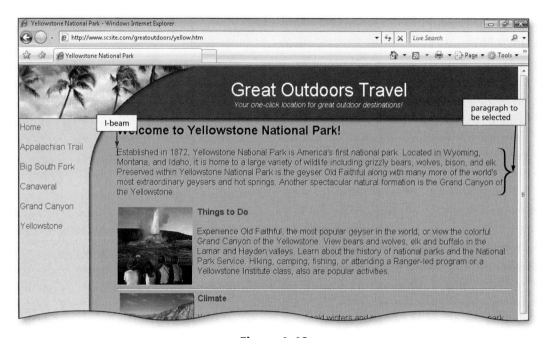

Figure 1–46

- Drag to select the text in the entire paragraph.

- Right-click the highlighted text to display a shortcut menu (Figure 1–47).

Figure 1–47

3

- Click Copy on the shortcut menu to copy the selected text to the Clipboard.

- Click the Document - WordPad button on the Windows taskbar to display the Document - WordPad window, and then right-click the empty text area in the Document - WordPad window to display a shortcut menu (Figure 1–48).

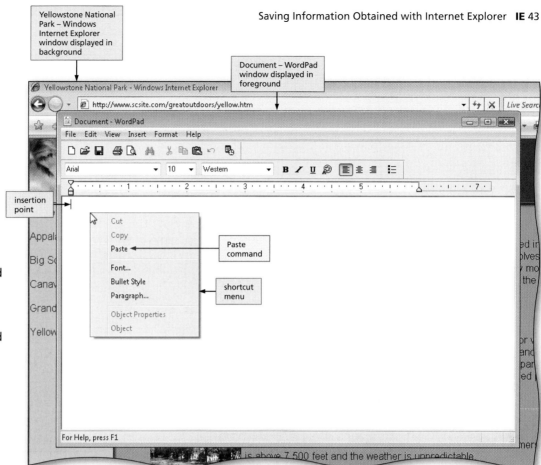

Figure 1–48

4

- Click Paste on the shortcut menu to paste the contents of the Clipboard in the Document - WordPad window (Figure 1–49).

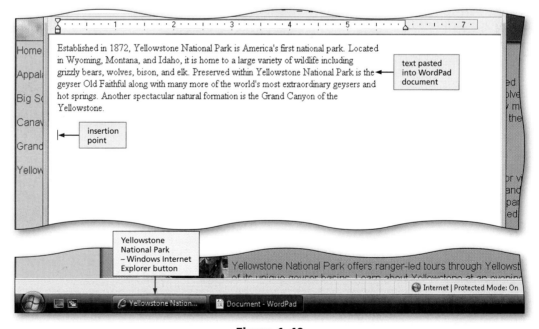

Figure 1–49

Other Ways
1. Select text, on Edit menu click Copy, select paste area, on Edit menu click Paste
2. Select text, on Page menu click Copy, select paste area, on Edit menu click Paste
3. Select text, press CTRL+C, select paste area, press CTRL+V
4. Select text, press ALT+E, press C, select paste area, press ALT+E, press P

Copy and Paste URLs
You can use the copy and paste operation to insert a URL that appears in the Address bar into a document or e-mail message. You also can copy a URL that appears in an e-mail message into the Address bar.

The text portion of the copy and paste operation is complete. The WordPad document contains a paragraph of text retrieved from a Web page.

To Copy and Paste a Picture from a Web Page into a WordPad Document

The steps to copy a picture from a Web page are similar to those used to copy and paste text. The following steps copy and then paste a picture from a Web page into a WordPad document.

1

- To activate the Yellowstone National Park Web page, click the Yellowstone National Park - Windows Internet Explorer button on the Windows taskbar.

- Click outside the selected text to deselect the text.

- Right-click the picture to the left of 'Things to Do' to display a shortcut menu (Figure 1–50).

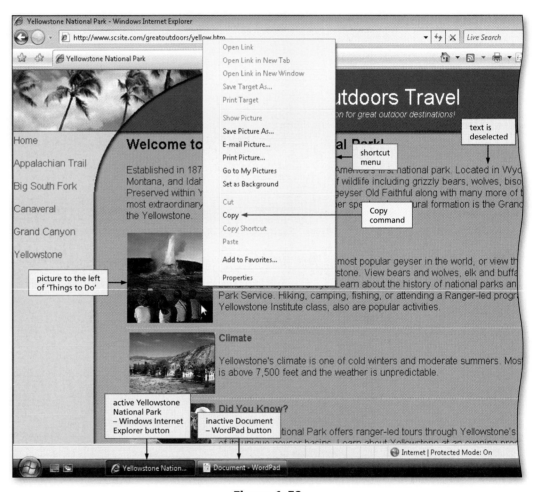

Figure 1–50

2

- Click Copy on the shortcut menu to copy the picture to the Clipboard.

- Activate the Document - WordPad window.

- Right-click an area below the insertion point in the Document - WordPad window to display a shortcut menu (Figure 1–51).

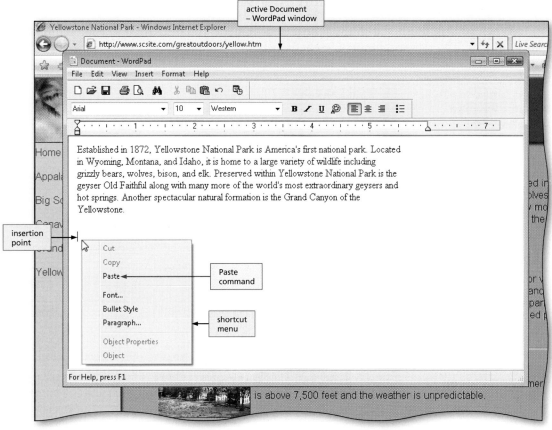

Figure 1–51

3

- Click Paste on the shortcut menu to paste the picture into the Document - WordPad window (Figure 1–52).

Figure 1–52

To Save the WordPad Document and Quit WordPad

When you are finished with the WordPad document, you can save it to your computer for later use and then quit WordPad. The following steps save the WordPad document using the Yellowstone National Park file name.

- Click the Save button on the WordPad toolbar in the Document - WordPad window to display the Save As dialog box (Figure 1–53).

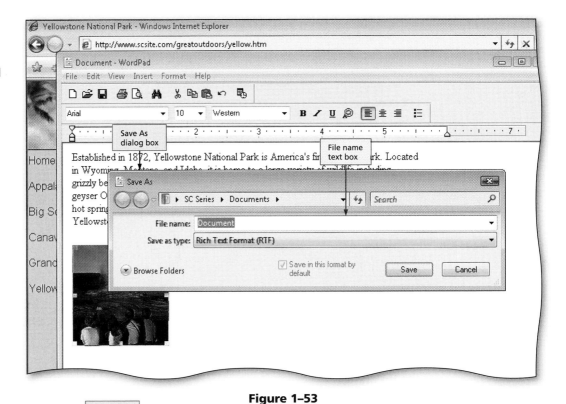

Figure 1–53

2

- Type Yellowstone National Park in the File name text box (Figure 1–54).

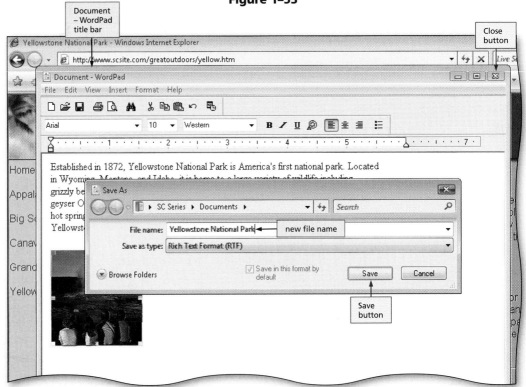

Figure 1–54

3

- Click the Save button in the Save As dialog box to save the WordPad document (Figure 1–55).

- Click the Close button on the Yellowstone National Park - WordPad title bar to quit WordPad.

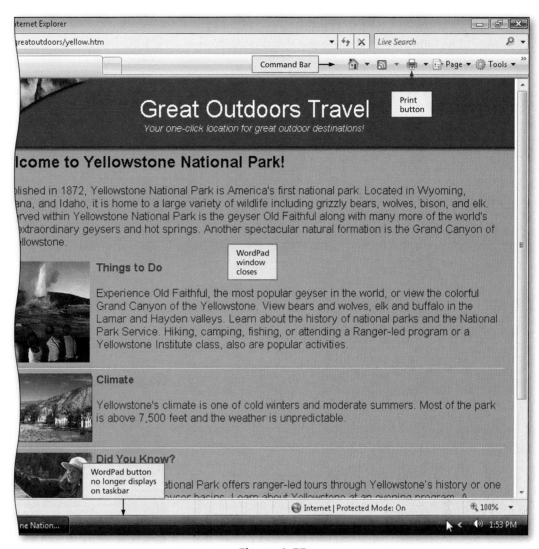

Figure 1–55

Printing a Web Page in Internet Explorer

As you visit Web sites, you may want to print some of the pages you view. A printed version of a Web page is called a **hard copy** or **printout**. You might want a printout for several reasons. First, to present the Web page to someone who does not have access to a computer, it must be in printed form. Second, people often like to keep Web page printouts for reference.

Other Ways

1. Press ALT+F, press A, type file name, press ENTER

2. Press CTRL+S, type file name, press ENTER

BTW

Printing
You can suppress the title and URL of a Web page that are displayed at the top of a printout using the Page Setup command on the File menu. The Header and Footer text boxes contain formatting codes that indicate what items are displayed.

To Print a Web Page

Internet Explorer's enhanced printing capability allows you to print both the text and picture portions of a Web page. The following steps print the Yellowstone National Park Web page.

- Ready the printer according to the printer instructions.

- Point to the Print button on the Command Bar (Figure 1–56).

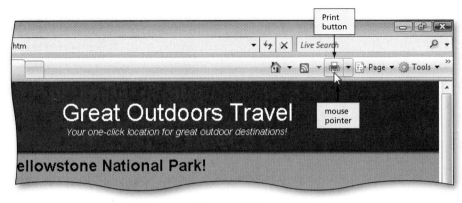

Figure 1–56

- Click the Print button on the Command Bar to begin printing the Web page.

- When the printer stops printing the document, retrieve the printouts, which should look like Figure 1–57.

Figure 1–57

Other Ways

1. On File menu click Print, click Print button

2. Press CTRL+P, click Print button

You also can click Print on the File menu to print a Web page. When you do this, a Print dialog box displays. The printing options available in the Print dialog box allow you to print the entire document, print selected pages of a document, print to a file, print multiple copies, change the printer properties, and cancel the print request.

BTW

Print Options
You can choose to print a table containing a list of all links on the Web page you are printing or all documents with links on the Web page. Click the Options tab in the Print dialog box and then click the Print all linked documents check box or Print table of links check box to print the documents or table.

Internet Explorer Help

Internet Explorer offers users many features and options. Although you will master some features and options quickly, it is not necessary for you to remember everything about all of them. Reference materials and other forms of assistance are available within **Internet Explorer Help**.

To Access Internet Explorer Help

The following steps use Internet Explorer Help to find more information about Uniform Resource Locators (URLs).

1

• To display the menu bar, press the ALT key.

• Click Help on the menu bar to display the Help menu (Figure 1–58).

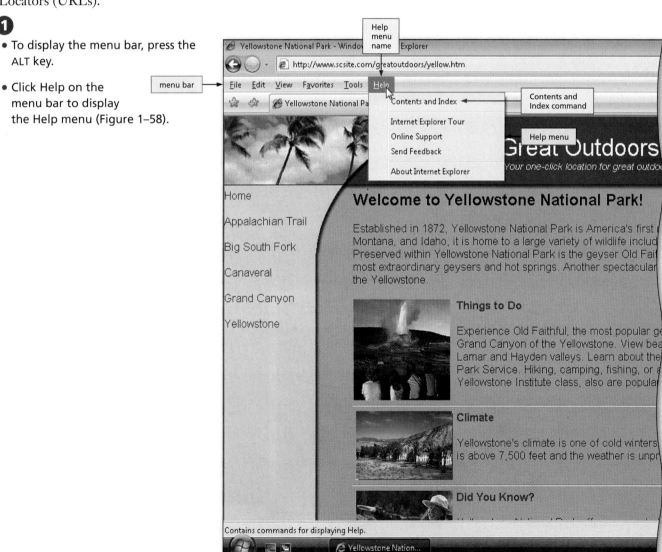

Figure 1–58

2

- Click Contents and Index on the Help menu to display the Windows Help and Support window (Figure 1–59).

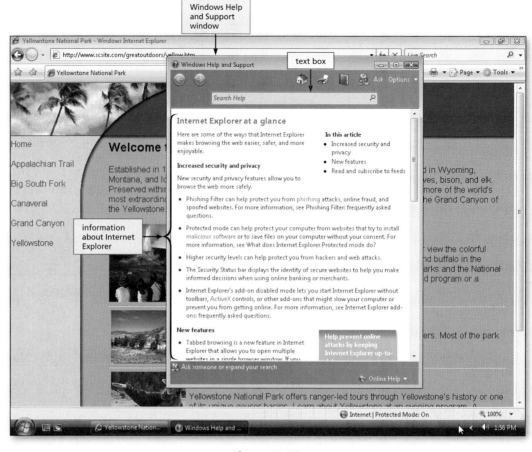

Figure 1–59

3

- Type `url` in the text box, and then press the ENTER key to display the search results matching your search text (Figure 1–60).

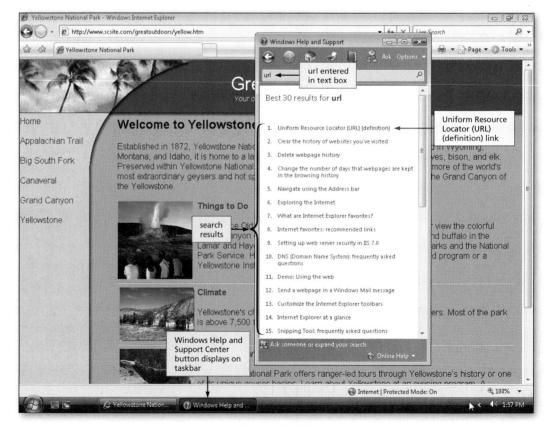

Figure 1–60

- Click the Uniform Resource Locator (URL) (definition) link in the list of Help topics to display information about uniform resource locators (Figure 1–61).

- When you are finished viewing the information, click the Close button on the right side of the title bar to close the Windows Help and Support window.

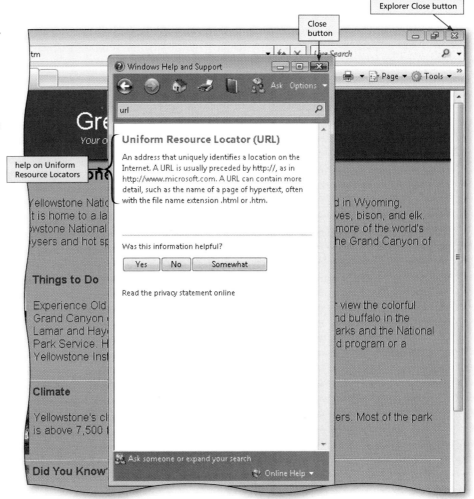

Figure 1–61

In Figure 1–59, buttons on the Help toolbar in the Windows Help and Support window allow you to perform activities such as going back to the most recent help topic, going forward to a help page you have visited prior to clicking the Back button, displaying the Windows Help and Support Center home page, printing the current page, requesting additional help, and changing Internet options.

The Help menu in Figure 1–58 on page IE 49 contains several other commands, which are summarized in Table 1–4.

Other Ways

1. Press ALT+H, press C
2. Press F1

Table 1–4 Commands on the Help Menu	
Menu Command	**Function**
Contents and Index	Displays Contents, Index, Search, and Favorites tabs
Internet Explorer Tour	Displays the Internet Explorer 7: Tour of new features Web page
Online Support	Displays Microsoft Help and Support Web site
Send Feedback	Displays Internet Explorer 7 support Web page containing answers to frequently asked questions and information for phone support
About Internet Explorer	Displays version, cipher strength, product ID, license information, and copyright information about Internet Explorer.

Quitting Internet Explorer

After browsing the World Wide Web and learning how to navigate Web sites, add favorites, copy and paste content, and print Web pages, Chapter 1 is complete.

To Quit Internet Explorer

The following steps quit Internet Explorer and return control to the Windows operating system.

- Click the Close button in the upper-right corner of the Windows Internet Explorer window to close the window (Figure 1–62).

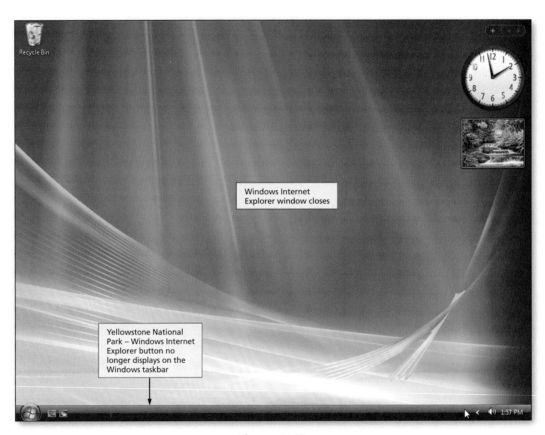

Windows Internet Explorer window closes

Yellowstone National Park – Windows Internet Explorer button no longer displays on the Windows taskbar

Figure 1–62

Other Ways

1. Double-click System menu icon at left end of title bar
2. On File menu click Exit
3. Press ALT+F, press X

Chapter Summary

Chapter 1 introduced you to the Internet and World Wide Web. You learned how to start Internet Explorer; use the History List, Favorites list, and buttons on the toolbar; and enter a URL to browse the Web. You learned how to add and remove Web pages on the Favorites list; copy and paste text from a Web page into a WordPad document; and print a Web page and save text, a picture, and an entire Web page to the hard drive. In addition, you learned how to use Internet Explorer Help to obtain help about Internet Explorer. The items listed below include all the new Internet Explorer skills you have learned in this chapter.

1. Start Internet Explorer (IE 11)
2. Browse the Web by Entering a URL (IE 16)
3. Refresh a Web Page (IE 21)
4. Use the Back and Forward Buttons to Find Recently Displayed Web Pages (IE 23)
5. Display a Web Page Using the Recent Pages List (IE 25)
6. Display a Web Page Using the History List (IE 27)
7. Add a Web Page to the Favorites Center (IE 30)
8. Display the Home Page Using the Home Button (IE 32)
9. Display a Web Page Using the Favorites Center (IE 33)
10. Remove a Web Page from the Favorites Center (IE 34)
11. Save a Web Page (IE 36)
12. Save a Picture on a Web Page (IE 37)
13. Start WordPad (IE 39)
14. Display the Yellowstone National Park Web Page (IE 41)
15. Copy and Paste Text from a Web Page into a WordPad Document (IE 42)
16. Copy and Paste a Picture from a Web Page into a WordPad Document (IE 44)
17. Save the WordPad Document and Quit WordPad (IE 46)
18. Print a Web Page (IE 48)
19. Access Internet Explorer Help (IE 49)
20. Quit Internet Explorer (IE 52)

Learn It Online

Test your knowledge of chapter content and key terms.

Instructions: To complete the Learn It Online exercises, start your browser, click the Address bar, and then enter the Web address `scsite.com/ie7/learn`. When the Internet Explorer 7 Learn It Online page is displayed, click the link for the exercise you want to complete and then read the instructions.

Chapter Reinforcement TF, MC, and SA
A series of true/false, multiple choice, and short-answer questions that test your knowledge of the chapter content.

Flash Cards
An interactive learning environment where you identify key terms from the chapter associated with displayed definitions.

Practice Test
A series of multiple-choice questions that test your knowledge of chapter content and key terms.

Who Wants To Be a Computer Genius?
An interactive game that challenges your knowledge of chapter content in the style of the television quiz show.

Wheel of Terms
An interactive game that challenges your knowledge of key terms from the chapter in the style of the television show *Wheel of Fortune*.

Crossword Puzzle Challenge
A crossword puzzle that challenges your knowledge of key terms presented in the chapter.

Apply Your Knowledge

Reinforce the skills and apply the concepts you learned in this chapter.

Browsing the World Wide Web Using URLs and Links
Problem: You work part-time for the Miami Herald, one of Florida's largest newspapers. Your editor has asked you to search for information on several informational Web sites and print the first page of each Web site.

Instructions: Perform the following tasks.

Part 1: Using the Instant Search Box to Find a Web Page
   1. If necessary, connect to the Internet and start Internet Explorer.

2. Click the Address bar, type www.fbi.gov in the box, and then press the ENTER key to display the Federal Bureau of Investigation's home page (Figure 1–63).

Figure 1–63

3. Click the Top Ten Fugitives link to display the Web page that contains the list of the ten most wanted fugitives.

4. Click the Print button on the Command Bar toolbar to print the Web page.

5. Use the Back button on the toolbar to display the FBI home page.

6. Click the Print button on the Command Bar to print the Web page.

7. Click the Address bar, type www.nbc.com in the box, and then press the ENTER key to display the NBC home page (Figure 1–64 on the next page).

Continued >

Apply Your Knowledge *continued*

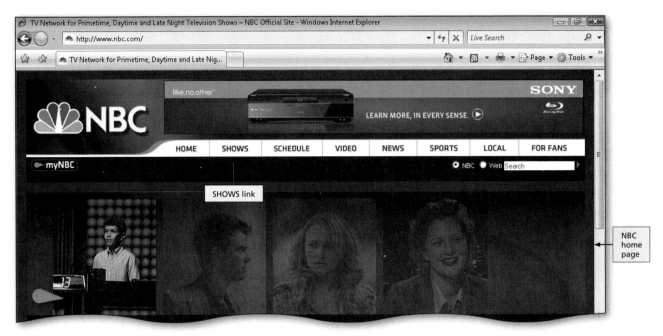

Figure 1–64

8. Point to the SHOWS link, and then click the Tonight Show | Jay link in the NBC Web site to display the Web page that lists the guest stars on the next Tonight Show.

9. Click the Print button on the Command Bar to print the Web page.

10. Click the Address bar, type www.weather.com in the box, and then press the ENTER key to display the weather.com home page (Figure 1–65).

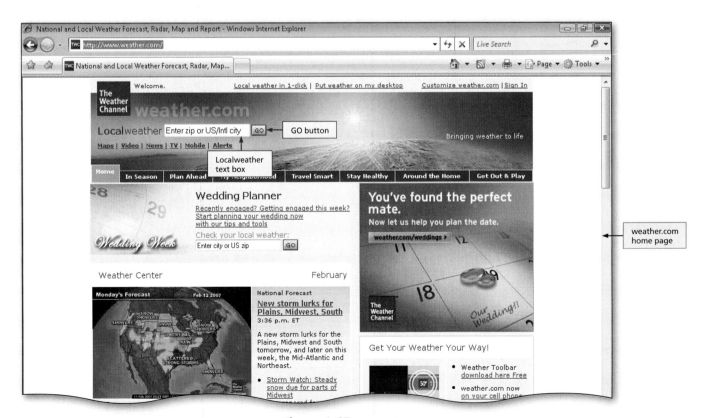

Figure 1–65

11. Type your ZIP code in the Localweather text box, and then click the GO button to display the Web page containing the weather report for your area.

12. Click the Print button on the Command Bar to print the Web page.

13. Click the Address bar, type www.cbs.com in the box, and then press the ENTER key to display the CBS home page (Figure 1–66).

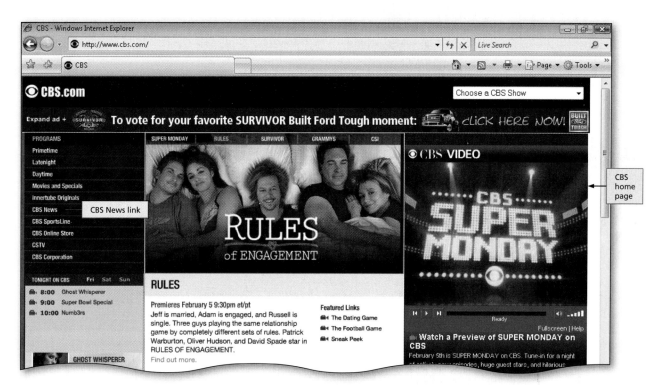

Figure 1–66

14. Click the CBS News link to display the page containing the top news stories.

15. Click the Print button on the toolbar to print the Web page.

Part 2: Using the History List to Find a Web Page
1. Click the Home button on the Command Bar to display your default home page.

2. Press the ALT key to display the menu bar, click the View menu, point to Explorer Bar, click the History command to display the History List, click Today, click nbc (www.nbc.com) folder name in the History List, and then click the TV Network for Primetime, Daytime and Late Night Television Shows - NBC Official Site entry to display the NBC home page.

3. Click the Print button on the Command Bar to print the Web page.

4. Click the Close button on the Explorer Bar.

Part 3: Using the Back Button Arrow to Find a Web Page
1. Click the Recent Pages arrow and then click the CBS home page entry on the menu to display the CBS home page.

2. Click the Print button on the Command Bar to print the Web page.

Continued >

Apply Your Knowledge *continued*

Part 4: Using the Address Bar Arrow to Find a Web Page

1. Click the Address bar arrow and then click http://www.weather.com in the Address list to display the weather.com home page.

2. Click the Print button on the Command Bar to print the Web page.

3. Click the Close button in the Internet Explorer window.

4. Discard the second page and subsequent pages of each Web site you printed. Organize the printed Web pages so that the home page is first and the Web page associated with the home page is second. Hand in the eight printed pages to your instructor.

Extend Your Knowledge

Extend the skills you learned in this chapter and experiment with new skills. You may need to use Help to complete the assignment.

Browsing the World Wide Web Using the Address Bar and Links

Perform the following tasks.

1. Use the Address bar to locate the official Symantec Corp. Home page. What did you have to type into the Address bar to locate this page?

2. Navigate to the Symantec Corp. Home page (Figure 1–67).

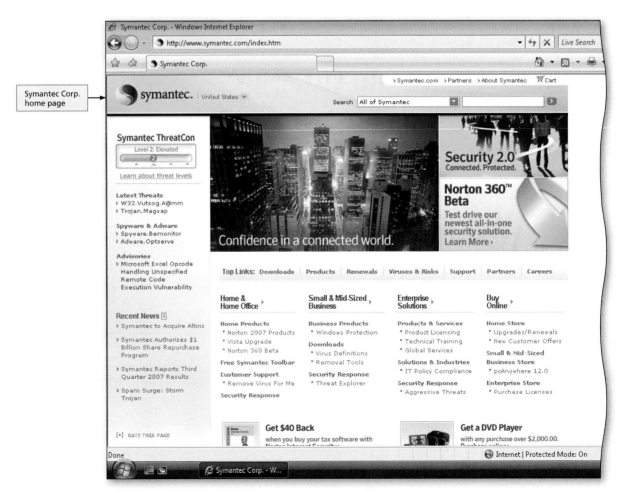

Figure 1–67

3. View the Web page in Print Preview. What buttons appear at the top of the Print Preview window? How many pages will it take to print this Web page?

4. Print the Symantec Corp. Home page from the Print Preview window, and then close the Print Preview window.

5. Use the links on the Symantec Corp. Home page to answer the following questions:

   a. What are five latest computer threats and risks?

   b. From looking at the list of latest threats and risks, about how long does it take Symantec to protect users from a threat once it has been detected?

   c. How does Symantec measure the severity of threats?

   d. What must you do to protect your computer from threats and risks? What programs does Symantec offer to help you protect your computer?

   e. What is Symantec ThreatCon?

   f. If your computer already has been infected by a threat, such as a virus or spyware, what should you do?

6. Use the History List to navigate back to the Symantec Corp. Home page.

7. Browse Symantec's Web site for a page that discusses the Netsky virus. Print the Web page.

8. Add the Web page to your Favorites Center.

9. Remove the Web page from your Favorites Center.

10. Organize your printed Web pages and submit them, along with the answers to the questions in this exercise, to your instructor.

In the Lab

Use Internet Explorer to navigate the World Wide Web by using the guidelines, concepts, and skills presented in this chapter. Labs are listed in order of increasing difficulty.

Lab 1: Using the History List to Locate Previously Viewed Pages

Problem: Your instructor would like you to practice browsing the Internet for Web sites and then adding them to the History List. As proof of completing this assignment, you should print the first page of each Web site you visit.

Instructions: Perform the following tasks.

Part 1: Clearing the History List

1. If necessary, connect to the Internet and start Internet Explorer.

Continued >

In the Lab *continued*

2. Click Tools on the Command Bar and then click Internet Options to display the Internet Options dialog box (Figure 1–68).

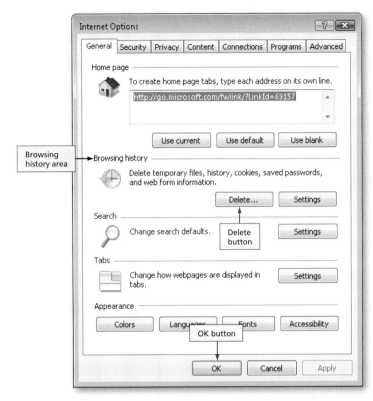

Browsing history area

Delete button

OK button

Figure 1–68

3. Click the Delete button in the Browsing history area, click the Delete history button in the Delete Browsing History dialog box, click the Yes button in the Delete History dialog box, and then click the Close button in the Delete Browsing History dialog box.

4. Click the OK button in the Internet Options dialog box.

Part 2: Browsing the World Wide Web
1. Click the Address bar, type www.mtv.com in the Address bar, and then press the ENTER key to display the MTV home page.
2. Click the Address bar, type www.ucf.edu in the Address bar, and then press the ENTER key to display the University of Central Florida home page.
3. Click the Address bar, type www.geocaching.com in the Address bar, and then press the ENTER key to display the Geocaching home page.

4. Click the Address bar, type www.espn.com in the Address bar, and then press the ENTER key to display the ESPN home page.

Part 3: Using the History List to Print a Web Page
1. Press the ALT key to display the menu bar, click the View menu on the menu bar, point to Explorer Bar, and then click the History command on the Explorer Bar submenu to display the History List (Figure 1–69).

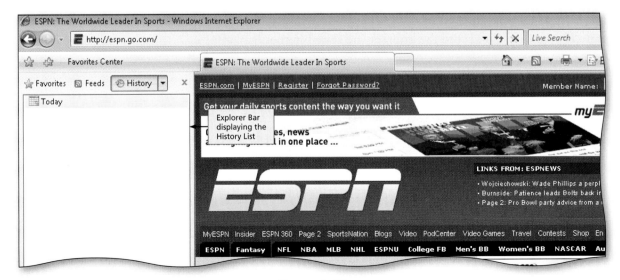

Explorer Bar displaying the History List

Figure 1–69

2. If necessary, click Today to view the list of Web sites you have visited today. Click the ucf (www.ucf.edu) folder in the History List and then click the University of Central Florida link. Print the Web page.

3. Click the mtv (www.mtv.com) folder in the History List and then click the MTV link. Print the Web page.

4. Click the espn.go (espn.go.com) folder in the History List and then click the ESPN link. Print the Web page.

5. Delete the geocaching (www.geocaching.com) folder by right-clicking the folder, clicking Delete on the shortcut menu, and then clicking the Yes button in the WARNING dialog box.

6. Click the Close button on the Explorer Bar.

Part 4: Clearing the History List
1. Click Tools on the Command Bar and then click Delete Browsing History to display the Delete Browsing History dialog box.

2. Click the Delete history button and then click the Yes button in the Delete History dialog box.

3. Click the Close button in the Delete Browsing History dialog box.

4. Click the Close button in the ESPN: The Worldwide Leader in Sports - Windows Internet Explorer window.

5. Hand in the printed Web pages to your instructor.

In the Lab

Lab 2: Adding, Viewing, Printing, and Removing Your Favorites
Problem: Your instructor would like you to practice browsing the Internet for Web sites and adding them to the Favorites Center. As proof of completing this assignment, print out the first page of each Web site you visit.

Instructions: Perform the following tasks.

Part 1: Creating a Folder in the Favorites Center
1. If necessary, connect to the Internet and start Internet Explorer.

Continued >

In the Lab *continued*

2. Press the ALT key to display the menu bar, click Favorites on the menu bar, and then click Organize Favorites on the Favorites menu to display the Organize Favorites dialog box. (Figure 1–70).

Figure 1–70

3. Click the New Folder button in the Organize Favorites dialog box to create a folder titled New Folder, type your first and last name as the folder name, and then press the ENTER key.

4. Click the Close button to close the Organize Favorites dialog box.

Part 2: Adding Favorites to Your Folder

1. Click the Address bar, type `www.state.gov` in the Address bar, and then press the ENTER key to display the U.S. Department of State home page.

2. Add the U.S. Department of State - Home Page favorite to the folder identified by your name by clicking the Add to Favorites button on the toolbar, and then click Add to Favorites. Click the Create in list arrow to display the Create in list (Figure 1–71).

Figure 1–71

3. Click your folder in the Create in list and then click the Add button.

4. Click the Address bar, type `www.expedia.com` in the Address bar, and then press the ENTER key to display the Expedia.com home page.

5. Add this Web page to your folder.

6. Click the Home button on the Command Bar to display your default home page.

Part 3: Displaying and Printing a Favorite from Your Folder

1. Click the Favorites button on the toolbar to display the Favorites Center. If necessary, click the Favorites button in the Favorites Center.

2. Click your folder in the Favorites Center and then click US Department of State - Home Page.

3. Print the Web page.

4. If necessary, click the Favorites button on the toolbar to display the Favorites Center.

5. Click Expedia Travel: Cheap Airfare, Hotels, Car Rental, Vacations & Cruises in the Favorites Center.

6. Print the Web page.

Part 4: Deleting a Folder in the Favorites Center

1. If necessary, display the Favorites Center.

2. Right-click your folder name, click the Delete command on the shortcut menu, and then click the Yes button in the Delete Folder dialog box.

3. If necessary, close the Favorites Center.

4. Verify that you have deleted your folder.

5. Click the Close button in the Windows Internet Explorer window.

6. Hand in the two printed pages to your instructor.

In the Lab

Lab 3: Printing and Saving the Current U.S. Weather Map

Problem: You are interested in finding a current United States weather map to use on a road trip starting in Seattle, Washington, and ending in Manchester, New Hampshire. You want to print the map and save it on your hard drive.

Instructions: Perform the following tasks.

1. If necessary, connect to the Internet and start Internet Explorer.

2. Type www.weather.com in the Address bar and then press the ENTER key to display the weather. com home page.

3. Scroll the home page to display the Select a Map drop-down. Select U.S. Current Temperatures from the list to display an enlarged weather map for the United States (Figure 1–72).

Figure 1–72

4. Right-click the weather map, click Print Picture on the shortcut menu, and then click the Print button in the Print dialog box to print the weather map.

5. Right-click the weather map and click Save Picture As on the shortcut menu to display the Save Picture dialog box. Click the Documents link in the left pane of the Save Picture dialog box, click the File name text box, type U.S. Weather map, and then click the Save button to save the picture on your hard drive.

6. Click the Close button to close the Windows Internet Explorer window.

7. Hand in the printed weather map to your instructor.

In the Lab

Lab 4: Collecting Biographical Information

Problem: To complete an assignment in history class, you must locate the Biography.com Web site and select an individual whose biography is on the Web site. When you find the biography of your chosen individual, copy his or her picture and the text of the biography into WordPad, and then print the WordPad document.

Instructions: Perform the following tasks.

Part 1: Retrieving a Web Page

1. If necessary, connect to the Internet and start Internet Explorer.

2. Type www.biography.com in the Address bar and then press the ENTER key to display the home page of the Biography.com Web site (Figure 1–73).

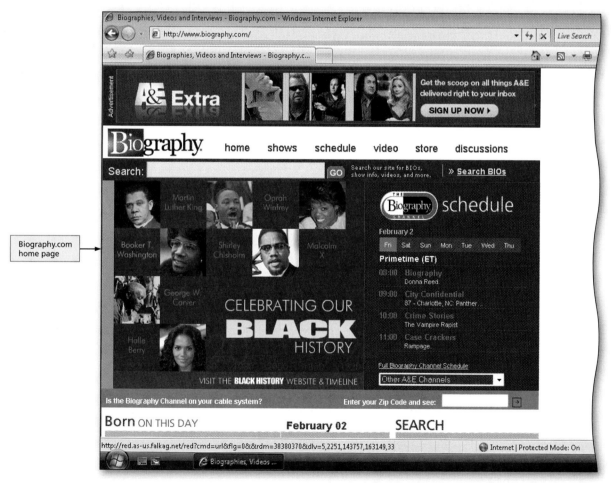

Figure 1–73

Continued >

In the Lab *continued*

3. Using the links on the Web site, search for the biography of an individual in whom you are interested. (Suggestions: Thomas Edison, Mia Hamm, Martin Luther King, Jennifer Lopez, Oprah, Elvis Presley, Eleanor Roosevelt, Tiger Woods)

Part 2: Copying a Picture and Text to Microsoft WordPad

1. If a picture of the individual is available, copy the picture to the Clipboard.

2. Start Microsoft WordPad.

3. Paste the picture from the Clipboard into the WordPad document, click anywhere off the picture, and then press the ENTER key.

4. Switch back to the Windows Internet Explorer window.

5. If necessary, click the link that contains the biography.

6. Copy the biography text to the Clipboard.

7. Click the Document - WordPad button on the taskbar.

8. Paste the text on the Clipboard into the WordPad document.

9. Save the WordPad document on your hard drive using the file name Biography Assignment.

10. Print the WordPad document.

11. Close the WordPad and Windows Internet Explorer windows.

12. Hand in the WordPad document to your instructor.

In the Lab

Lab 5: Searching the Web for a Job in E-Commerce

Problem: You are job hunting for a position that uses your expertise in e-commerce. Instead of using the newspaper to find a job, you decide to search for jobs on the Internet. You decide to visit three Web sites in hopes of finding the perfect job.

Instructions: Perform the following tasks.

1. If necessary, connect to the Internet and start Internet Explorer.

2. Click the Address bar, type www.computerjobs.com, and then press the ENTER key to display the computerjobs.com home page (Figure 1–74).

Figure 1–74

3. When the computerjobs.com home page displays, type `e-commerce` in the keyword search text box and then press the ENTER key. When the first page of the e-commerce listings displays, print it.

4. Type `www.monster.com` in the Address bar and then press the ENTER key.

5. When the Monster home page appears, click the Find Jobs link. If you are asked to sign up for a Monster account, click "No, thank you" and then click the Next button. Type `e-commerce` in the Keyword(s) box and then press the ENTER key. If a special offer displays, click the "No, thank you" link. When the first page of the e-commerce listings displays, print it.

6. Type `www.careerbuilder.com` in the Address bar and then press the ENTER key.

7. When the careerbuilder.com page displays, type `e-commerce` in the Keywords box, and then press the ENTER key. When the first page of the e-commerce listings displays, print it.

8. Close the Windows Internet Explorer window.

In the Lab

Lab 6: Using Windows Help and Support to Find Information about Internet Explorer

Problem: Because you do not know much about Windows Help and Support, you decide to learn more by using it to search for the following topics: cookies, AutoComplete, certificates, content advisor, and shortcut keys.

Instructions: Use Windows Help and Support to perform the following tasks.

1. If necessary, connect to the Internet and start Internet Explorer.

2. Press the F1 key to display the Windows Help and Support window, which contains general information about Internet Explorer (Figure 1–75).

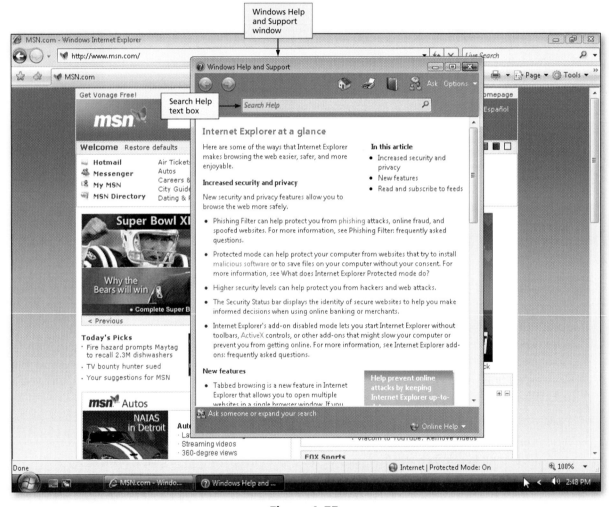

Figure 1–75

3. Type cookies in the Search Help text box, press the ENTER key, and browse the topics necessary to answer the following questions.

   a. What is a cookie?

   b. What does a cookie contain?

4. Select the text in the text box, type `autocomplete` in the box, and browse the search results to answer the following questions.

    a. What does the AutoComplete feature save?

    b. What does AutoComplete do?

5. Select the text in the text box, type `certificates` in the box, and browse the search results to answer the following questions.

    a. List two types of certificates.

    b. What is EFS?

6. Select the text in the text box, type `content advisor` in the box, and browse the search results to answer the following question.

    a. What is the purpose of Content Advisor?

7. Select the text in the text box, type `shortcut keys` in the box, and browse the search results to answer the following questions.

    a. What is the shortcut key to go to the next Web page?

    b. What is the shortcut key to refresh the current Web page?

    c. What is the shortcut key to stop downloading a Web page?

8. Click the Close button in the Windows Help and Support window.

9. Click the Close button in the Windows Internet Explorer window.

10. Submit the answers to the questions to your instructor.

Cases and Places

Apply your creative thinking and problem solving skills to use the Internet to find the information you need.

● Easier ●● More Difficult

● 1: Browse the Web for a New Car

Your old car broke down and you are in the market for a new one. Type the URL autos.msn.com to display the MSN Autos home page. Select your favorite make and model and then click the Go button to search for a new car. Select two competitors of the car you chose. Print the information on your favorite car and its two competitors.

● 2: Browse the Web for Stock Information

Your uncle would like to invest in the stock market. He has asked you to find fundamental stock information about Microsoft Corporation (MSFT), Netflix (NFLX), FuelCell Energy Inc. (FCEL), and TiVo Inc. (TIVO). Use the Yahoo! Finance Web site (finance.yahoo.com) to obtain today's stock price, dividend rate, daily volume, 52-week range, and the P/E (price earnings ratio). To display this information, enter the stock symbol and click the Get Quotes button to display the information. Print the detailed results for each stock. In addition, when the stock information for Microsoft displays, click the first Headline and print the page.

●● 3: Browsing the Web for Vacation Specials

You are planning a vacation to Montego Bay, Jamaica. You want to leave exactly one month from today and plan to stay seven days, including the travel days. Check with at least two different travel Web sites such as orbitz.com and expedia.com for travel specials to Montego Bay. Print any Web pages containing flight information and then summarize the information you find in a brief report.

●● 4: Shopping Online for a Computer

You have decided to purchase a computer online. You plan to spend between $800 and $1,200 for a computer with a monitor and a printer. Visit three online computer stores, such as HP (hp.com), Dell (dell.com), and Gateway (gateway.com). On each site, find a computer that sells for the amount you plan to spend. For each site, print the page that provides the computer features and price. Compare the three computers. Which one is the best buy? Why?

●● 5: Browsing the Web for Product Information

Although Internet Explorer may be the most widely used Web browser, it is not the only Web browser in use today. Using the Internet, computer magazines, newspapers, or other resources, prepare a brief report about three other Web browsers in use today. Describe their features, differences, and similarities.

●● 6: Comparing Newspaper Web Sites

Working Together

Have each member of your group visit a daily newspaper Web site, such as the *New York Times* (nytimes.com), *Chicago Tribune* (chicagotribune.com), *Los Angeles Times* (latimes.com), *Miami Herald* (miamiherald.com), and a local newspaper's Web site. Print at least one page from each newspaper site. Compare the latest headline news. Navigate through each site. How are the newspaper sites similar and dissimilar? Which newspaper has the best Web site? Why? Present your findings to the class.

2 Web Research Techniques and Search Engines

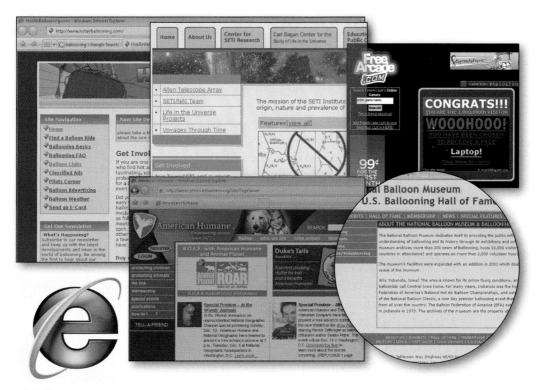

Objectives

You will have mastered the material in this chapter when you can:

- Describe the twelve general categories of Web sites
- Evaluate a Web resource
- Describe the three basic types of search tools
- Search the Web using both a directory and keywords
- Use tabbed browsing to view multiple Web pages in one window
- Customize and refine a search
- Describe the techniques used for successful keyword searches

- Describe how to create a working bibliography
- Compile a list of works cited for Web resources
- Search the Web for addresses, maps, definitions, and pictures
- Use the Instant Search box to search for a Web page
- Use the Address bar to search for a Web page or view folders on the computer

2 | Web Research Techniques and Search Engines

Introduction

Research is an important tool for success in an academic career. Writing papers, preparing speeches, and doing homework assignments are all activities that rely heavily on research. When researching, you are seeking information to support an idea or position, to prove a point, or to learn about a topic or concept. Traditionally, research was accomplished using books, newspapers, periodicals, and other materials found in libraries. The World Wide Web provides a new and useful resource for supplementing the traditional print materials found in the library. There currently are billions of Web pages, up from just a few million pages in 1994.

While the Web is a valuable resource, you should not rely solely on the Web for your research. The information found on Web pages is not always up-to-date, accurate, or verifiable. In addition, Web sites change quite frequently, which means Web pages may become unavailable.

This chapter demonstrates successful techniques for locating information about hot air ballooning on the Web and then evaluating the information for its usefulness as a source.

Overview

As you read this chapter, you will learn how to search the Web and use Internet Explorer by performing these general tasks:

- Search the Web, using directories and keywords
- Use tabbed browsing
- Refine a Web search, using advanced search techniques
- Evaluate a Web resource
- Create a working bibliography

Plan Ahead

Internet Research Guidelines
Internet research involves searching for Web sites using appropriate search engines and search criteria as well as evaluating your search results for timeliness and accuracy. Understanding search techniques will help you find relevant Web sites. Before starting your research, you should consider these general guidelines:

1. **Determine the information you need.** Before you can effectively search the Internet for information and locate relevant Web sites, you must determine what information you will need. You should also consider whether you are looking for factual information or an opinion. If you are seeking factual information, be sure to search credible Web sites.

2. **Determine an appropriate search method.** Many search resources exist on the Internet. Before deciding on a site or sites to perform your search, you should learn about the types of searches that each search engine offers. You also can search the Internet from your Web browser, without navigating first to a Web site that is designed to perform searches.

(continued)

(continued)

**Plan
Ahead**

3. **Determine a search engine that will find Web sites matching your search criteria.** The Internet contains Web sites that allow you to search for information, addresses, maps, pictures, and so on. Some Web sites may be better for performing certain types of searches than others. For example, some users may prefer to find the definition of a word using the dictionary.com Web site. If you have never searched the Internet, you may consider experimenting with various search engines before finding the one that you prefer.

4. **Determine whether the information you find is accurate, up-to-date, and valid.** Anyone can post information on the Internet, so it is important that you evaluate the accuracy of any information you plan to use from an Internet source. In addition, because some Web pages on the Internet date back many years, you should also evaluate the information for currency. The Web can be an extremely valuable resource for information, but you must know where to look.

5. **Determine how you will need to cite your work.** If you are performing research on the Internet to write a paper for a class or to submit a report to your boss, you should plan to cite the sources you utilize. When you submit a report with information from various outside sources, you typically will need to follow a standard documentation style such as **Modern Language Association (MLA)** or **American Psychological Association (APA).** It might be helpful to first obtain information on the style that you are required to use before beginning your Internet research.

When necessary, more specific details concerning the above guidelines are presented at appropriate points in the chapter.

Types of Web Resources

Web sites are organized by content into twelve categories: portal, news, informational, business/marketing, educational, entertainment, advocacy, blog, wiki, online social network, content aggregator, and personal (Figure 2–1 on the next page). In addition, the Web provides other resources through which you can access useful information when doing research. The following sections describe the types of Web sites and other resources.

Portals

A **portal** is a Web site that offers a variety of Internet services from a single, convenient location (Figure 2–1a on the next page). Most portals offer the following free services: search engine and/or directory; news, sports, and weather; Web publishing; reference tools such as yellow pages, stock quotes, and maps; shopping; and e-mail and other forms of online communications. See Table 2–1 on page IE 75 for a list of popular portals.

Many portals have online communities. An **online community** is a Web site that joins a specific group of people with similar interests or relationships. These communities may offer online photo albums, chat rooms, and other services to facilitate communications among members. A wireless portal is a portal designed for Internet-enabled mobile devices.

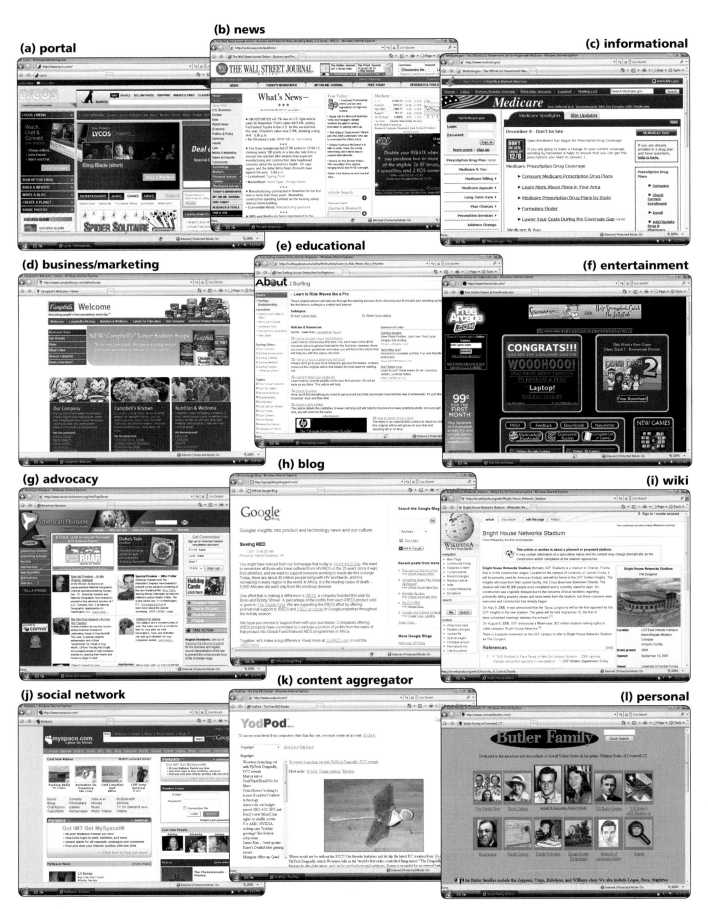

Figure 2–1 Types of Web sites

Table 2–1 Popular Portals and Their URLs

Portal	URL	Portal	URL
AltaVista	altavista.com	HotBot	hotbot.com
America Online	aol.com	LookSmart	looksmart.com
Euroseek.com	euroseek.com	Lycos	lycos.com
Excite	excite.com	Microsoft Network	msn.com
Go.com	go.com	Netscape	netscape.com
Google	google.com	Yahoo!	yahoo.com

News Web Sites

A news Web site contains newsworthy material including stories and articles relating to current events, life, money, sports, and the weather (Figure 2–1b). Many magazines and newspapers have Web sites that provide content that has appeared in the print edition as well as additional online-only content. Television and radio stations also maintain news Web sites.

Informational Web Sites

An informational Web site contains factual information (Figure 2–1c). Many United States government agencies have informational Web sites that provide information about such topics as the census, tax codes, and the federal budget. Other organizations provide information such as public transportation schedules and published research findings.

Business/Marketing Web Sites

A business/marketing Web site contains content that promotes or sells products or services (Figure 2–1d). Nearly every business has a business/marketing Web site. Allstate Insurance Company, Dell Inc., General Motors Corporation, Kraft Foods Inc., and Walt Disney Company all have Web sites to promote their businesses and market products and services. Many of these companies also allow you to purchase products or services online.

Educational Web Sites

An educational Web site offers exciting, challenging avenues for formal and informal teaching and learning (Figure 2–1e). On the Web, you can learn how airplanes fly or how to cook a meal. For a more structured learning experience, companies provide online training to employees, and colleges offer online classes and degrees. Instructors often use the Web to enhance classroom teaching by publishing course materials, grades, and other pertinent class information online.

Entertainment Web Sites

An entertainment Web site offers an interactive and engaging environment (Figure 2–1f). Popular entertainment Web sites offer music, videos, sports, games, sweepstakes, chats, and more. Sophisticated entertainment Web sites often partner with other technologies. For example, you can cast your vote about a topic on a television show on the show's accompanying Web site.

Advocacy Web Sites

An advocacy Web site contains content that describes a cause, opinion, or idea (Figure 2–1g on page IE 74). These Web sites usually present views of a particular group or association. Sponsors of advocacy Web sites include such organizations as the Democratic National Committee, the Republican National Committee, and the Society for the Prevention of Cruelty to Animals.

Blogs

A **blog**, short for Web log, is an informal Web site consisting of time-stamped articles, or posts, in a diary or journal format, usually listed in reverse chronological order (Figure 2–1h on page IE 74). A blog that contains video clips is called a video blog, or vlog. The term blogosphere refers to the worldwide collection of blogs, while vlogosphere refers to all vlogs worldwide. A photo blog contains a collection of photographs. An individual may choose to post pictures of his or her most recent vacation to a photo blog for everyone to see.

Blogs reflect the interests, opinions, and personalities of the author, called the blogger or vlogger (for vlog author), and sometimes of individuals viewing the blogs. It is important to note that because blogs represent opinions, the content may not be factual.

Blogs have become an important means of worldwide communication. Businesses create blogs to communicate with employees, customers, and vendors. Teachers create blogs to collaborate with other teachers and students. Home users create blogs to share aspects of their personal life with family, friends, and others.

Wikis

A **wiki** is a collaborative Web site that allows users to create, add to, modify, or delete the Web site content via their Web browser. While most wikis are open to modification by the general public, some nonpublic wikis exist that are used by project teams to communicate on large, complex projects. Wikis usually collect recent edits on a Web page so a moderator can review them for accuracy. The difference between a wiki and a blog is that readers of blogs cannot modify original posts made by the blogger. However, a person viewing a wiki may have the option to change the content originally posted by an author. A popular wiki is Wikipedia, a free Web encyclopedia (Figure 2–1i on page IE 74).

Online Social Networks

An **online social network**, also called a **social networking Web site**, is a Web site that encourages members in its online community to share their interests, ideas, stories, photos, music, and videos with other registered users (Figure 2–1j on page IE 74). Most include chat rooms, newsgroups, and other communications services. Popular social networking Web sites include Facebook, Friendster, and MySpace, which alone has more than 12 million visitors each day. A **media sharing Web site** is a specific type of online social network that enables members to share media such as photos, music, and videos. Flickr, Fotki, and Webshots are popular photo sharing communities; Yahoo! Video and YouTube are popular video sharing communities.

Content Aggregators

A **content aggregator** is a business that gathers and organizes Web content and then distributes, or feeds, the content to subscribers for free or a fee. Examples of distributed content include news, music, video, and pictures. Subscribers select content in which they are interested. Whenever this content changes, it is downloaded automatically (pushed) to the subscriber's computer or mobile device.

RSS 2.0, which stands for Really Simple Syndication, is a specification that content aggregators use to distribute content to subscribers (Figure 2–1k on page IE 74). Atom is another specification sometimes used by content aggregators to distribute content. You also may find that online news outlets and blogs offer RSS. Chapter 3 covers RSS in greater detail.

Personal Web Sites

A private individual or family not usually associated with any organization may maintain a personal Web site or just a single Web page (Figure 2–1l on page IE 74). People publish personal Web pages for a variety of reasons. Some are job hunting. Others simply want to share life experiences with the world. Some authors of personal Web sites may now add updates to their Web pages in a blog-type format. It may be advantageous to post a personal Web page if you have a large family and would like an easy way to keep in touch or post updates about yourself. In addition, individuals seeking jobs that have a computer requirement may choose to post an online resume for their employers to view. Because the Web is accessible to everyone, you should not post too much personal information on your personal Web site.

Other Web Resources

A number of other resources where you will find useful information are available on the Web. File transfer protocol (FTP) sites, newsgroups, and for-profit database services all contain information and files that you can use for research purposes.

Papers, documents, manuals, and complete ready-to-execute programs are available using FTP. **File transfer protocol (FTP)** is an Internet standard that permits file uploading and downloading (transferring) with other computers on the Internet. **Downloading** is the process of transferring documents, graphics, and other objects from a computer on the Internet to your computer. Uploading is the opposite of downloading; that is, **uploading** is the process of transferring documents, graphics, and other objects from your computer to another computer on the Internet.

A **newsgroup** is an online area in which users have written discussions about a particular subject. Many experts and professionals read the threads in newsgroups pertaining to their areas of expertise and are willing to answer questions and supply information. To participate in a discussion, or **thread**, a user sends a message to the newsgroup, and other users in the newsgroup read and reply to the message. While some newsgroups may require that you access them through a special program, other newsgroups are available simply by visiting a Web site. For example, Yahoo! Groups and Google Groups provide easy access to discussions about almost any topic. Some major topic areas include news, recreation, society, business, science, and computers.

Newsgroups
For more information about accessing newsgroups, see Chapter 3 of this book.

A number of **database services**, such as Dow Jones and LexisNexis (Figure 2–2) are now available on the Web. Previously, users of these services needed specialized software to access these databases. For a fee, these database services allow you to search a wide variety of sources, including publications and journals, financial and public records, and legal documents. Colleges and universities often subscribe to database services and make the search services available to faculty, staff, and students. Ask a librarian how to access these database services.

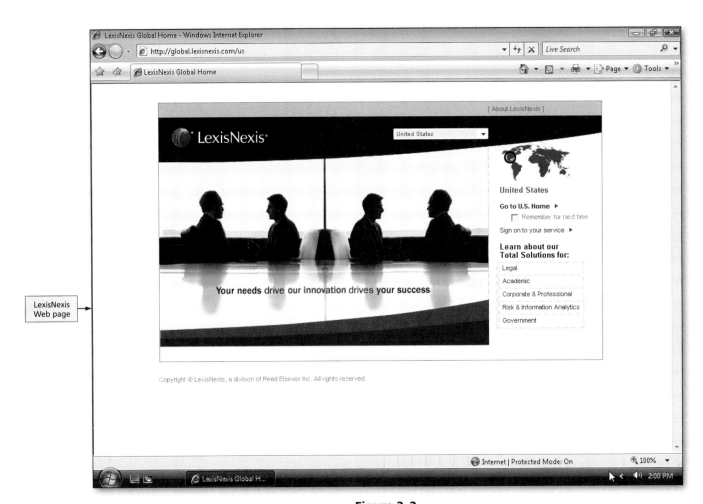

Figure 2–2

Summary of Types of Web Resources

Determining the category of a particular Web resource is sometimes difficult, because many Web sites have multiple objectives. You will find advertising on news Web pages. Personal Web pages may advocate a cause or opinion. A business/marketing Web page may contain factual information that is verifiable from other sources. In spite of this overlap, identifying the general category in which the Web page falls can help you evaluate the usefulness of the Web page as a source of information for a research paper.

Evaluating a Web Resource

Once a promising Web page is found, you should evaluate it for its reliability, significance, and content. Remember, anyone can put a page on the Web, and Web pages do not have to be reviewed for accuracy or verified by editors. You have an obligation to ensure that the information and other materials you use are accurate, attributable, and verifiable.

Just as criteria exist for evaluating printed materials, criteria also exist for evaluating Web pages. These criteria include authorship, accuracy of information, currency of information, and topic and scope of coverage. Table 2–2 shows the information you should look for within each criterion when evaluating Web resources.

Table 2–2 Criteria for Evaluating Web Pages

Criterion	Information to Evaluate
Authorship	• Is the name of the person or organization publishing the page legitimate? • Does a link exist to a page that describes the goals of the organization? • Does the page include a statement of official approval from the parent organization? • Is there a copyright notice? • What are the author's qualifications? • Are any opinions and biases clearly stated? • Does the page contain advertising? If so, is it differentiated from content? • Is the information provided as a public service?
Accuracy of Information	• Are any sources used and are they listed on the page? • Does the page contain links to other Web sites that verify the information on the page? • Are data and statistics clearly displayed and easy to read? • Is the page grammatically correct?
Currency of Information	• When was the page written? • When was the page placed on the Web? • When was the page last updated? • Does the page include dates associated with the information on the Web page?
Topic and Scope of Coverage	• What is the purpose of the Web page? • Does the page declare a topic? • Does the page succeed in describing or discussing the declared topic? • Are points clear, well-stated, and supported? • Does the page contain links to related resources? • Is the page under construction?

You may want to create an evaluation worksheet to use as an aid in consistently evaluating the Web pages you find as potential resources. Figure 2–3 shows a sample evaluation worksheet template created from the criteria listed in Table 2–2 on the previous page. You can make copies of this worksheet, or create a new worksheet to use each time you find a possible research source.

Web Resource Evaluation Worksheet

Web Page Title:

Web Page URL:

Type of Web Resource

   Advocacy Blog Business/Marketing Content Aggregator Educational

   Entertainment Informational News Personal Portal Social Network Wiki

Authorship

   What are the author's qualifications?

   Is there a sponsoring organization? Does the page link to the organization?

   Are any opinions and biases clearly stated?

   Does the page contain a copyright notice?

Accuracy of Information

   What sources verify the information on the Web page? Does the page link to those sources?

   Is the page grammatically correct?

Currency of Information

   What date was the page placed on the Web?

   What date was the page last updated?

   What date did you visit the page?

Topic and Scope

   What is the purpose of the page?

   Does the page succeed in describing and discussing the topic?

   Are points clear, well-stated, and supported?

   Does the page include links to other related pages?

Figure 2–3

Web Search Resources

Finding a valuable resource among the many Web pages available on the World Wide Web can be quite a challenge. The most efficient way to find a relevant resource from among all those pages is to use one of the many Web search tools to guide you to the information you are seeking.

The World Wide Web includes many Web pages, and bibliographic control does not exist. To find information for a term paper, learn more about a topic of interest, or locate the Web site of a governmental agency, you must know either the URL of the Web page with the information you are after or you must use a search tool. A **search tool** is a specialized Web site that helps you find Web pages relevant to your research. Search tools fall into three general categories.

- Directory
- Search engine
- Keyword system

The first type of search tool, called a **directory**, uses a directory to organize related Web resources. Figure 2–4 shows a directory (Yahoo! Directory) that is organized into broad categories. You must decide which category would include your search topic and then click the corresponding link. When you click the link, another page of links is displayed that contains more specific categories from which to choose. You continue following the links until you find the information you want.

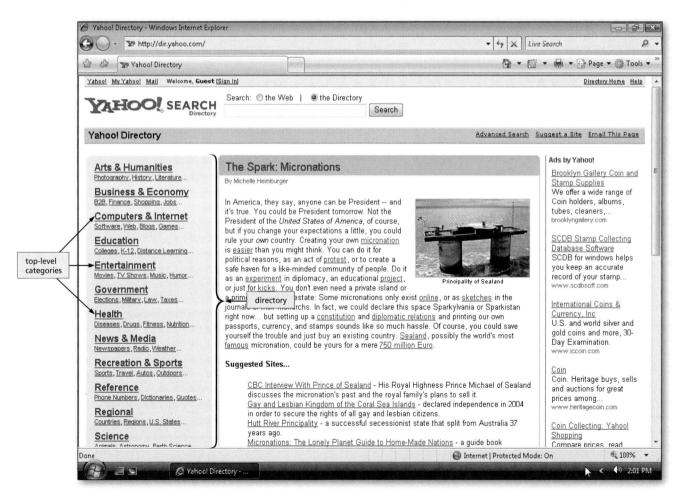

Figure 2–4

One of the benefits of using a directory is that since you select topics from a list of categories, you do not have to determine which terms to use to find the most relevant Web sites. On the other hand, it's possible that you may navigate through several levels of categories only to discover that there are no links on your topic.

A second type of search tool, called a **search engine**, retrieves and displays a list of links to Web pages based on a query. A **query** is a **keyword** or **search term** (a word, set of words, or phrase) you enter to tell the search engine the topic about which you are searching. The search engine uses the keyword to search an index of Web resources in its database. Some of the more popular search engines are Google, Yahoo, Windows Live, Ask.com, AltaVista, and Excite.

When you use a search engine that performs searches based upon keywords, instead of a directory, you can explore the Web and display links to Web pages without having to maneuver through any intermediate pages. You provide one or more relevant words, or **keywords**, about the topic in which you are interested, and the search engine returns links that point directly to pages containing those keywords.

Figure 2–5 shows a **keyword search form** (Google Advanced Search) used to enter keywords to search the Web. You provide one or more relevant keywords about the topic, and the search engine will return links that point directly to Web pages that contain those keywords.

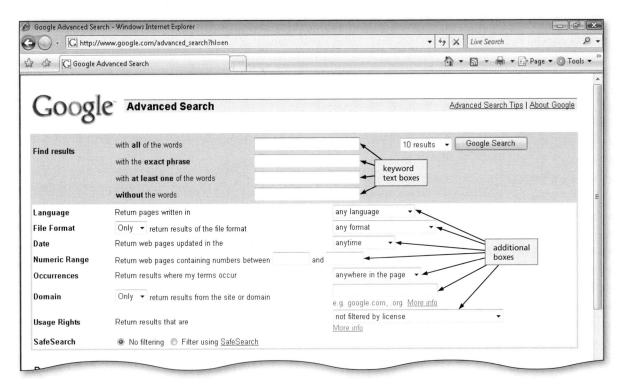

Figure 2–5

The index used by a search engine is created using several techniques. An automated program, called a **robot** or **spider**, travels around the Web, automatically following links and adding entries to the index. Individuals also can request that their Web pages be added to a directory or index, usually for a fee. Many businesses pay a fee to advertise on search engines. For example, if you perform a search on Google using the keyword "cruises", you will notice that a link to Expedia.com, a popular travel Web site, displays in the Sponsored Links area at the top of the page, indicating that the company pays a fee for its Web site to show up at the top of the search results.

Most of the popular portal Web sites listed in Table 2–1 on page IE 75 have both a search engine and a directory. Most portals also include specialized search tools that display maps and directions (Expedia), provide information about businesses (Yellow Pages), and help find people (People Finder).

Internet Explorer's Address bar also can be used as a search tool known as a **keyword system**. If you type a keyword into the Address bar, Windows Live Search (or the search engine you have designated as your default search provider) automatically will display a Web page containing a list of search results. While some people prefer using this method because it does not require navigating to a search engine's Web page to initiate a search, Internet Explorer now provides an easier, more flexible method for searching. The Instant Search box offers quick access to multiple search providers, and also allows you to change your Search Defaults.

To Start Internet Explorer

The following step starts Internet Explorer using the method described at the beginning of Chapter 1.

1

- To start Internet Explorer, click the Start button on the Windows taskbar, click All Programs on the Start menu, and then click Internet Explorer on the All Programs list (Figure 2–6).

- If the Internet Explorer window is not maximized, double-click its title bar to maximize it.

Figure 2–6

Searching the Web Using a Directory

Yahoo! is respected for its directory because it is created and maintained by real people, rather than by using an automated system. Starting with general categories and becoming increasingly more specific as links are selected, the Yahoo! directory provides a menu-like interface for searching the Web. Because the Yahoo! directory uses a series of menus to organize links to Web pages, you can find information without entering keywords.

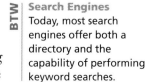

BTW

Search Engines
Today, most search engines offer both a directory and the capability of performing keyword searches.

To Display the Yahoo! Directory Home Page

The following step displays the Yahoo! Directory home page.

1

- Click the Address bar, type dir.yahoo. com as the URL, and then press the ENTER key to display the Yahoo! Directory Web page (Figure 2–7).

Figure 2–7

When you type a URL in the Address bar and then press the ENTER key, **AutoComplete** remembers the URL you typed. As a result, when you type the URL for the Yahoo! home page in the Address bar in Figure 2–7, AutoComplete may display a list of previously entered URLs in a box below the Address bar. If this happens, you can select a URL from the list in the Address bar by clicking the URL, or you can continue to type the URL from the keyboard.

The Search text box and Search button next to the Yahoo! title allow you to perform a keyword search. Several links appear along the left side of the Web page. Scrolling the Web page displays the Yahoo! Directory (Figure 2–8). Web pages in the Yahoo! Directory are organized into the broad categories.

To Search Using the Yahoo! Directory

You decide to start your search on hot air ballooning with the major category Recreation & Sports. The following steps navigate through the Yahoo! Directory to retrieve information about hot air balloon museums.

- If necessary, scroll the display area to display the Recreation & Sports link (Figure 2–8).

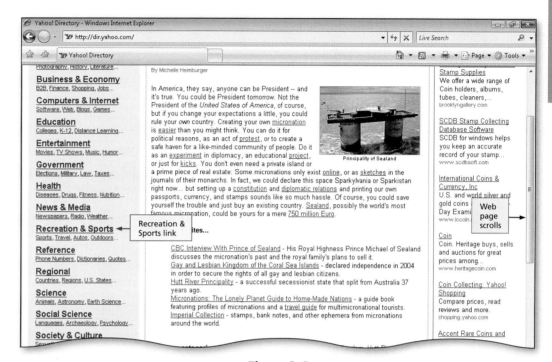

Figure 2–8

- Click Recreation & Sports to view the links in the Recreation & Sports category (Figure 2–9).

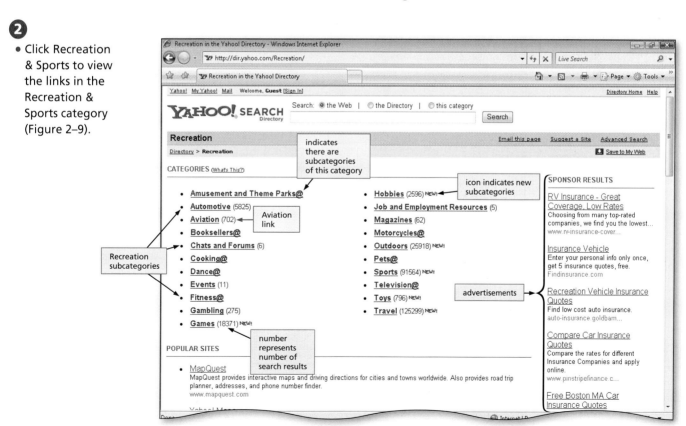

Figure 2–9

3
- Click Aviation to view the links in the Aviation subcategory (Figure 2–10).

Q&A

What are the numbers that appear in parentheses?

The numbers in parentheses represent the number of search results found in that category.

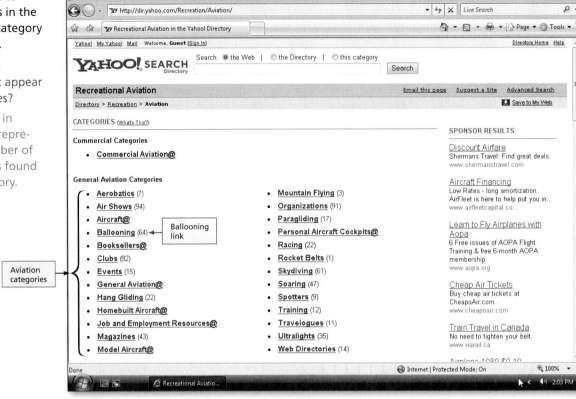

Figure 2–10

4
- Click Ballooning to view the links in the Ballooning subcategory (Figure 2–11).

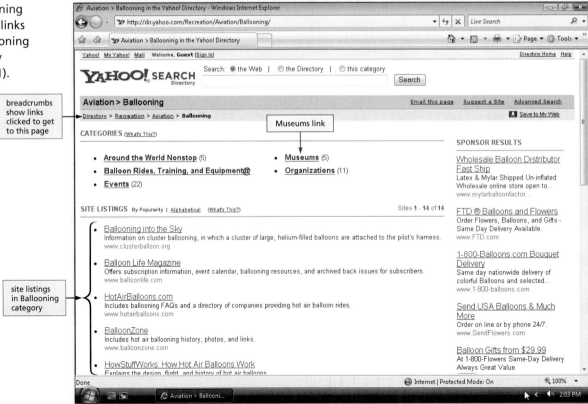

Figure 2–11

- Click Museums to
  view the links in
  the Museums
  subcategory
  (Figure 2–12).

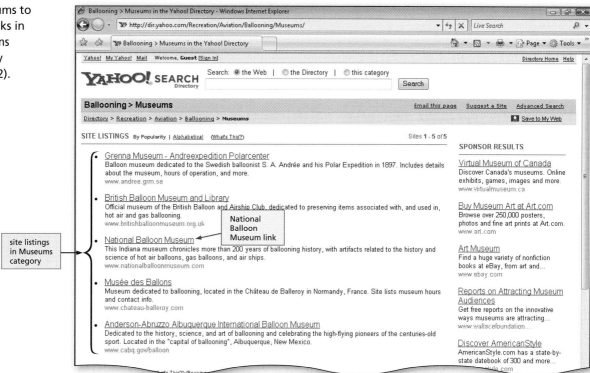

Figure 2–12

- Click the National
  Balloon Museum
  link to display the
  National Balloon
  Museum and
  Ballooning Hall of
  Fame Web page
  (Figure 2–13).

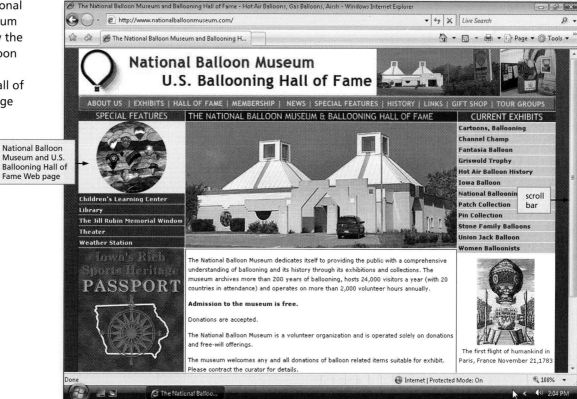

Figure 2–13

To Evaluate a Web Resource

Now that you have located a potentially informative Web site, you need to evaluate the Web page to see if it can be used as a source. The following steps use the sample evaluation worksheet (Figure 2–3 on page IE 80) to evaluate the National Balloon Museum page for accuracy, validity, and reliability.

- If necessary, scroll the display area to display the bottom of the National Balloon Museum Web page (Figure 2–14).

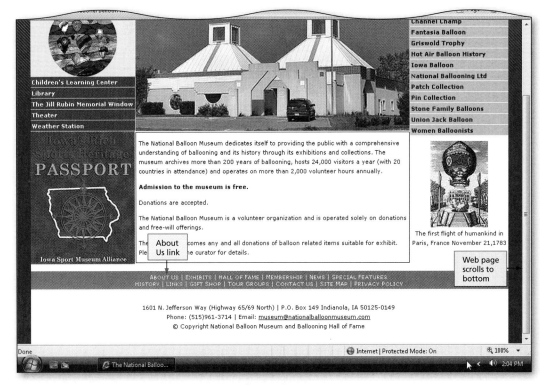

Figure 2–14

- Click the About Us link at the bottom of the Web page to display the About the National Balloon Museum & Ballooning Hall of Fame Web page (Figure 2–15). Use this information to complete the evaluation worksheet.

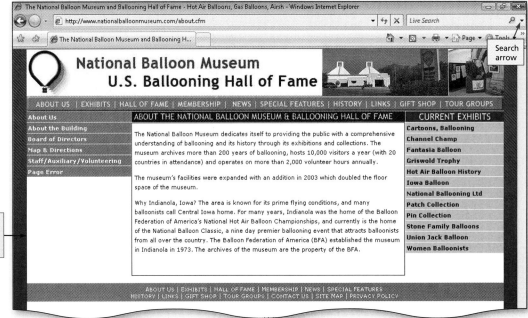

Figure 2–15

The information gathered so far is summarized on the worksheet illustrated in Figure 2–16. Based on the current worksheet criteria, The National Balloon Museum and Ballooning Hall of Fame Web page is an exceptionally strong resource.

Web Resource Evaluation Worksheet

Web Page Title: **The National Balloon Museum and Ballooning Hall of Fame**

Web Page URL: **http://www.nationalballoonmuseum.com**

Type of Web Resource

    Advocacy Blog Business/Marketing Content Aggregator Educational

    Entertainment (Informational) News Personal Portal Social Network Wiki

    Reasons **Contains information about ballooning and the museum**

Authorship

    What are the author's qualifications?

    Is there a sponsoring organization? Does the page link to the organization? **Yes – The National Balloon Museum and Ballooning Hall of Fame; Yes**

    Are any opinions and biases clearly stated? **Yes**

    Does the page contain a copyright notice? **Yes**

Accuracy of Information

    What sources verify the information on the Web page? Does the page link to those sources?

    Is the page grammatically correct? **Yes**

Currency of Information

    What date was the page placed on the Web?

    What date was the page last updated?

    What date did you visit the page? **November 11, 2008**

Topic and Scope

    What is the purpose of the page? **The sport of ballooning**

    Does the page succeed in describing and discussing the topic? **Yes**

    Are points clear, well-stated, and supported? **Yes**

    Does the page include links to other related pages? **Yes**

Figure 2–16

BTW

Evaluating a Web Resource
Many Web pages do not meet the necessary criteria to be a source for a research paper. You will find that you discard many promising Web pages because after evaluating the site, you find that the information on the site cannot be considered reliable, accurate, and verifiable.

BTW

Google Products
In addition to providing search capabilities for various resources, Google also offers productivity tools such as a calendar and programs that create documents and spreadsheets. To view a list of Google products, navigate to the Google Web page, click the more link, and then click the even more link.

If you are doing a large amount of Web research, consider creating an electronic version of the worksheet. Then you can record the evaluation details for each Web resource you use and save the document using a filename that identifies the Web site.

Searching the Web

In addition to performing an Internet search using a question, you can also search the Internet using one or more keywords. A search engine uses a keyword to find relevant Web pages. The following section discusses how to search the Web using keywords and how to use tabs in Internet Explorer while doing so.

Google is one of the more widely used search engines. It has an index of billions of Web pages. Each day, its robots visit millions of sites, capturing URLs and corresponding text to update its index. Robot programs also check for dead links, the term used for URLs that no longer work. Google not only is capable of locating Web sites containing textual information that matches your search criteria; it also can return results for various other resources such as images, video, maps, books, items for sale, and patents.

To Search Using the Google Simple Search Form

As with most search engines, Google has both a simple search form and an advanced search form. The simple search form is displayed on its home page and consists of a text box, the Google Search button, and the I'm Feeling Lucky button. When you type a keyword in the text box and click the Google Search button, Google will search for the keyword and display a list of links to Web pages that contain the keyword. The following steps use Google to search for Web pages that contain the keyword "ballooning".

1

- Click the Address bar, type www.google.com, and then press the ENTER key to display the Google Web page (Figure 2–17).

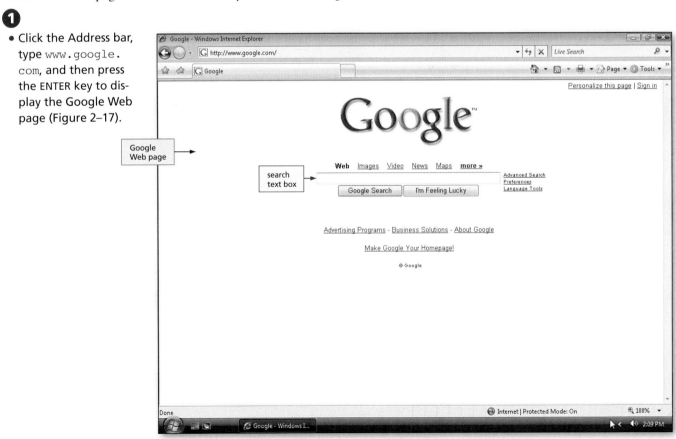

Figure 2–17

2

- Type balloooning in the search text box (Figure 2–18).

What will happen if I click the I'm Feeling Lucky button?

If you click the I'm Feeling Lucky button instead of the Google Search button after entering your search text, Google will display the Web page for the first search result it locates.

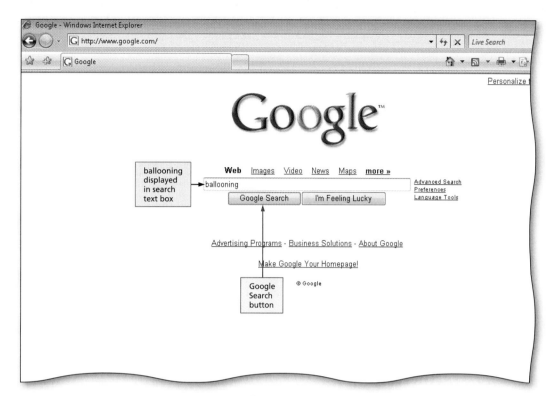

ballooning displayed in search text box

Google Search button

Figure 2–18

3

- Click the Google Search button to initiate Google's search and to display a Web page containing the search results (Figure 2–19). Your search results may differ.

search results

this search returned 4,290,000 results

search text

HotAirBallooning.com link

Figure 2–19

Using Tabbed Browsing to Help Search the Web

Searching the Web for an exact topic is not always easy when search engines return numerous hits. A **hit** is the term used when a search engine returns a Web page that matches the search criteria. The **tabbed browsing** feature provides a way to navigate between the search results and associated Web page(s) within a single browser window. In previous versions of Internet Explorer, it would be necessary to open a new browser window if you wanted to have multiple Web pages open simultaneously. When a Web page opens in a new tab, the tab is added in the tab row, which appears to the left of the Command Bar.

To Open a Link in a New Tab

Because the first Web page you view may not contain the information you are looking for, it may be necessary to return to the Google Search results page to continue evaluating additional Web pages. Internet Explorer's tabbed browsing feature allows you to open multiple Web pages within the same browser window using tabs, instead of opening multiple browser windows for each page. The following steps open a link in a new tab.

- Right-click the HotAirBallooning.com link to display a shortcut menu (Figure 2–20).

Figure 2–20

2

- Click the Open in New Tab command to open the HotAirBallooning.com Web page in a new tab.

- If necessary, click the HotAirBallooning.com tab to make it the active tab (Figure 2–21).

How can I open a new tab and manually navigate to a Web page of my choice?

Clicking the New Tab button on the tab row, or pressing CTRL+T, will open a new tab. Once the new tab opens, you can type the URL of the Web page you wish to visit in the Address bar, and then press the ENTER key to display the Web page.

Figure 2–21

Other Ways

1. While holding down the CTRL key, click the HotAirBallooning.com link

To Switch Between Tabs

Currently, the ballooning - Google Search tab is inactive and the HotAirBallooning.com tab is active. A tab is considered active when the contents of the tab are displayed in the display area and when the tab is light blue. When you want to switch to another tab, click the tab. The clicked tab becomes the active tab and the contents of the tab are displayed in the display area. The following steps switch between the two open tabs.

- Click the ballooning - Google Search tab to display the Web page containing the Google search results (Figure 2–22).

Figure 2–22

- Click the HotAirBallooning.com tab to return to the HotAirBallooning.com Web page (Figure 2–23).

Figure 2–23

Other Ways

1. Press CTRL+TAB, press CTRL+TAB

2. Press CTRL+1, press CTRL+2

To Switch Between Tabs by Using the Tab List Button

As you add additional tabs to the tab row in Internet Explorer, the size of the tabs decreases, and it may not be possible for you to read all of the text displayed on each tab — making it difficult to identify which Web page corresponds to which tab. When you click the Tab List button on the tab row, Internet Explorer displays a menu that contains the title of each Web page currently open in a tab. Clicking a Web page title in this menu will switch to the tab that contains the Web page you selected. The following steps switch between tabs by using the Tab List button.

1

- Right-click the Balloon Clubs button on the HotAirBallooning.com Web page to display the shortcut menu.

- Click the Open in New Tab command on the shortcut menu to open the Balloon Clubs Web page in a new tab.

- If necessary, click the HotAirBallooning.com tab on the right side of the tab row to display the Balloon Clubs Web page in the display area (Figure 2–24).

Figure 2–24

- Click the Tab List button to display a menu containing a list of tabs that currently are open (Figure 2–25).

Figure 2–25

- Click ballooning - Google Search in the menu to switch back to the tab containing the Google search results (Figure 2–26).

Q&A

Why is the HotAirBallooning.com link red?

The red link is the last link opened from a given Web page. It may not still be open in a tab, but it was recently visited.

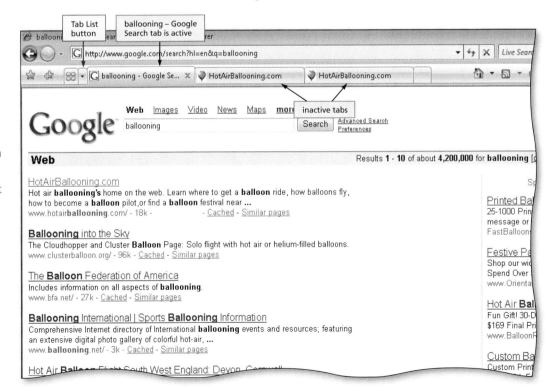

Figure 2–26

4

- Click the Tab List button to display the Tab List menu.

- Click the second HotAirBallooning.com menu item to display the Balloon Clubs Web page (Figure 2–27).

Figure 2–27

To Switch Between Tabs by Using the Quick Tabs Button

If the Web page titles are not descriptive enough to identify the Web pages they represent, you may have a hard time locating the tab you want to display. For example, the Web page currently displayed contains a list of balloon clubs. However, the title of this Web page (Hot Air Ballooning) does not specifically describe the contents. The Quick Tabs button displays a thumbnail version of each open Web page so that you can visually identify the tab for the Web page you want. The following steps switch between tabs by using the Quick Tabs button.

- Click the Quick Tabs button to display thumbnail versions of each open Web page in the display area (Figure 2–28).

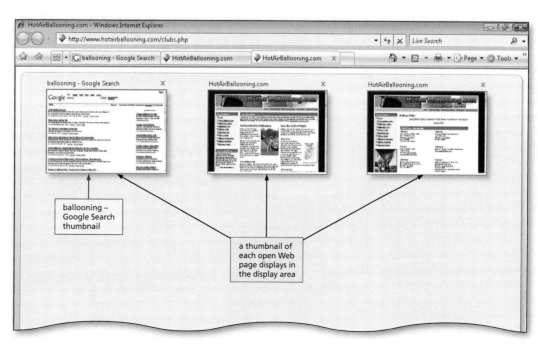

Figure 2–28

2

- Click the balloning - Google Search thumbnail to open the Web page containing the Google search results (Figure 2–29).

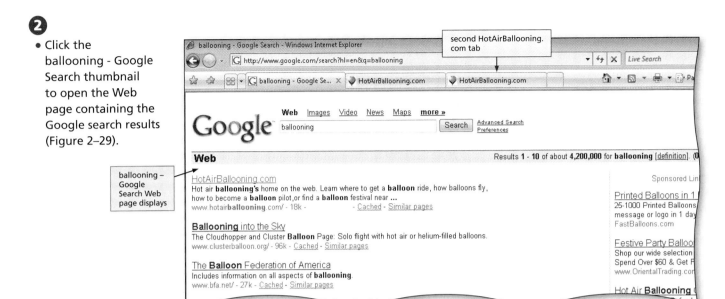

Figure 2–29

To Close a Tab

When you are finished viewing the contents of a Web page in a tab, you should close the tab to keep the tab bar free from clutter. Having too many tabs open at one time makes it difficult to locate a particular tab. The following steps close open tabs.

- To make the second HotAirBallooning.com tab the active tab, click the second HotAirBallooning.com tab (Figure 2–30).

Figure 2–30

2

• Click the Close Tab button on the second HotAirBallooning.com tab to close the second HotAirBallooning.com tab (Figure 2–31).

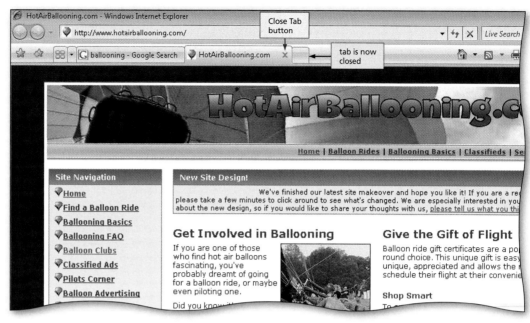

Figure 2–31

3

• Click the Close Tab button on the remaining HotAirBallooning.com tab to close the tab (Figure 2–32).

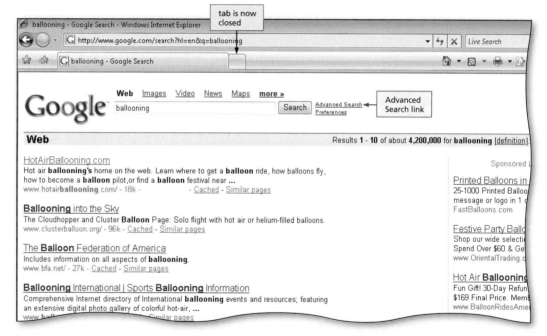

Figure 2–32

Other Ways

1. Right-click tab to close, click Close

2. Select tab to close, press CTRL+W

Using the Instant Search Box

Internet Explorer allows you to search the Web using either the Address bar or Instant Search box. The Address bar allows you to search for Web pages on the Internet and to search for files and folders on the local computer. The Address bar will be discussed later in this chapter. The Instant Search box allows you to search for Web pages directly from the browser interface without first navigating to a search engine's Web page. The Instant

Search box uses search engines such as AOL, Ask.com, Lycos, Windows Live Search, Yahoo!, and Google. In addition, Internet Explorer allows you to customize the Instant Search box by adding other search engines. Table 2–3 lists additional topic search engines that you can add to the Instant Search Box.

Table 2–3 Additional Topic Search Engines Available for the Instant Search Box	
Topic Search	**Description**
About.com	Search consumer advice and information
Amazon	Search Amazon's online stores
CNET	Search tech news, reviews and downloads
EBay	Search Online Auctions
ESPN	Search Sports Online
Expedia.com	Search your favorite travel destinations
Microsoft	Search Microsoft.com
Monster	Search today's top jobs
MTV	Search music, videos, and TV shows
Shopzilla.com	Shop for clothes, computers, toys, and more
SuperPages.com	Search Verizon's Online Yellow Pages
Target	Search Target.com
Wal-Mart	Search Walmart.com
Weather.com	Search local weather, forecasts, news, & video
Wikipedia.com	Search the free encyclopedia
USATODAY.com	Search news online

To Customize the Instant Search Box by Adding a Search Engine

The following steps add the Ask.com search engine to the Instant Search box.

- Click the Search arrow on the Instant Search box to display the Search menu (Figure 2–33).

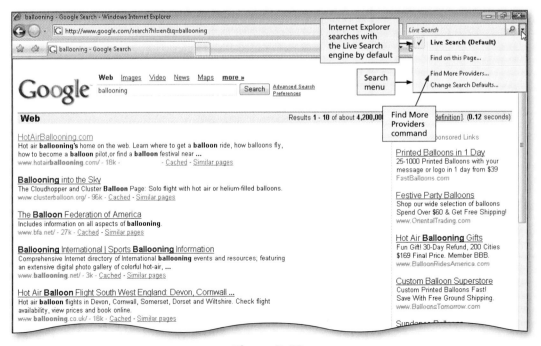

Figure 2–33

2
- Click Find More Providers on the Search menu to display the Add Search Providers to Internet Explorer 7 Web page (Figure 2–34).

Figure 2–34

3
- Click the Ask.com link to display the Add Search Provider dialog box (Figure 2–35).

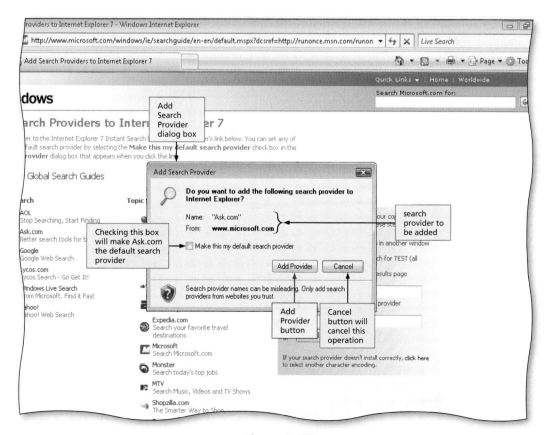

Figure 2–35

- Click the Add Provider button in the Add Search Provider dialog box to add the Ask.com search engine to the Instant Search box (Figure 2–36).

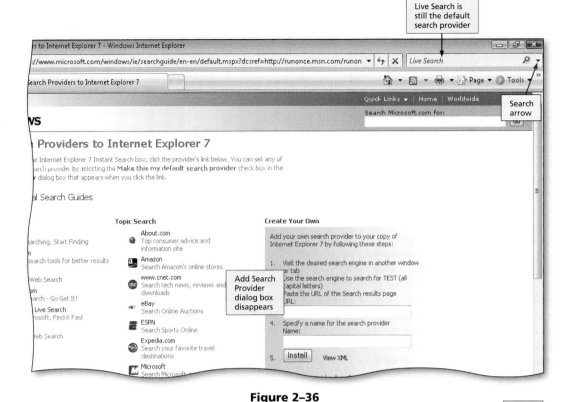

Figure 2–36

- Click the Search arrow on the Instant Search box to display the Search menu containing the Ask.com command (Figure 2–37).

- Click the Search arrow on the Instant Search box to close the Search menu.

Figure 2–37

To Search for Web Pages Using the Ask.com Search Engine

The Ask.com search engine finds answers to questions entered by users. Ask.com allows you to perform a search by using natural language as your search criteria, whereas other search engines expect you only to enter key-words. For instance, you can enter a statement (Give me a list of places to go ballooning.) or a question (What is the biggest hot air balloon?). The search engine searches for and displays a list of links to Web pages that pertain to the words, phrase, statement, or question.

The following steps use the Instant Search box to search Ask.com for Web pages on how hot air balloons work.

1
- To display the Search menu, click the Search arrow on the Instant Search box (Figure 2–38).

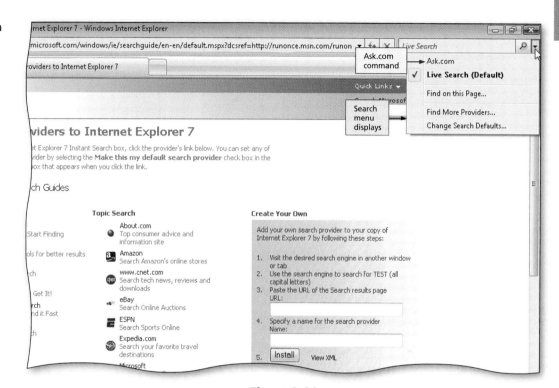

Figure 2–38

2
- Click the Ask.com entry on the Search menu to make the Ask.com search engine the active search engine in the Instant Search box (Figure 2–39).

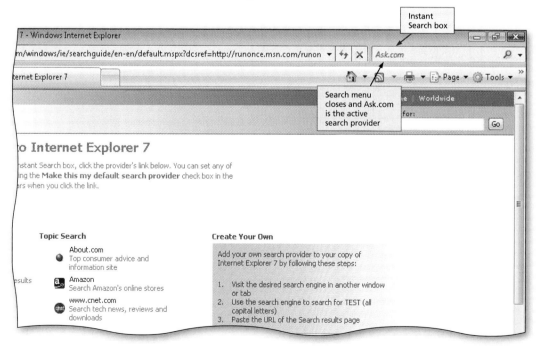

Figure 2–39

3

- **Type** How does a Hot Air Balloon Work? in the Instant Search box. (Figure 2–40).

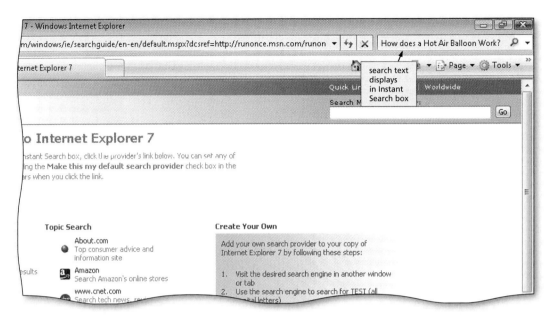

Figure 2–40

4

- Press the ENTER key to display the Ask.com Web page containing the search results (Figure 2–41).

Experiment

- Hold the CTRL key and click a search result to open a new tab containing a Web page that discusses how a hot air balloon works. After you view the Web page, close the tab and return to the search results.

Q&A

How can I open the page containing my search results in a new tab?

After you enter your search text, hold down the ALT key while pressing the ENTER key to display your search results in a new tab.

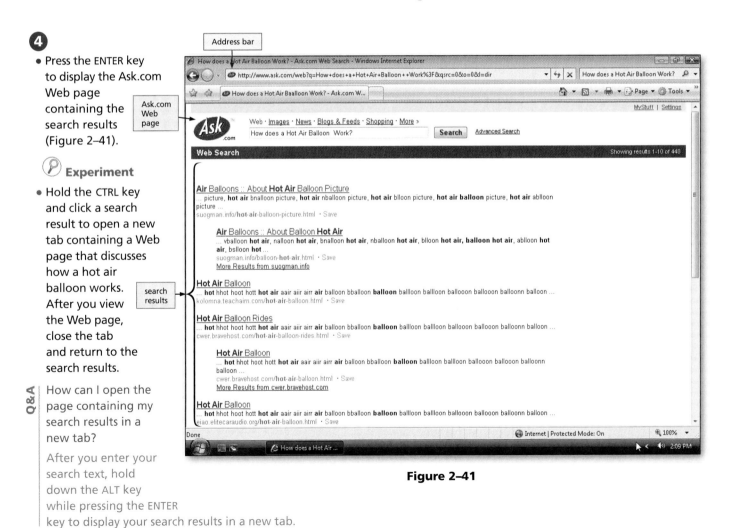

Figure 2–41

Refining a Web Search

You **refine** a search by providing more information for the search engine to use to return a narrower, more focused set of results. Most search engines, when performing a search using multiple keywords, will give each word the same weight, or level of importance. When each keyword contains the same weight, Web pages containing any one of a set of these keywords or any combination of a set of these keywords will satisfy the search engine and be returned as a successful match. Any Web page that contains the word ballooning, for example, will be included in the hundreds of thousands of links returned by the search, even though some of those pages will have nothing to do with hot air ballooning. To eliminate these Web pages, the keywords you use to search need to be more specific and better organized.

In addition to entering keywords, Google, along many other search engines, allows the use of operators, advanced operators, and some compound search criteria to refine a search.

Operators increase the accuracy of a search by fine-tuning the keywords in the search. Operators include the + (plus), – (minus), and ~ (tilde) symbols and the OR logical operator. Typing the **+ (plus) symbol** before a keyword guarantees the keyword will be included in the search results. Alternatively, placing quotation marks around two or more keywords also includes the keywords in the search, but the search engine will search for those keywords in that same order. Placing the **– (minus) symbol** before a keyword guarantees that the keyword is excluded from the search. Placing the **~ (tilde) symbol** immediately preceding a keyword causes a search for the keyword and any synonyms.

The **OR operator**, also referred to as a **Boolean operator**, is a compound search criteria that allows you to control how individual words in a keyword phrase are used. For example, the phrase, computer OR technology, finds Web pages containing either computer or technology. The resulting Web pages can contain both keywords or just one of the keywords.

Although the Google search engine only allows the OR operator, other search engines allow the use of additional Boolean operators. These logical operators include AND, NOT, and NEAR. The **AND operator**, like the OR operator, allows you to create keyword searches containing compound conditions. The **NOT operator** is used to exclude keywords from the resulting Web pages. The **NEAR operator** is used to find pages in which two keywords appear within close proximity of each other.

Table 2–4 describes the Boolean operators and gives an example of each one.

Table 2–4 Boolean Operators and Examples	
Boolean Operator	**Example**
AND	Finds only those Web pages that contain all of the specified words or phrases. Peanut AND butter finds Web pages where both the word peanut and the word butter appear.
OR	Finds Web pages containing at least one of the specified words or phrases. Peanut OR butter finds Web pages containing either peanut or butter. The Web pages found can contain both words, but only have to contain one of the words.
NOT	Excludes Web pages containing the specified word or phrase. Peanut AND NOT butter finds Web pages where the word peanut appears but the word butter does not. With some search engines, NOT cannot be used alone. It must be used in conjunction with another operator, such as AND.
NEAR	Finds Web pages containing both specified words or phrases within ten words of each other. Peanut NEAR butter would find Web pages on peanut butter, but probably not any other kind of butter such as apple butter.
( )	Use parentheses to group complex Boolean phrases. For example, (peanut AND butter) AND (jelly OR jam) finds Web pages with the words 'peanut butter and jelly' or 'peanut butter and jam' or both.

Another useful feature is the **wildcard character**. Several search engines allow you to use the asterisk (*) to replace zero, one, or more characters in a word. For example, searching for immun* will return hits for immune, immunize, immunization, immunology, immunologist, and any other word beginning with the letters, i-m-m-u-n. Use wildcards if the spelling of a keyword is unknown or may be incorrectly specified on the Web page. Table 2–5 offers useful search tips.

Table 2–5 Successful Search Techniques	
Tip or Wildcard	**Example**
Use parentheses to group items	Use parentheses ( ) to specify precedence in a search. For example, to search for Web pages that contain information about both President Clinton and President Bush, try this advanced query: president AND ((George NEAR Bush) AND ((Bill OR William) NEAR Clinton)).
Use wildcard characters	Use an asterisk (*) to broaden a search. To find any words that start with gold, use gold* to find matches for gold, goldfinch, goldfinger, golden, and so on. Use this character if the word you are searching for could have different endings (for example, do not search for dog, search for dog* to include the plural).
Use quotes to surround a phrase	If you know a certain phrase will appear on the page you are looking for, put the phrase in quotes (for example, try entering song lyrics such as "you ain't nothin' but a hound dog").
Use either specific or general keywords	Conduct searches using specific keywords to obtain fewer, more precise links, or general keywords to obtain numerous, less precise links.

Advanced operators are query words that have special meaning in search engines. The advanced operators modify a search or perform a different type of search. Google's advanced operators include: cache, link, related, info, define, stocks, site, allintitle, intitle, allinurl, and inurl. For example, entering link:www.google.com in the Google search box finds all Web pages that have links to the www.google.com Web page.

Most search engines have a link on their search pages to access advanced search options. The Google **Advanced Search** link appears to the right of the Google Search text box on the Google home page and to the right of the Search button on other pages. In addition, clicking the **Advanced Search Tips** link on the Google Advanced Search page (Figure 2–42) displays information about advanced searching.

To Display the Google Advanced Search Form

The following steps display the Google Advanced Search form.

1

- To display the Google home page, type www.google.com in the Address bar and then press the ENTER key.

- Click the Advanced Search link to the right of the Google Search button to display the Advanced Search form (Figure 2–42).

Figure 2–42

The **Find results area** contains four descriptions and four text boxes. Table 2–6 describes the text box descriptions and gives an example of each search rule.

Table 2-6 Find Results Area	
Text Box Description	**Search Rules**
with all of the words	Web pages must contain all the words you typed in the text box.
with the exact phrase	Web pages must contain the exact words in the order they were typed in the text box.
with at least one of the words	Web pages must contain at least one of the words in the text box.
without the words	Web pages must not contain the word or words in the text box.

To Search Using Google Advanced Search

The following steps use the Google Advanced Search form to refine the search and find information about Bruce Comstock, a recent inductee into the U.S. Ballooning Hall of Fame.

- Type Bruce Comstock in the with all of the words text box.

- Click the with the exact phrase text box.

- Type hot air balloon flight in the text box (Figure 2–43).

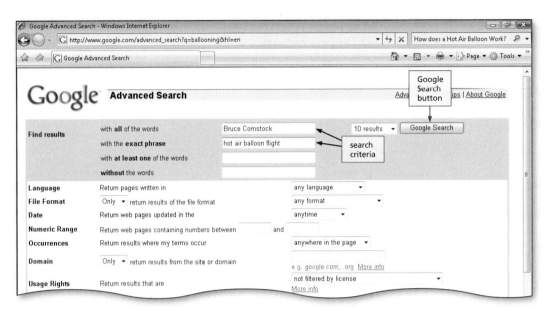

Figure 2–43

- Click the Google Search button to display the search results.

- If necessary, scroll down to locate the first appearance of The National Balloon Museum and Ballooning Hall of Fame - Hot Air... link (Figure 2–44).

Figure 2–44

3

- Click the The National Balloon Museum and Ballooning Hall of Fame - Hot Air... link to display The National Balloon Museum and Ballooning Hall of Fame Web Page (Figure 2–45).

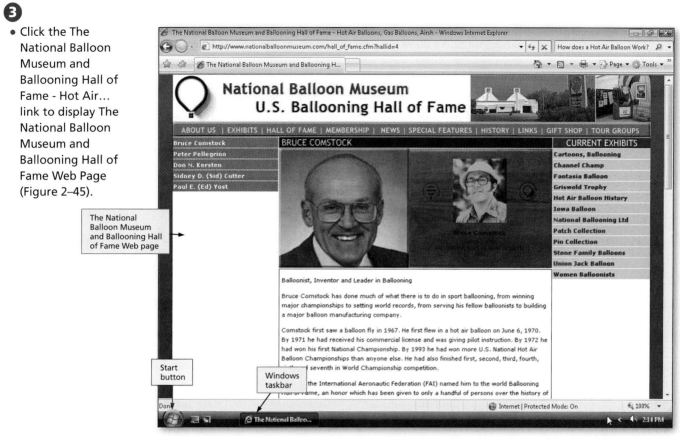

The National Balloon Museum and Ballooning Hall of Fame Web page

Start button

Windows taskbar

Figure 2–45

Searching using the names Bruce and Comstock in the 'with all of the words' text box results in a search for both names and displays Web pages that contain both names. The phrase, hot air balloon flight, in the 'with the exact phrase' text box results in a list of Web pages that contain the exact phrase.

Recall that the initial search for ballooning using the Google simple search form returned hundreds of thousands of links. The second attempt using the Google Advanced Search form returned 18 links, and the pages were more useful because they met more-specific search criteria. This illustrates the first successful searching technique: **be as specific as possible with keywords**. Put some thought into what small group of words most represents the topic or is used frequently with it. Choose the best words from this group to use with the search engine.

If you receive only a couple or no useful links, make the keywords slightly more general and try again. For example, if you wanted to find information about tax-exempt municipal bonds, a general-to-specific list of keywords might include: *investments*, *bonds*, *tax-free investments*, *municipal bonds*, or *tax-exempt bonds*.

Most search engines support the use of Boolean operators, such as AND, OR, NOT, and NEAR, and parentheses for grouping. Use the operators to specify complex phrases and conditions. For example, you might use the keywords (rocket OR shuttle) AND experiment to search for rocket experiments or shuttle experiments. Remember to use the search engine's Help feature to learn which Boolean operators are available and how to use them.

BTW

Choosing Search Engines
With the Web growing and changing every day, it is impossible for one search engine to catalog all the available Web pages. Despite this limitation, many people use one favorite search engine exclusively. This exclusivity makes it easier to have successful searches because they are familiar with the search engine's advanced techniques.

Creating a Working Bibliography

Once you find a good Web source, how do you record it? A **working bibliography** will help you organize and compile the resources you find, so that you can record them as sources in the list of works cited. For Web resources, you should note the author or authors, title of the page, URL, date of publication, date of the last revision, date you accessed the resource, heading of any part or section where the relevant information is located, navigation instructions necessary to find the resource, and other pertinent information.

When you are compiling the information, you often will need to locate the name of the person who authored the material on the Web page. If the author's information is not readily available, you may have to write to the person responsible for the Web site, or **Webmaster**, and ask for the author's name. First, display the home page of the Web site to see if a directory or contact section is listed. If you do not find a directory or contact section, display the bottom of the Web page or other pages in the Web site. Many Web pages include the e-mail address of the Webmaster at the bottom of the page.

In the past, index cards were used to record relevant information about a work, and you still can use index cards to record Web research. There are a variety of ways you can keep track of the Web sites you use and the information you gather.

- You can e-mail the information that you need to yourself and store the messages in separate folders. Use one folder for each point or category you are researching.
- You can store the information in separate document files using copy and paste techniques. Use a separate file for each point or category you research.
- You can create a folder in the Favorites list and then place related favorites you find on the Web in that folder.
- You can print the Web page.

To Record Relevant Information about a Web Research Source in WordPad

To demonstrate how to record relevant information about a Web resource, the following steps copy information from The National Balloon Museum and Ballooning Hall of Fame Web page and paste it into a WordPad document.

1

- Open WordPad by clicking the Start button on the Windows taskbar, clicking All Programs on the Start menu to display the All Programs list, clicking Accessories on the All Programs list to display the Accessories list, and then clicking WordPad on the Accessories list (Figure 2–46).

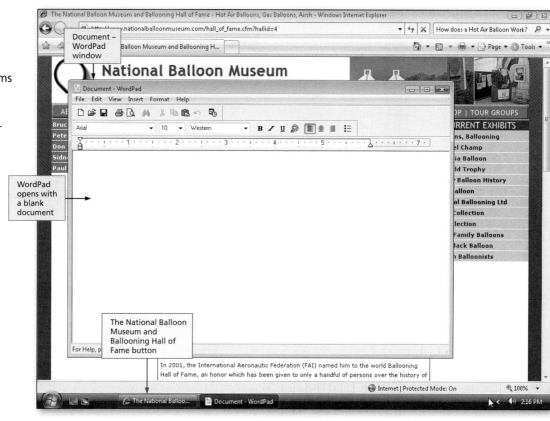

Figure 2–46

2

- Click the The National Balloon Museum and Ballooning Hall of Fame button on the taskbar to move the Document - WordPad window to the background and display the Internet Explorer window in the foreground.

- If necessary, scroll to display the beginning of the article (Figure 2–47).

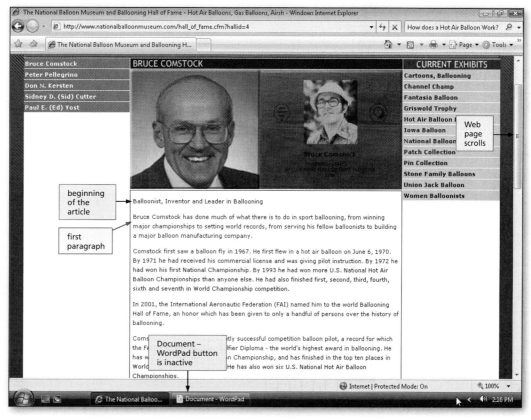

Figure 2–47

3

- Select the entire first paragraph.

- Right-click the selected text to display a shortcut menu (Figure 2–48).

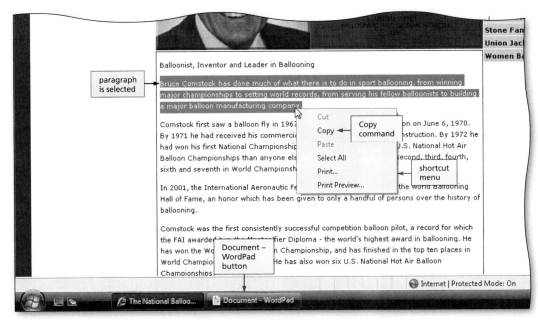

Figure 2–48

4

- Click Copy on the shortcut menu to copy the selected text to the Clipboard.

- Click the Document - WordPad button on the taskbar to display the Document - WordPad window (Figure 2–49)

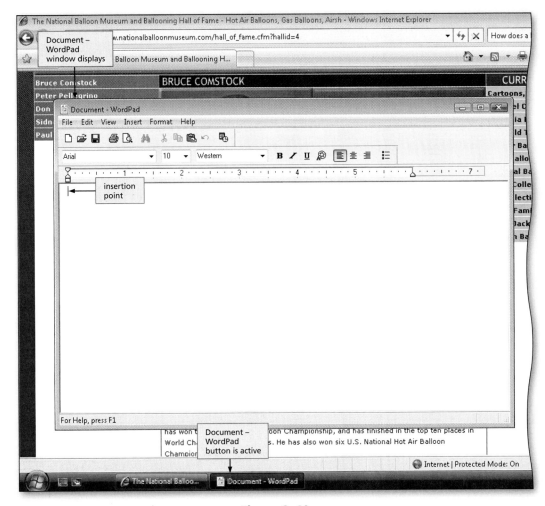

Figure 2–49

5

- Type http://www.
nationalbal
loonmuseum.com/
hall_of_fame.
cfm?hallid=4 in
the WordPad
document.

- Press the ENTER key
and then type The
National Balloon
Museum and
Ballooning Hall
of Fame in the
WordPad document.

- Press the ENTER
key and then type
today's date in the
WordPad document.

- Press the ENTER key
twice (Figure 2–50).

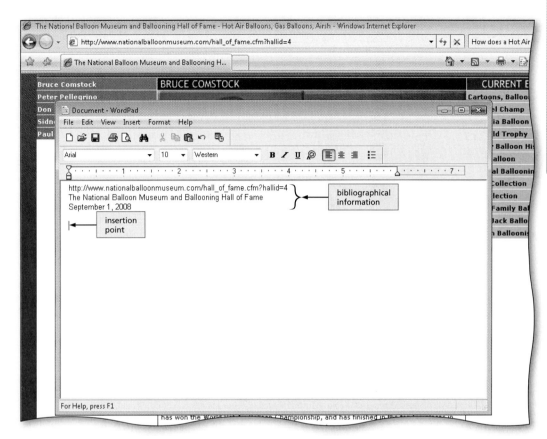

Figure 2–50

6

- Right-click a blank
area of the docu-
ment and then click
Paste on the short-
cut menu to paste
the contents of the
Clipboard in the
WordPad window
at the location of
the insertion point
(Figure 2–51).

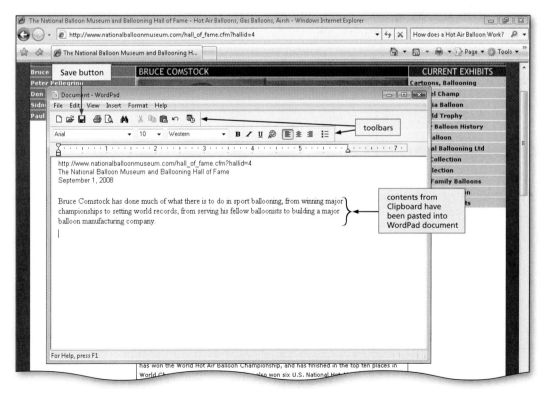

Figure 2–51

To Save a WordPad Document

The following steps save the WordPad document in the Documents folder on your computer using the file name, Bruce Comstock - Ballooning.

1 Click the Save button on the toolbar.

2 If necessary, select the Documents folder under Favorite Links.

3 Type `Bruce Comstock - Ballooning` in the File name box.

4 Click the Save button in the Save As dialog box to save the new file to the Documents folder on your computer.

5 Click the Close button on the WordPad title bar to quit WordPad.

If you have a lot of research to do, consider saving both the evaluation criteria and the research information for a particular Web site in the same document.

Citing Web Sources

Standards for citing Web resources have been developed and published by most of the documentation style authorities, like the **Modern Language Association (MLA)** and the **American Psychological Association (APA).** You can find these guides to documentation style at a library or on the Web at www.mla.org and www.apa.org.

An example of citing a Web resource using the MLA documentation style appears in Figure 2–52. The example documents the source of the criteria for Bruce Comstock's contributions to the sport of ballooning.

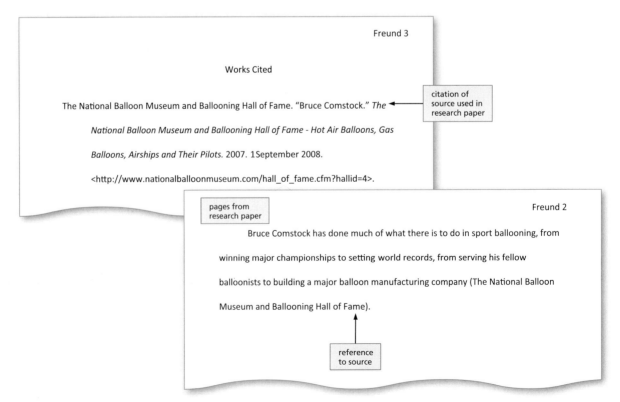

Figure 2–52

As you have learned in this chapter, the World Wide Web can be an informative and valuable source of information. By using proper searching and note-taking techniques, and asking the right questions about the usefulness of a Web resource, you can add to the information base you use to write a paper or speech. Always remember, however, that Web sources should complement, not replace, printed sources for locating information.

BTW

Citing Web Sources
Both of the style guides mentioned in the text differ slightly from one another on the format of the citation of a Web source. Check with your instructor for your school's accepted format.

Searching the Web for Other Information

In this chapter, you first searched for Web pages using the Yahoo! Directory and then searched for Web pages using the Instant Search box and the keyword-based Google search engine. You can also use the Web to search for mailing addresses and e-mail addresses, business names and business categories, maps, words, encyclopedia articles, and pictures.

To Search the Web for an Address

You can use Web sites such as InfoSpace and BigFoot to find addresses of businesses or individuals. The following steps use InfoSpace to search for the address of the National Balloon Museum when you know only the company's name and the state in which the company is located.

1

- If necessary, maximize the Internet Explorer window.

- Type www. infospace.com in the Address bar and then press the ENTER key to display the InfoSpace Web page (Figure 2–53).

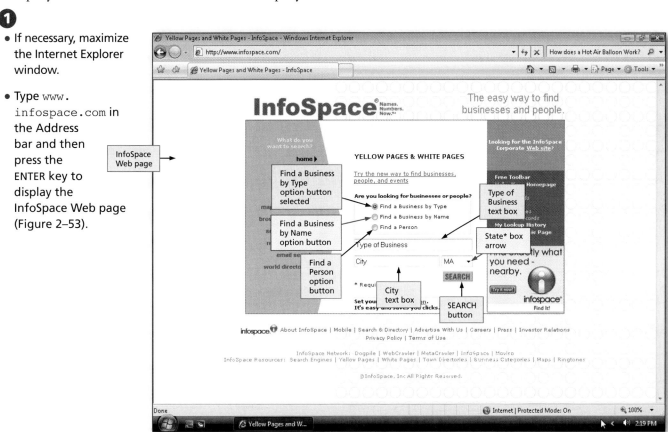

Figure 2–53

2

- Click the Find a Business by Name option button.

- Click the Name of Business text box to remove the text and then type National Balloon Museum in the text box.

- Click the arrow in the State* box to display a list of state names and then click IA in the list (Figure 2–54).

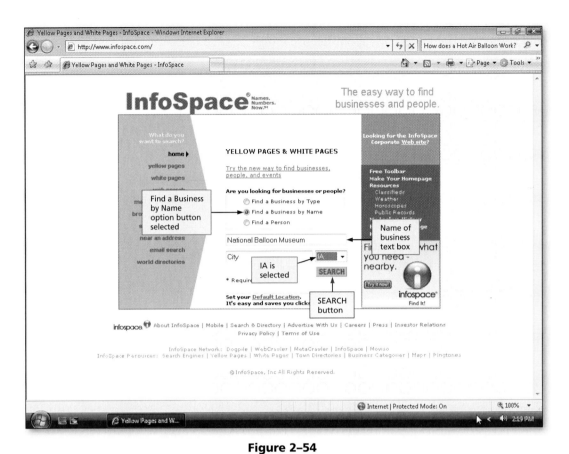

Figure 2–54

3

- Click the SEARCH button.

- If necessary, scroll the display area to display the search results (Figure 2–55).

Figure 2–55

To Search the Web for a Map of a Place or Landmark

When you plan to visit a new landmark, city, or state, you can use the Internet to provide a map of the area you plan to visit. Many people like the Google Maps Web site for finding maps. The next steps use Google Maps to search for a map of the National Balloon Museum in Indianola, IA.

1

• Type maps.google.com in the Address bar and then press the ENTER key to display the Google Maps Web page (Figure 2–56).

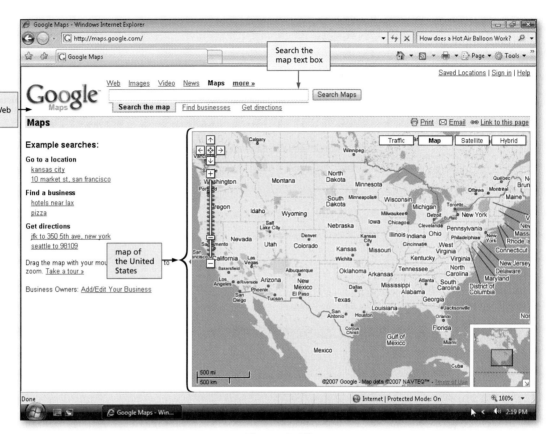

Figure 2–56

2

• Type National Balloon Museum in the Search the map text box (Figure 2–57).

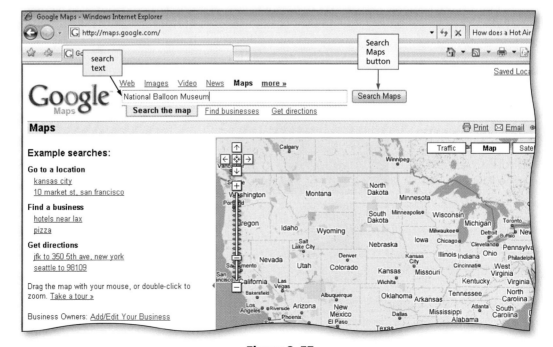

Figure 2–57

3

- Click the Search Maps button to search the Google Maps database and display the search results (Figure 2–58).

🔍 **Experiment**

- In the National Balloon Museum - Google Maps window, click the Zoom In and Zoom Out buttons multiple times to zoom the map in and out.

🔍 **Experiment**

- Click the Satellite button to view satellite imagery of the area surrounding the National Balloon Museum.

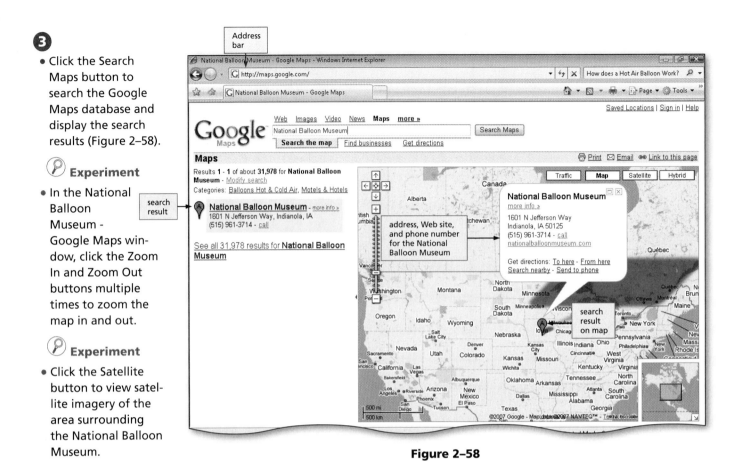

Figure 2–58

To Search the Web for a Definition of a Word

The Dictionary.com Web page allows you to search for an encyclopedia article, definition, or synonym and antonym. When you enter a word and then click the Search button, the word's definition is displayed. The following steps use Dictionary.com to find the definition of the word "ballooning."

1

- Type www. dictionary.com in the Address bar and then press the ENTER key to display the Dictionary.com Web page (Figure 2–59).

Figure 2–59

❷

- Type `ballooning` in the text box at the top of the Dictionary. com Web page (Figure 2–60).

Figure 2–60

❸

- Click the Search button.

- If necessary, scroll down to display the first definition. (Figure 2–61)

Dictionary.com
When you look up a definition on the Dictionary.com Web site, you may notice a Cite This Source link that appears immediately above the definition. If you click this link, a new Web page will open that specifically tells you how to cite the Web page containing your definition.

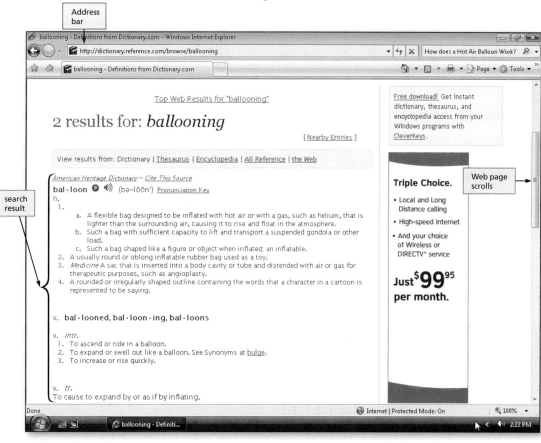

Figure 2–61

To Search the Web for a Picture

When you want to search for an image, many search engines are available to provide convenient access to millions of images. The following steps use Windows Live to search for images related to ballooning.

1

• Type www.live.com in the Address bar and then press the ENTER key to display the Live Search Web page (Figure 2–62).

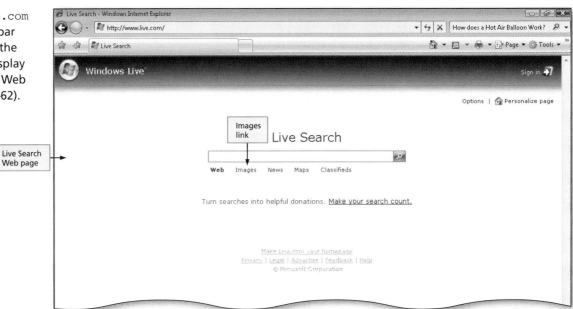

Figure 2–62

2

• Click the Images link to display the Live Search Images Web page (Figure 2–63).

Figure 2–63

3

• Type ballooning in the Live Search text box (Figure 2–64).

Figure 2–64

4

• Click the Search button to initiate the Windows Live search and display the search results (Figure 2–65).

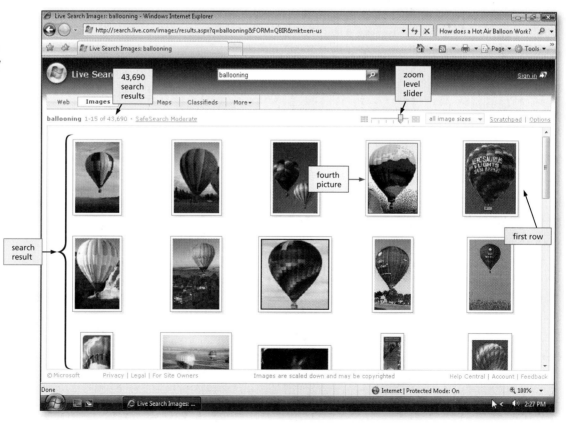

Figure 2–65

5

- Click the fourth picture in the first row to display the Web page containing the picture (Figure 2–66). The location of this picture in your listing may be different than in Figure 2–65.

Q&A

Can I use the pictures that a search engine returns for personal or business-related use?

You always should obtain permission from the person or company hosting the Web site containing the image before using it for your own purposes. Many images on the Internet are protected by copyright regulations and are unavailable for use without permission.

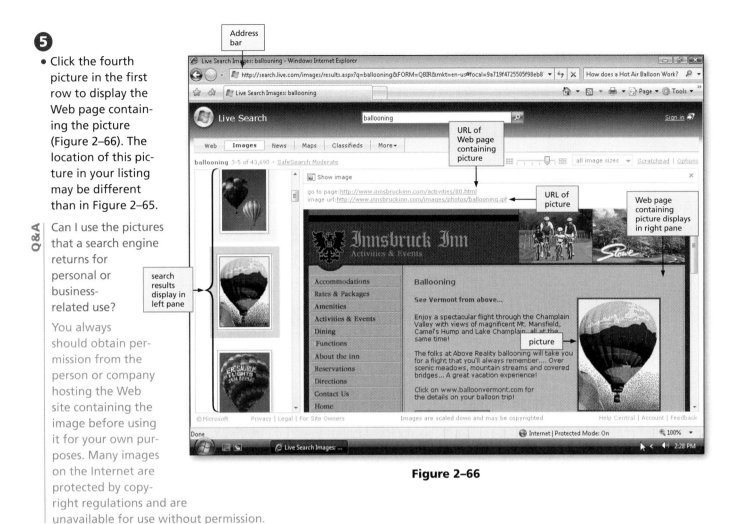

Figure 2–66

Using the Address Bar to Search the Web

Previously, this chapter used various Web sites to search for information (Web page, mailing address, place or landmark, definitions, pictures, and so on). Using the Address bar also allows you to search for information on the Web. You can use the Address bar to type an address (URL) and display the associated Web page or to type a keyword or phrase (search inquiry) to display a list of Web pages relating to the keyword or phrase. Using the Address bar to search for a keyword or phrase is known as a **Keyword system**.

Additionally, you can use the Address bar to navigate your local computer. Typing a folder location (path) in the Address bar will display a new window that contains the contents of the folder, typing an application program name will start a program, and typing a document name will start an application and display the document in the application window.

To Search for a Web Page Using the Keyword System

If you type a specific product, trademark, company name, or institution name in the Address bar and then press the ENTER key, Windows Live Search will search for and display a list of Web pages relating to the entry in the Address bar. Any Address bar entry that does not look like a URL is passed to the Keyword system.

You are looking for information on the National Balloon Museum, but do not know the museum's URL. After entering the phrase, National Balloon Museum, Windows Live Search searches for and displays a list of Web pages. The following steps use the Keyword system to display the home page of the National Balloon Museum.

1

- Click the Address bar and then type National Balloon Museum in the Address bar (Figure 2–67).

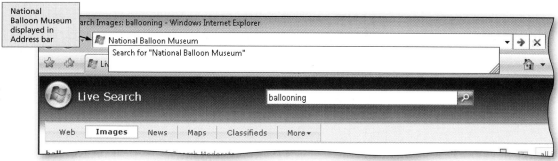

Figure 2–67

2

- Press the ENTER key to display the Windows Live search results in the display area (Figure 2–68).

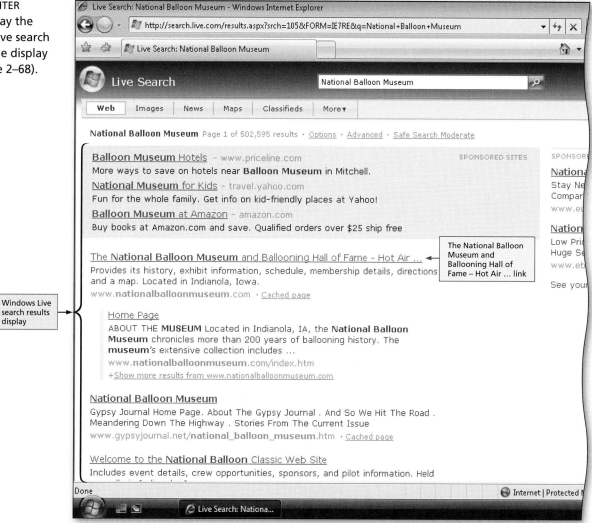

Figure 2–68

3

- Click the The National Balloon Museum and Ballooning Hall of Fame – Hot Air ... link to display the home page for The National Balloon Museum (Figure 2–69).

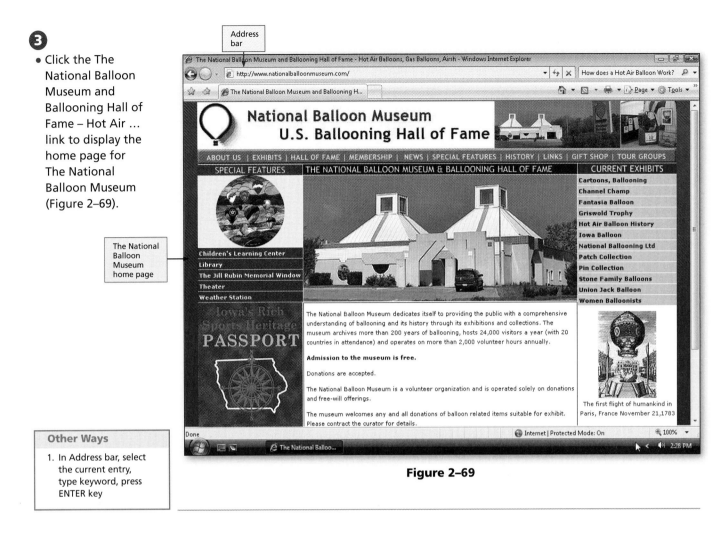

Figure 2–69

Other Ways

1. In Address bar, select the current entry, type keyword, press ENTER key

To Search for Related Web Pages Using the Keyword System

More often than not, the topic on which you want information is much more general than the name of a company or institution. If you enter a general keyword, such as music, surfing, or education, the Keyword system passes the keyword to Windows Live Search, which returns a Web page with several related links from which you can choose. Windows Live Search is Internet Explorer's default search engine.

You are looking for information on the topic, aviation, for a term paper. The following steps show how the Keyword system passes the general topic, aviation, to Windows Live Search, which displays a page of links from which you can choose.

1

• Click the Address bar and then type `aviation` in the Address bar (Figure 2–70).

Figure 2–70

2

• Press the ENTER key to display the search results (Figure 2–71).

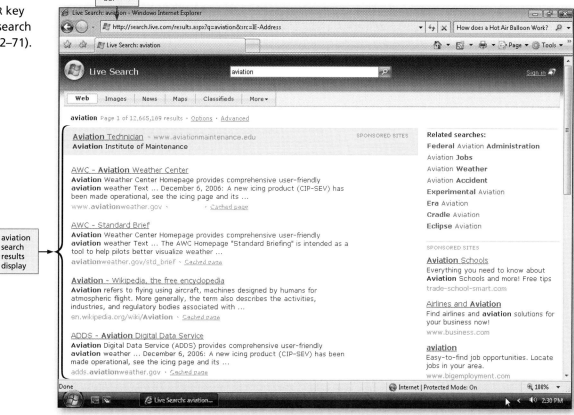

Figure 2–71

Other Ways

1. In Address box press TAB key to select entry, type keywords, press ENTER key

To Search for a Folder and Its Contents

To display the contents of a folder on the local computer or on the network using the Address bar, you type the path of the folder and then press the ENTER key. A **path** is the means of navigating to a specific location on a computer or network. To specify a path, you must type the drive letter, followed by a colon (:), a backslash (\), and the folder name. For example, the path for the Windows folder on drive C is C:\Windows. The following steps use the path of the Windows folder on the local computer to display the contents of the Windows folder in the display area of the browser window.

1
- Click the Address bar and then type c:\windows in the Address bar (Figure 2–72).

Figure 2–72

2
- Press the ENTER key to display a new window containing the contents of the Windows folder (Figure 2–73). If the Internet Explorer Security dialog box displays, click the Allow button.

3
- Click the Close button on the C:\Windows window to close the window.

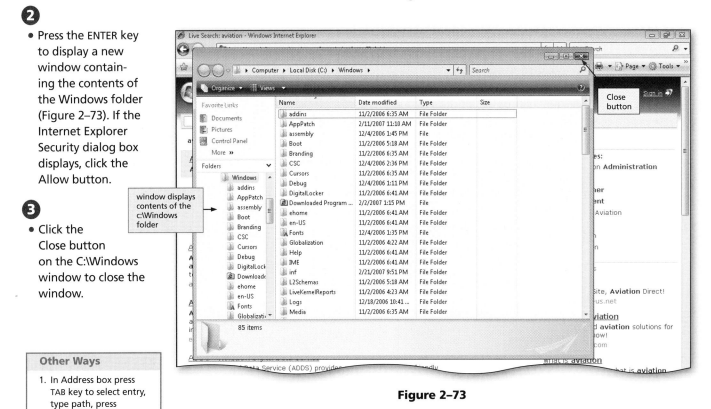

Figure 2–73

Other Ways
1. In Address box press TAB key to select entry, type path, press ENTER key

In addition to using the Address bar to display a Web page, search for information on the Web, and display the contents of a folder, you also can use the Address bar to start a program and open a document. To start an application, such as the Notepad application, you type the path and application name (C:\Windows\notepad.exe) in the Address bar and then press the ENTER key. The Untitled - Notepad window will appear on the desktop. To display a document, you type the document name in the Address bar and then press the ENTER key. The document will appear in a separate window.

Why study different search tools? Just as it is impossible for a card catalog to contain an entry for every book in the world, it is impossible for each search tool to catalog every Web page on the World Wide Web. In addition, different search tools on the Web perform different types of searches. Some search for keywords in the title of a Web page, while others scan links for the keywords. Still others search the entire text of Web pages. Because of the different searching techniques, the results of a search vary surprisingly.

Chapter Summary

In this chapter, you have learned about the twelve general types of Web pages and the three general types of search tools. You learned how to evaluate a Web page as a potential source for research. You learned how to search the Internet using the Yahoo! Directory. You learned the techniques for using the Windows Live Search and Google search engines to enter keywords and use advanced search techniques. You learned how to record relevant information about a potential source for future reference and how to write a citation for a Web resource. You also saw how to use various Web sites to search the Internet for an address, a map, a definition, and a picture. In addition, you learned how to search the Web using the Address bar and the Keyword system.

The items listed below include all the new Internet Explorer skills you have learned in this chapter.

1. Start Internet Explorer (IE 83)
2. Display the Yahoo! Directory Home Page (IE 84)
3. Search Using the Yahoo! Directory (IE 85)
4. Evaluate a Web Resource (IE 88)
5. Search Using the Google Simple Search Form (IE 90)
6. Open a Link in a New Tab (IE 92)
7. Switch Between Tabs (IE 93)
8. Switch Between Tabs by Using the Tab List Button (IE 95)
9. Switch Between Tabs by Using the Quick Tabs Button (IE 97)
10. Close a Tab (IE 98)
11. Customize the Instant Search Box by Adding a Search Engine (IE 100)
12. Search for Web Pages Using the Ask.com Search Engine (IE 103)
13. Display the Google Advanced Search Form (IE 107)
14. Search Using Google Advanced Search (IE 108)
15. Record Relevant Information About a Web Research Source in WordPad (IE 110)
16. Save a WordPad Document (IE 114)
17. Search the Web for an Address (IE 115)
18. Search the Web for a Map of a Place or Landmark (IE 117)
19. Search the Web for a Definition of a Word (IE 118)
20. Search the Web for a Picture (IE 120)
21. Search for a Web Page Using the Keyword System (IE 123)
22. Search for Related Web Pages Using the Keyword System (IE 124)
23. Search for a Folder and Its Contents (IE 126)

Learn It Online

Test your knowledge of chapter content and key terms.

Instructions: To complete the Learn It Online exercises, start your browser, click the Address bar, and then enter the Web address scsite.com/ie7/learn. When the Internet Explorer 7 Learn It Online page is displayed, click the link for the exercise you want to complete and then read the instructions.

Chapter Reinforcement TF, MC, and SA
A series of true/false, multiple-choice, and short-answer questions that test your knowledge of the chapter content.

Flash Cards
An interactive learning environment where you identify chapter key terms associated with displayed definitions.

Practice Test
A series of multiple-choice questions that test your knowledge of chapter content and key terms.

Who Wants To Be a Computer Genius?
An interactive game that challenges your knowledge of chapter content in the style of the television quiz show.

Wheel of Terms
An interactive game that challenges your knowledge of chapter key terms in the style of the television show *Wheel of Fortune*.

Crossword Puzzle Challenge
A crossword puzzle that challenges your knowledge of key terms presented in the chapter.

Apply Your Knowledge

Reinforce the skills and apply the concepts you learned in this chapter.

Searching the Web for Art Exhibits Using the Yahoo! Directory
Problem: To practice using the Yahoo! Directory you will search for an art exhibit. You will need to print a Web page containing a graphic image to complete this assignment.

Instructions: Perform the following tasks.

Part 1: Displaying the Yahoo! Directory
1. If necessary, connect to the Internet and start Internet Explorer.
2. Click the Address bar, type dir.yahoo.com, and then press the ENTER key to display the Yahoo! Directory.

Part 2: Finding Art Departments Using the Yahoo! Directory
1. Click the Arts & Humanities link to display the Arts & Humanities category.
2. Click the Museums, Galleries, and Centers link to display the Museums, Galleries, and Centers subcategory.
3. Click the Exhibits link to display the Exhibits subcategory.
4. Click the Universities@ link to display the Universities subcategory.
5. Click the Hittin' the Roofs link to display the ASU Art Museum Web page.
6. Click the Current Exhibitions link at the top of the page to display the ASU Art Museum Current Exhibitions and Events Web page (Figure 2–74).

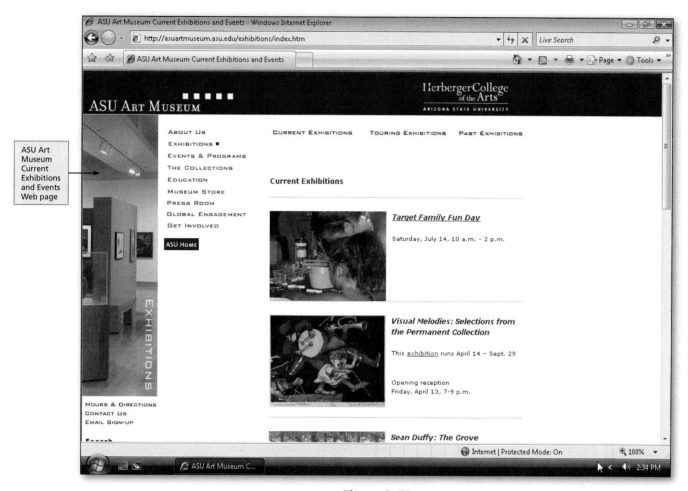

ASU Art Museum Current Exhibitions and Events Web page

Figure 2–74

7. Print the page, write your name and a brief description of the contents on the printed page, and submit it to your instructor.

Extend Your Knowledge

Extend the skills you learned in this chapter and experiment with new skills. You may need to use Help to complete the assignment.

Searching the Web for Various Information Using the Web Directories

Instructions: Connect to the Internet and start Internet Explorer. You will use various search tools to find answers to the questions below. Hand in the printed Web pages to complete the assignment.

Instructions: Perform the following tasks.

1. Navigate to the Google Directory (Figure 2–75). Using the Health category, locate information on Neuromuscular Integrative Action (Nia). Answer the following questions:

Figure 2–75

 a. List the URLs of three Web sites that discuss Nia.

 b. Who developed Nia?

 c. What are the benefits of Nia?

 d. Print the Web page(s) containing the answers to these questions.

2. Using the Yahoo! Directory, locate the home page of the only private college in Cherokee County, South Carolina. Answer the following questions:

 a. What is the college name?

 b. In what city is the college located?

 c. What team name does the Athletic department use?

 d. Print the home page of the college.

3. Using the search.com directory and the Recreation category, locate information about water parks in Canada and answer the following questions:

 a. What is the name of a water park in Canada?

 b. What are at least two rides or attractions at the park?

 c. Where is the park located?

 d. Print the Web page(s) containing the answers to these questions.

4. Using the Yahoo! Directory and the Science category, locate information about the periodic table of elements and answer the following questions:

 a. What is the symbol for Gold?

 b. Which element is associated with the symbol Ca?

 c. What is the atomic weight of Californium?

 d. Print the Web page containing the periodic table.

5. Submit the printed Web pages to your instructor.

In the Lab

Use Internet Explorer to navigate the World Wide Web by using the guidelines, concepts, and skills presented in this chapter. Labs are listed in order of increasing difficulty.

Lab 1: Searching the Web Using the Google Directory

Problem: Your instructor would like you to use the Google Directory to find Web pages that contain information on games, antiques, and recreational activities. To complete this assignment, you will need to print the first page of each Web site you visit that supplies the requested information.

Instructions: Perform the following tasks.

Part 1: Starting Internet Explorer and Displaying the Google Directory

 1. If necessary, connect to the Internet and start Internet Explorer.

 2. Display the Google home page.

Continued >

In the Lab *continued*

3. Click the more link, click the even more link (Figure 2–76), and then click Directory on the resulting page.

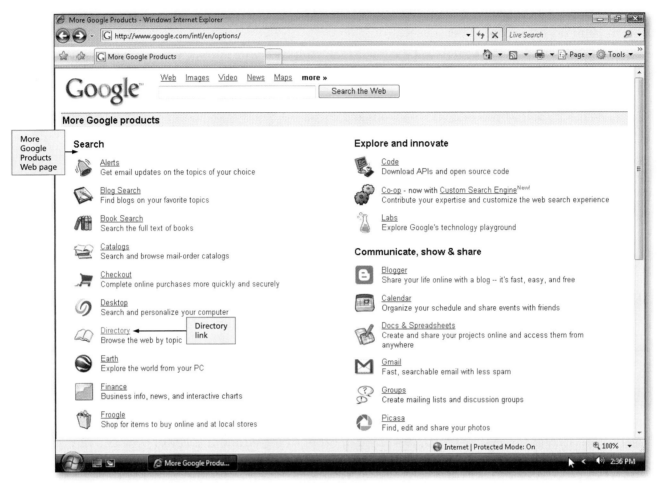

Figure 2–76

Part 2: Finding Antiques Using the Google Directory

1. Using the Google Directory and the Arts category, locate a Web page that contains information on antique Canon cameras. Print the Web page.

2. Locate a Web page that contains information about antique bicycles, and print the Web page.

3. Locate a Web page that contains information about antique phonographs, and print the Web page.

Part 3: Finding Games Using the Google Directory

1. Using the Google Directory and the Games category, locate a Web page that contains the rules for the Cribbage card game. Print the Web page.

2. Locate a Web page that contains the rules for the Canasta card game, and print the Web page.

3. Locate a Web page that contains rules for the Pinochle card game, and print the Web page.

Part 4: Finding Recreational Activities Using the Google Directory
1. Using the Google Directory and the Recreation category, locate a Web page that contains images of Squash. Print the Web page.

2. Locate a Web page that contains images of greyhounds, and print the Web page.

3. Locate a Web page that contains information about archery, and print the Web page.

4. Submit all printed Web pages to your instructor.

In the Lab

Lab 2: Searching the Web Using AltaVista and Keywords

Problem: Your instructor would like you to use the AltaVista search engine to search for Web pages on two of the topics listed below. You will need to record the URL of each Web page and develop a short report on each topic using WordPad.

Instructions: Perform the following tasks.

Part 1: Displaying the AltaVista Home Page
1. Click the Address box, type www.altavista.com, and then press the ENTER key to display the AltaVista home page. The home page contains the AltaVista simple search form.

Part 2: Performing an AltaVista Simple Search
1. Use the text box and the FIND button in the AltaVista simple search form to search for two of the following topics: bungee jumping, ice climbing, snowboarding, hang gliding, skydiving, or any other extreme sport. Figure 2–77 shows a Web page about bungee jumping.

Figure 2–77

Continued >

In the Lab *continued*

2. For both topics you selected, find two informational Web sites.

3. Using WordPad, copy information about each topic from the Web pages into a WordPad document and develop a short report about each topic. Add the URLs of the Web sites you used and your name to the end of the report.

4. Submit the WordPad document to your instructor.

Part 3: Performing an AltaVista Advanced Search
1. Click the Advanced Search link in the AltaVista simple search form.

2. Use the Advanced Search form to find three Web pages that contain information about three companies that provide training in the extreme sport you chose previously.

3. Print the three Web pages and write your name on each.

4. Submit the printed Web pages to your instructor.

In the Lab

Lab 3: Searching the Web Using Google and Keywords
Problem: You want to use both the Google simple search and advanced search to find Web pages relating to several topics. To complete this assignment, print the first page of each Web page you visit.

Instructions: Perform the following tasks.

Part 1: Starting the Google Search Engine
1. Navigate to the Google home page.

Part 2: Searching for a Web Page
1. Find a Web page containing inspirational quotations about children. Print the Web page.

2. Find the Web page containing the address, phone number, and e-mail address of your representative in the U.S. House of Representatives. Print the Web page.

3. Find the Official Web site of David Eckstein, and print the Web page.

Part 3: Searching for Information
1. Find the current temperature in Atlanta, Georgia. Print the Web page, circle the temperature, and write your name on it.

2. Using the keywords, movie database, find who played Irene Kritski in the movie The Super. Print the Web page and write the actor's name and your name on the printed Web page.

3. Locate a URL and address of a company or school that offers ballooning lessons, and print the Web page.

Part 4: Using the Google Advanced Search

1. Click Advanced Search on the Google home page to display the Google Advanced Search form (Figure 2–78).

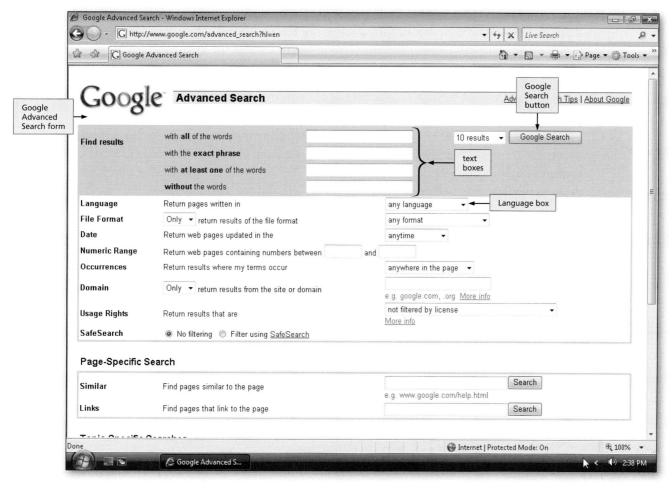

Figure 2–78

2. Find the number of Web pages that contain the keyword, airplane. Print the Web page and circle the number of search results that were returned.

3. Find the number of Web pages that contain the keywords, airplane and Boeing. Print the Web page and circle the number of search results that were returned.

4. Find the number of Web pages that contain the keywords, airplane, Boeing, and engines. Print the Web page and circle the number of search results that were returned.

5. Find the number of Web pages that contain the exact phrase, geographic map. Print the Web page and circle the number of search results that were returned.

6. Find the number of Web pages that contain the exact phrase, geographic map, and the keyword, Brazil. Print the Web page and circle the number of search results that were returned.

7. Find the number of Web pages that contain an exact phrase (geographic map), keyword (Brazil), and are written in the Portuguese language. Print the Web page and circle the number of search results that were returned.

8. Submit all printed Web pages to your instructor.

In the Lab

Lab 4: Searching the Web Using Excite and Keywords

Problem: Your instructor would like you to use the Excite search engine to research one of topics listed below. You will need to copy information about the topic into a WordPad document and develop a short report to complete this assignment. Remember to include the URLs of each Web site you used.

Instructions: Perform the following tasks.

1. Click the Address bar, type `www.excite.com`, and then press the ENTER key to display the Excite home page. The home page contains the Excite simple search form.

2. Perform a search using Excite for any one of the following topics: government spending, a historical event, the life of a current political figure, an extreme weather event, milestones in aviation, an extraterrestrial sighting, or genetic engineering. Figure 2–79 shows the Web page of an organization that explores, understands, and explains the origin, nature, and prevalence of life in the universe.

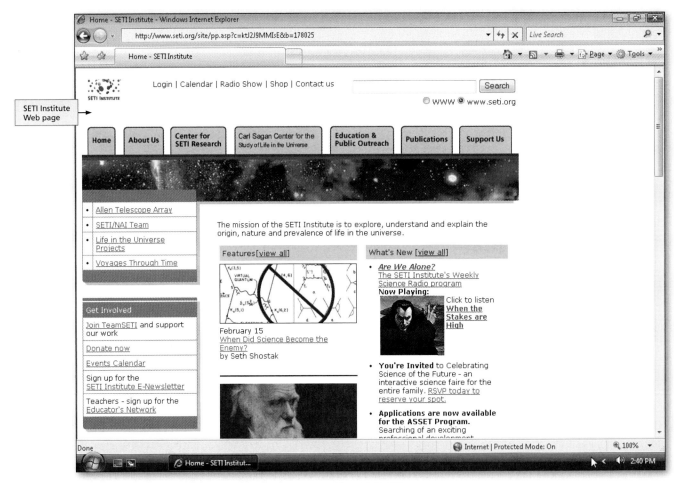

Figure 2–79

3. Find two informative Web pages about the topic you selected. Using WordPad, copy information about the topic from the Web pages into a WordPad document and develop a short report about the topic.

4. Add the URLs of the Web sites you used and your name to the end of the report.

5. Submit the WordPad document to your instructor.

In the Lab

Lab 5: Searching the Web Using Multiple Search Engines

Problem: You would like to become more familiar with search engines and be able to search for pictures, addresses, and maps. You will need to print the first page of each Web site you visit to complete this assignment.

Instructions: Perform the following tasks.

Part 1: Searching for Web Pages using Google
  1. Using Google, search for the following and print a Web page for each:
     a. A Web page containing a picture of a Red Ear Slider.
     b   A Web page containing a picture of Simon Cowell or Jay Leno.
     c. A Web page containing a picture of the northern lights (aurora borealis).

Part 2: Searching for a Business Address
  1. Enter www.infospace.com in the Address bar to display the Infospace home page.
  2. Use WordPad to create a list of business names, addresses, and telephone numbers for each of the following businesses: Specialty Supplies, Inc., Microsoft Corporation (Redmond, Washington), Flagler Museum (Palm Beach, Florida), and Recreational Equipment, Inc. (Sumner, Washington).

Part 3: Searching for a Map
  1. Enter maps.google.com in the Address bar to display the Google Maps Web page.
  2. Find and print a map for each of the following places or landmarks: Eiffel Tower (France), Key West (Florida), and White House (District of Columbia).
  3. Circle the place or landmark on the map and write your name on each map.

Part 4: Searching for a Picture
  1. Enter www.corbis.com in the Address bar to display the Corbis home page (Figure 2–80).

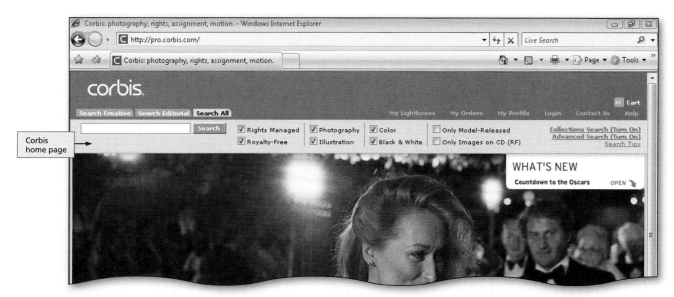

Figure 2–80

Continued >

In the Lab *continued*

2. Find and print a picture of the Golden Gate Bridge.

3. Find and print a picture of the Seattle Space Needle.

4. Find and print a picture of the Statue of Liberty.

5. Submit all the printed Web pages and the WordPad document to your instructor.

In the Lab

Lab 6: Searching for Home Pages Using the Address Bar

Problem: You are currently searching for an educational institution where you can complete your master's degree. Since you know the names of the institutions you wish to research, you will use the Address bar to find their home pages to assist with your research.

Instructions: Use the Address bar in Internet Explorer to find the URL for each of the educational institutions listed below, and use the search tools within each institution's Web site to answer the following questions.

Part 1: Learning about the University of New Hampshire

1. What is the URL for the University of New Hampshire?

2. What are the names of the three colleges in the University of New Hampshire?

3. What can a student expect to find in the Memorial Union building?

Part 2: Learning about the University of Michigan

1. What is the URL for the University of Michigan?

2. What is the URL for the Ross School of Business?

3. In which city is the University of Michigan's central campus located?

Part 3: Learning about the University of Miami

1. What is the URL for the University of Miami?

2. What are the names of at least four schools in the University of Miami?

3. What is the current student-faculty ratio?

Part 4: Compiling Results

1. Open WordPad and type a short report answering the questions listed above.

2. Submit the answers to the above questions to your instructor.

3. Quit WordPad and Internet Explorer.

Cases and Places

Apply your creative thinking and problem-solving skills to use the Internet to find the information you need.

• EASIER   •• MORE DIFFICULT

• 1: Search the Web for Concert Tour Locations and Dates

Many bands have their own home pages on the Web. Using the search engine of your choice, find out when and where the Dave Matthews Band will be performing next. Find and print their home page. Next, find out when and where your favorite performer, band, or musical group will be playing next. Find and print their home page. Do these pages qualify as informational Web pages? Write your answer and the reasons supporting your position and submit the report to your instructor.

• 2: Searching for and Comparing Skate Shops Online

You have been hired by a local skate shop to compare their store prices with the prices available on the Internet. Search the Internet for Web pages that sell skateboards and skateboard parts. Find at least five items being sold by three different online skate shops. Develop a price list to compare the prices of the five items and submit the price list to your instructor.

• 3: Searching For and Comparing Online Stock Brokers

You recently graduated from college and took a job at a small investment firm. Your first job is to search for and compare the services of the major online brokers. Find five online brokers and compare their services, costs to buy and sell stocks, Web sites, and any other pertinent information. Summarize your findings in a report.

•• 4: Designing Your Ideal Search Engine

Web search engines use different techniques for searching Web resources. If you were designing a search engine, what would you have the engine look for when determining whether a Web page successfully matches the keywords? Visit the Help page of a few search engines to get an idea of what criteria they use, and then write a list containing the criteria you would have your search engine use to determine whether a Web page is a successful match for keywords. Include an explanation for each item, such as the relative importance assigned, and then submit the list and explanations.

•• 5: Locating and Comparing Search Engines

Many search engines exist on the Internet. Locate at least five current search engines, and prepare a report for your instructor that compares and contrasts these search engines. Your report should discuss the different types of searches that each search engine is capable of performing. For example, the Google search engine can search for Web sites, images, news articles, maps, and more. You also should discuss how easy it is to use each search engine as well as the relevance of the search results returned by each search engine.

•• 6: Identifying Good Security Measures and Citing Your Sources

Working Together

Computer security is a major concern for systems administrators. An important first line of defense is an account name or username and password. Choosing good passwords is important for security issues. Have each member of your group select a different search engine and then find three different Web sites that describe criteria for creating a good password. Each member should record the relevant information necessary for citing the sources using the MLA or APA style. Print the three Web pages and write the citation on each page using either the MLA or APA style. As a group, each member should present their findings to the class.

3 Communicating Over the Internet

Objectives

You will have mastered the material in this project when you can:

- Open, read, print, reply to, and delete electronic mail messages
- Open a file attachment
- Compose and format an electronic mail message
- Attach a file to an e-mail
- Send an e-mail
- Add and delete a Windows contact
- Display newsgroups
- Subscribe to a newsgroup

- Read and print newsgroup articles
- Unsubscribe from a newsgroup
- Locate and subscribe to an RSS feed
- Identify other communication methods available on the Internet
- Start and sign in to Windows Live Messenger
- Add and remove a Windows Live Messenger contact
- Send an instant message

3 | Communicating Over the Internet

Introduction

In Chapters 1 and 2, you used Internet Explorer to search for information on the World Wide Web. In addition to searching for information, you also can use the Internet to communicate with other individuals. Web services available from Microsoft that are designed for communicating over the Internet include Windows Mail, which allows you to send and receive electronic mail and to read and post messages to a newsgroup; Windows Live Messenger, which allows you to communicate with other Windows Live Messenger members by sending and receiving instant messages; and Internet Explorer, which allows you to subscribe to RSS feeds and to visit various Web sites for other methods of communication such as blogs, chat rooms, bulletin boards and forums, and groups. In this chapter, you will use Windows Mail, Windows Live Messenger, and Internet Explorer to explore other methods of Web-based communications.

Overview

As you read this chapter, you will learn how to communicate over the Internet and use Internet Explorer, Windows Mail, and Windows Live Messenger by performing these general tasks:

- Send and receive e-mail
- Subscribe to and read newsgroup articles
- Subscribe to and read RSS feeds
- Send and receive instant messages

Plan Ahead

> **Internet Communication Guidelines**
>
> To communicate effectively, you should understand the general guidelines for using e-mail, instant messaging, and newsgroups. Before communicating via the Internet, consider these general guidelines:
>
> 1. **Determine the information you need.** The Internet provides access to a wealth of information, whether it is current news, a note from a friend stating whether she can join you for dinner Friday, or an instant message from a colleague who is asking a question for a customer at his desk. The type of information and the speed at which you need it will help you choose the most effective method of communication.
>
> 2. **Consider who is most likely to have the information you need.** Some applications, such as e-mail or instant messaging, allow you to communicate easily with friends and family, while others, such as newsgroups, provide you with access to people you may not know. If the information you are seeking is not available from those who are close to you, you will need to use a communication method that enables you to reach a broader audience.
>
> *(continued)*

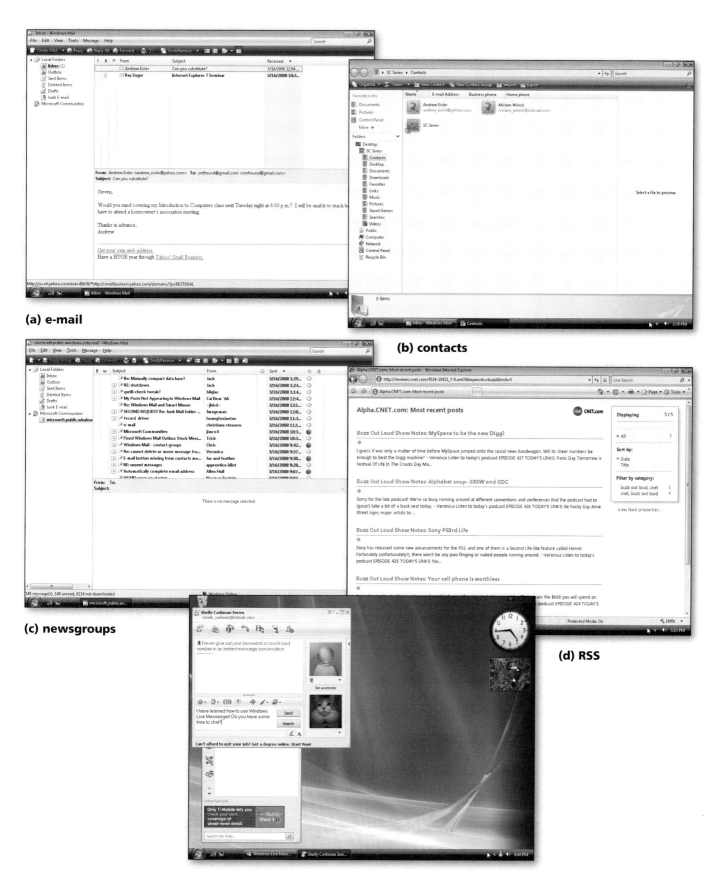

(a) e-mail

(b) contacts

(c) newsgroups

(d) RSS

(e) Instant Messaging

Figure 3–1

(continued)

3. **Communicate with people you trust.** The Internet enables anyone to communicate with you. In fact, it is possible to receive a large amount of unsolicited communication as well as harmful e-mail attachments. Communicate with individuals you trust or through exchanges that you initiate, and be cautious when communicating with strangers.

4. **Do not open unsolicited file attachments.** If you receive a file via an e-mail or an instant message, do not open it unless you are expecting it from someone you know and trust. Some viruses that travel via file attachments are able to appear as if they originated from someone you know and trust, so it is especially important for you to be careful. If you receive a file that you suspect to be infected with a virus, contact the sender of the file immediately.

5. **Determine whether your communication should be formal or informal.** If you are communicating with a potential employer or a colleague at work, you should use proper spelling, grammar, and etiquette. If you are communicating with friends and family, you can be less formal, and you might not bother checking for spelling and grammatical errors.

6. **Gather e-mail and instant messaging addresses.** Before you can send e-mail or instant messages to your friends, family, and colleagues, you will need to obtain their e-mail or instant messaging addresses. Without this information, you will be unable to communicate with them.

Electronic (E-Mail) Messages

Electronic mail (e-mail) has become an important means of exchanging messages and files between business associates and friends. Businesses find that using e-mail to send files electronically saves both time and money. Parents with students away at college or relatives who are scattered across the country find that exchanging e-mail messages is an inexpensive and easy way to stay in touch with family members. In fact, exchanging e-mail messages is one of the more widely used features of the Internet. E-mail is so popular nowadays that many individuals have multiple e-mail accounts. For instance, you might have an e-mail account for your job, and an e-mail address for personal use. It is important to recognize that if your employer supplies you with an e-mail account, all messages sent to and from that account are the property of, and accessible by, your employer. If you plan to send personal e-mail messages, it is recommended that you do not use the e-mail account provided by your employer. Some individuals also find it useful to have multiple personal e-mail accounts. They may give one e-mail address to their friends and family, and use another e-mail address when signing up for mailing lists, filling out registration forms, or entering a sweepstakes. This way personal e-mail is kept separate from bulk or junk e-mail.

E-mail can be accessed by using an e-mail program that is installed on your computer, such as Microsoft Outlook, Eudora, or Microsoft Windows Mail, or by using a Web-based e-mail service. A **Web-based e-mail service** allows you to send and receive e-mails by logging into a Web site, instead of installing an e-mail program on your computer. By using a Web-based e-mail service, you are able to check your e-mail on any computer that has an Internet connection and a Web browser. Free Web-based e-mail services include Windows Live Hotmail (www.hotmail.com), Gmail (www.gmail.com), Yahoo Mail (www.yahoo.com), and AIM Mail (www.aim.com). These companies are able to provide free Web-based e-mail services by placing advertisements on their Web sites or directly in the e-mail messages sent from their Web site. While all e-mail services offer the same basic functionality, such as sending and receiving e-mails and storing contact information, some features, such as the amount of storage space each service offers, may differ. Before choosing a Web-based e-mail service, compare the different options to determine which one might work best for you. Appendix B discusses how to sign up for a Windows Live Hotmail account.

If you work for an employer who provides you with an e-mail account, you most likely access your e-mail account by using an e-mail program installed on your computer. Some companies also provide Web-based access to their e-mail system, enabling employees to send and receive e-mail messages from a location other than the office. It is common for the Web-based interface to resemble the interface of the e-mail program you use in the office to access your e-mail account. While the interfaces and functionality may be similar between Web-based e-mail services and e-mail programs installed on your computer, some differences do exist. For example, if you are accessing your e-mail account by using an e-mail program installed on your computer, the e-mail messages are transferred to and stored on your computer before you can read them. If you are accessing your e-mail account using a Web-based e-mail service, the e-mail messages are stored remotely on the e-mail server.

Microsoft Windows Mail is an e-mail program that allows you to receive and store incoming e-mail messages, compose and send e-mail messages, access your Windows contacts and your Windows Calendar, and read and post messages to Internet newsgroups. Although the steps in this chapter are for Microsoft Windows Mail, other e-mail programs, whether they are installed on your computer or are Web-based, contain very similar functionality.

To Start Windows Mail

The following steps, which illustrate how to start Windows Mail, assume that you have Windows Mail installed on your computer and an e-mail account configured. For more information about configuring an e-mail account in Windows Mail, see your instructor.

1

• Display the Start menu.

• Click All Programs on the Start menu to display the All Programs list (Figure 3–2).

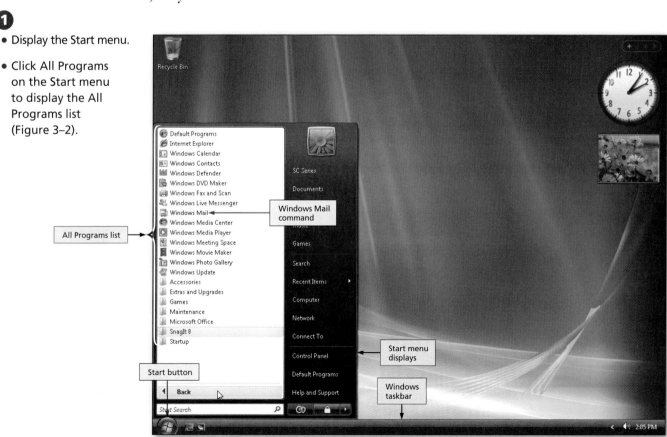

Figure 3–2

2
- Click Windows Mail to start the Windows Mail application.

- If necessary, maximize the Inbox - Windows Mail window (Figure 3–3).

Q&A

Why does my screen look different?

Because you are accessing your own e-mail account, Windows Mail will display different e-mail messages in the message list. However, you can still follow the steps presented in this chapter by using the e-mails displayed in your message list.

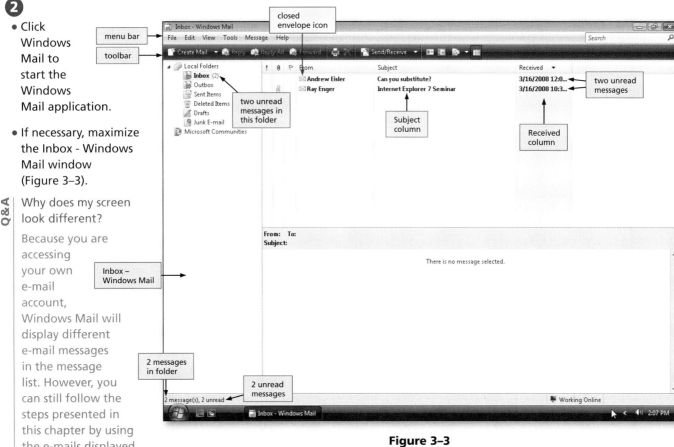

Figure 3–3

Other Ways

1. Press CTRL+ESC, type `windows mail`, click Windows Mail

BTW

Windows Mail
Windows Mail, like many other e-mail programs, allows you to change the appearance of e-mail by using different fonts and formatting, changing the background graphic, attaching files, and adding links to Web pages.

The Windows Mail Window

The Inbox - Windows Mail window shown in Figure 3–3 contains a number of elements. The title bar contains the folder name (Inbox) and the application name (Windows Mail). A toolbar below the title bar and menu bar contains buttons specific to Windows Mail (Create Mail, Reply, Reply All, Forward, and so on). Table 3–1 contains the toolbar buttons and a brief explanation of their functions.

Table 3–1 Toolbar Buttons and Functions

Button	Function
Create Mail	Displays the New Message window used to compose a new e-mail message.
Reply	Displays a window used to reply to an e-mail message. The recipient's name, original subject of the e-mail message preceded by the Re: entry, and the original e-mail message appear in the window.
Reply All	Displays a window used to reply to an e-mail message. The names of all recipients, subject of the e-mail message preceded by the Re: entry, and the original e-mail message appear in the window.
Forward	Displays a window used to forward an e-mail message to another recipient. The original subject of the e-mail message preceded by the Fw: entry and the original e-mail message appear in the window.

Table 3–1 Toolbar Buttons and Functions (continued)	
Button	**Function**
	Prints the highlighted e-mail message in the message list.
	Deletes the highlighted e-mail message in the message list by moving the message to the Deleted Items folder.
	Displays the Windows Mail dialog box, contacts the mail server, sends any e-mail messages in the Outbox folder, and places new e-mail messages in the Inbox folder.
	Displays the Contacts window containing a list of frequently used contacts.
	Displays the Windows Calendar, containing a list of appointments and tasks you may have scheduled.
	Displays the Find Message window that allows you to search for an e-mail message in the message list based on sender name, recipient name, e-mail subject, e-mail message, date, whether the e-mail has an attachment, and whether the e-mail is flagged.
	Displays or hides the Folder list in the left pane.

The Inbox - Windows Mail window is divided into three areas. The **Folder list** contains, in a hierarchical structure, the Local Folders folder and the six mail folders contained within it. The six standard mail folders (Inbox, Outbox, Sent Items, Deleted Items, Drafts, and Junk E-mail) are displayed when you first start Windows Mail. Although you cannot rename or delete these folders, you can create additional folders.

The **Inbox folder** in Figure 3–4 on the next page is the destination for incoming mail. The **Outbox folder** temporarily holds messages you send until Windows Mail delivers them. The **Sent Items folder** retains copies of messages that you have sent. The **Deleted Items folder** contains messages that you have deleted. As a safety precaution, you can retrieve deleted messages from the Deleted Items folder if you later decide you want to keep them. Deleting messages from the Deleted Items folder removes the messages permanently. The **Drafts folder** retains copies of messages that you are not yet ready to send. The **Junk E-mail folder** contains e-mail messages that have been flagged as junk e-mail. Windows Mail contains a feature that can automatically detect junk e-mail, otherwise known as unsolicited commercial e-mail, or spam. Although Windows Mail can identify most junk e-mail, it cannot detect it all. Similarly, Windows Mail may incorrectly flag an incoming message as junk e-mail. For this reason, it is important that you check your Junk E-mail folder regularly to ensure that no legitimate messages have been filed there.

Folders can contain e-mail messages, faxes, and files created in other Windows applications. Folders in bold type followed by a blue number in parentheses indicate the number of messages in the folder that are unopened. Other folders may appear on your computer in addition to the folders shown in Figure 3–4.

The contents of the Inbox folder automatically appear in the **message list** shown in Figure 3–4 when you start Windows Mail. The first three columns in the message list contain icons that provide information about the e-mail. The second three columns contain the e-mail author's name or e-mail address, subject of the message, and date and time the message was received. Collectively, these three entries are referred to as the **message heading**.

An exclamation point icon appearing in the first column indicates that the e-mail message has been marked high priority by the sender, suggesting that it should be read immediately. A paper clip icon appearing in the second column indicates that the e-mail message contains an attachment. In Figure 3–4, the second e-mail message in the message list (Ray Enger) contains an attachment, as indicated by the paper clip icon. A flag icon in the third column indicates the e-mail message has been flagged. You may choose to flag an important message that you want to revisit at a later time.

BTW

Mail Folders
You can create additional folders in the Local Folders folder. To do so, right-click the Local Folders icon, click New Folder, type the folder name in the Folder name text box, and then click the OK button.

A closed envelope icon in the From column and a message heading that appears in bold type identifies an unread e-mail message. In Figure 3–4, the second e-mail message, from Ray Enger, contains a paper clip icon, a closed envelope icon, and a message heading that appears in bold type. The closed envelope icon and bold message heading indicate that the e-mail message has not been read (opened) and the paper clip indicates that the message has an attachment.

The first e-mail message, from Andrew Eisler, contains an opened envelope icon and a message heading that appears in normal type. The icon and message heading indicate that the e-mail message has been read. Because you will be accessing Windows Mail with a different e-mail account, other e-mail messages will display on your computer in place of these messages.

The closed envelope icon is one of several icons, called **message list icons**, that display in the From column. Different message list icons may display in the From column to indicate the status of the message. The icon may indicate an action that was performed by the sender or one that was performed by the recipient. The actions may include reading, replying to, forwarding, digitally signing, and encrypting a message. The **Preview pane** in Figure 3–4 contains the text of the highlighted e-mail message (Andrew Eisler) in the message pane. The **message header** is displayed at the top of the Preview pane and contains the sender's name and e-mail address, recipient's e-mail address, and the subject of the e-mail. The text of the e-mail message appears below the message header.

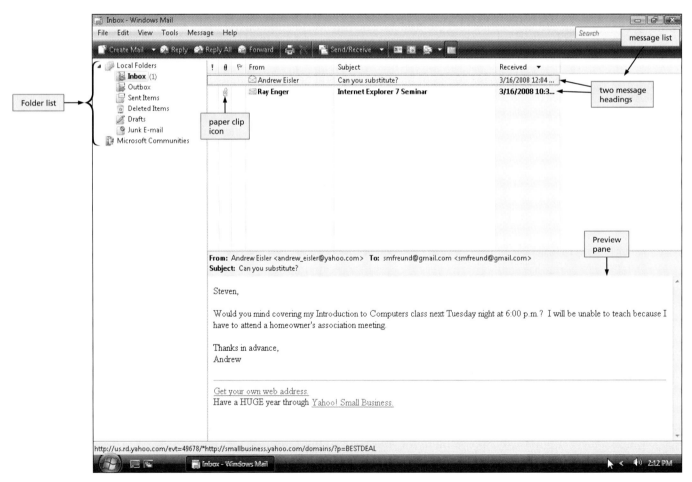

Figure 3–4

Opening and Reading E-Mail Messages

In Figure 3–4, the message headings for Andrew Eisler and Ray Enger are displayed in the message list. Double-clicking the closed envelope icon in either heading opens the e-mail message in a separate window, as opposed to opening it in the Preview pane.

BTW

Reading E-Mail Messages
Many people minimize the Inbox - Windows Mail window. When they receive a new e-mail message, an envelope icon is displayed in the status area on the Windows taskbar and a notification sound is played.

To Open (Read) an E-Mail Message

The following step opens an e-mail message in a new window so you can read it.

1

- Double-click anywhere on the message heading of the message from Andrew Eisler, which has the closed envelope icon. If the envelope icon for Andrew Eisler is not displayed in the message list, double-click another message with a closed envelope icon.

- Maximize the Can you substitute? window (Figure 3–5).

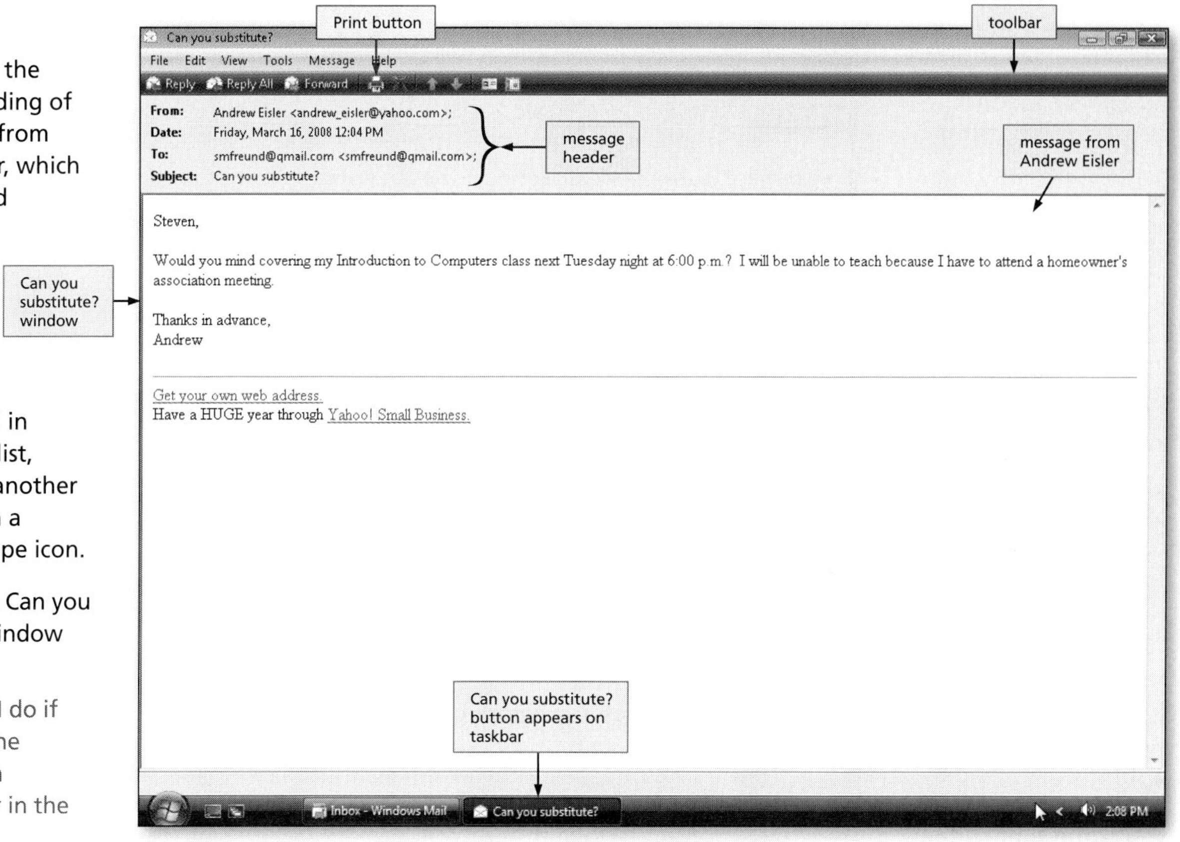

Q&A

What should I do if I do not see the message from Andrew Eisler in the message list?

If you do not see the message from Andrew Eisler, double-click any message in the message list and then maximize the window that opens.

Figure 3–5

When you double-click a closed envelope icon in the message list, Windows Mail displays the message in a separate window, changes the closed envelope icon to an opened envelope icon, and no longer displays the message heading in bold type. The number of unread e-mails next to the Inbox folder in the Folder list also decreases by one.

Other Ways

1. Right-click message heading with a closed envelope icon, click Open on shortcut menu
2. Click message heading with a closed envelope icon, on File menu click Open
3. Select message heading, press CTRL+O

The Windows Mail toolbar (Figure 3–6) contains the buttons needed to work with opened e-mail messages (Reply, Reply All, Forward, and so on). Table 3–2 contains the toolbar buttons and a brief explanation of their functions.

Figure 3–6

Table 3–2 Toolbar Buttons and Functions

Button	Function
Reply	Displays a window used to reply to an e-mail message. The e-mail address, original subject of the e-mail message preceded by the Re: entry, and original e-mail message appear in the window.
Reply All	Displays a window used to reply to an e-mail message. The e-mail addresses of all recipients, subject of the e-mail message preceded by the Re: entry, and original e-mail message appear in the window.
Forward	Displays a window used to forward an e-mail message to another recipient. The original subject of the e-mail message preceded by the Fw: entry and the original e-mail message appear in the window.
	Prints the e-mail message in the window.
	Deletes the e-mail message in the window by moving the message to the Deleted Items folder and displays the next e-mail message in the message list.
	Displays the previous e-mail message in the message list.
	Displays the next e-mail message in the message list.
	Displays the Contacts window containing a list of frequently used contacts.
	Displays the Windows Calendar containing a list of your appointments and tasks.

To Print an Opened E-Mail Message

You can print the contents of an e-mail message before or after opening the message. The following steps print an opened e-mail message.

1

• Click the Print button on the toolbar to display the Print dialog box (Figure 3–7).

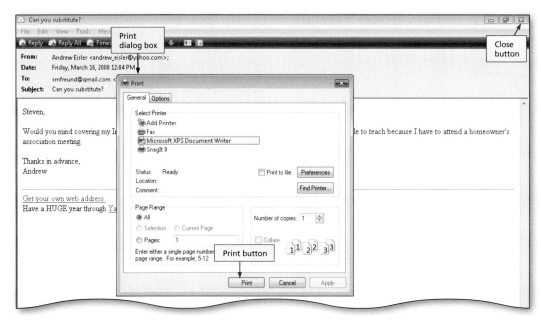

Figure 3–7

2

- Click the Print button in the Print dialog box (Figure 3–8).

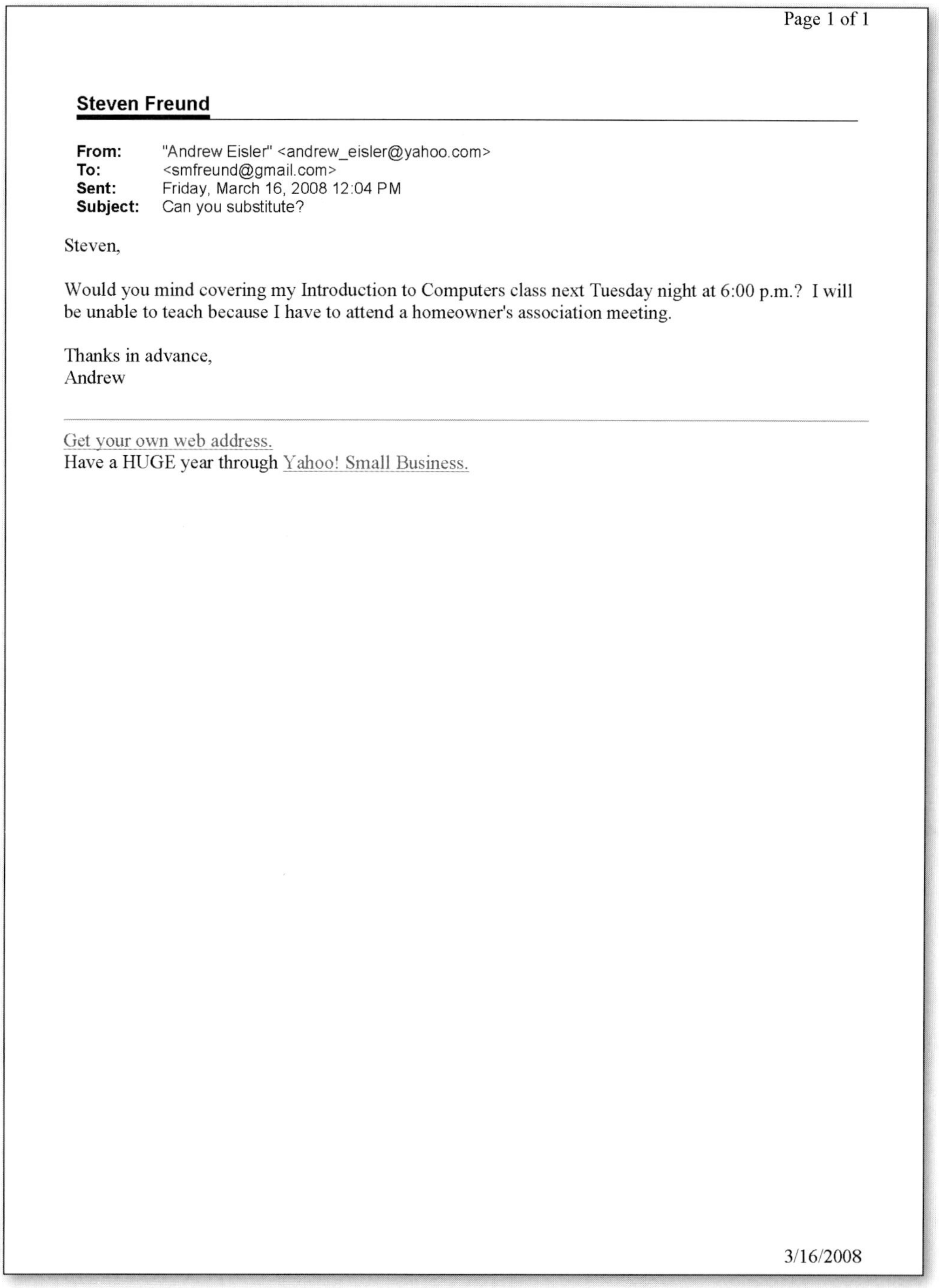

Page 1 of 1

Steven Freund

From: "Andrew Eisler" <andrew_eisler@yahoo.com>
To: <smfreund@gmail.com>
Sent: Friday, March 16, 2008 12:04 PM
Subject: Can you substitute?

Steven,

Would you mind covering my Introduction to Computers class next Tuesday night at 6:00 p.m.? I will be unable to teach because I have to attend a homeowner's association meeting.

Thanks in advance,
Andrew

Get your own web address.
Have a HUGE year through Yahoo! Small Business.

3/16/2008

Figure 3–8

Other Ways

1. On File menu click Print, click Print button in Print dialog box
2. Press ALT+F, press P, press ENTER
3. Press CTRL+P, press ENTER

To Close an E-Mail Message

When you have finished opening and reading an e-mail message, you can close the window containing the message by following this step.

1

- Click the Close button on the title bar to close the window containing the e-mail message (Figure 3–9).

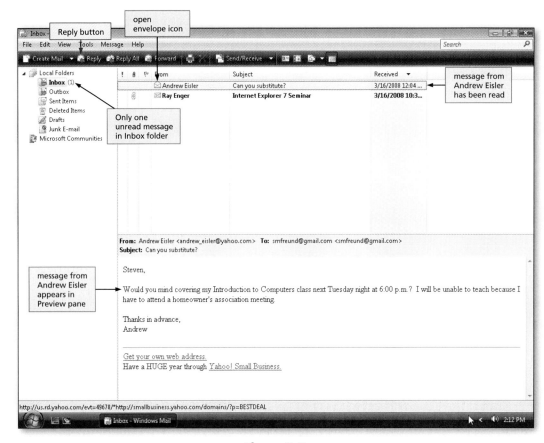

Figure 3–9

Other Ways

1. On File menu click Close   2. Press ALT+F4

To Reply to an E-Mail Message

One method of composing and sending an e-mail reply uses the Reply button, located on the toolbar. The Reply button opens a new message and pre-fills the To: with the e-mail address of the sender and the Subject: with the subject line of the original message preceded by Re: (regarding). The following steps compose and send an e-mail reply to a sender, in this case, Andrew Eisler, using the Reply button.

1

- Click the Reply button on the toolbar.

- Maximize the Re: Can you substitute? window (Figure 3–10).

If I am replying to a message that was sent to multiple recipients, will each recipient see my reply?

No. Your reply only will be sent to the sender of the original message. If you want all recipients to see your reply, you click the Reply All button instead of the Reply button.

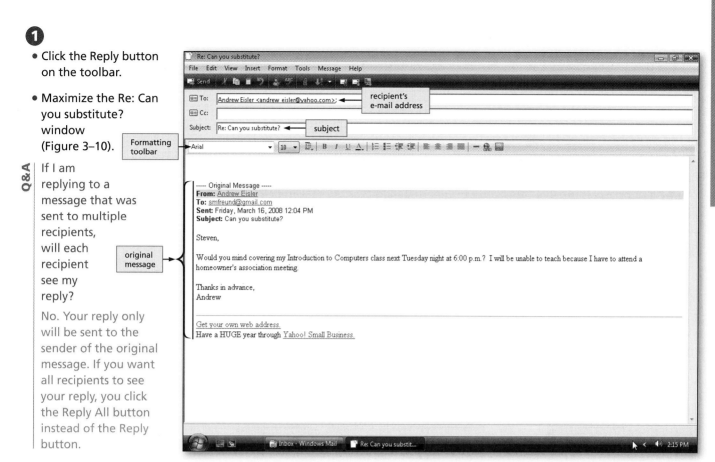

Figure 3–10

2

- Type I will be happy to cover your class. Please let me know what I will have to cover. (Figure 3–11).

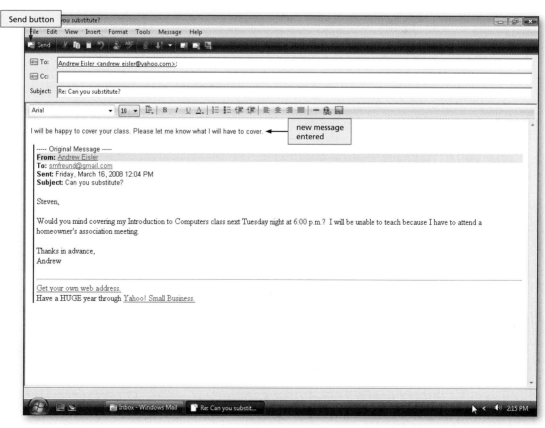

Figure 3–11

3

• Click the Send button on the toolbar to send the message (Figure 3–11).

How can I be sure that the intended recipient will receive my e-mail message?

The best way to verify that the recipient has received your e-mail message is to ask him or her for a response. If an e-mail address is incorrect, you often will receive an e-mail stating that your message was unable to be delivered. If this happens, confirm the e-mail address of your recipient and try to send the e-mail message again.

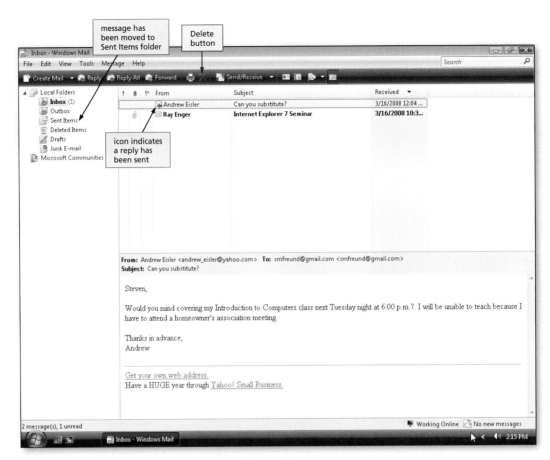

Figure 3–12

Other Ways

1. On Message menu click Reply to Sender
2. Press ALT+M, Press R
3. Press CTRL+R

BTW

Replying to an E-Mail Message
Some people who receive reply e-mail messages find it awkward that the original e-mail message appears with the reply message. To remove the original message from all e-mail replies, the person who sends the e-mail replies should click Tools on the menu bar, click Options, click the Send tab, click to deselect the Include message in reply check box, and then click the OK button.

In Figure 3–11 on the previous page, the underlined Andrew Eisler name appears in the To text box and the original e-mail message is identified by the words Original Message and the From, To, Sent, and Subject entries in the message list. In addition, the window contains a toolbar (Figure 3–13) below the menu bar. The buttons on the toolbar (Send, Cut, Copy, Paste, and so on) are useful when replying to a message. Table 3–3 shows the toolbar buttons and their functions.

Figure 3–13

Table 3–3 Toolbar Buttons and Functions

Button	Function
Send	Places the e-mail message in the Outbox folder temporarily, sends the message and then moves the message to the Sent Items folder.
	Moves a selected item in an e-mail message to the Clipboard.
	Copies a selected item in an e-mail message to the Clipboard.
	Copies an item from the Clipboard to an e-mail message.

Button	Function
Table 3–3 Toolbar Buttons and Functions (continued)	
	Undoes the previous operation.
	Checks the recipient's name against the Contacts list.
	Spell checks the e-mail message.
	Attaches a file to the e-mail message.
	Sets the priority (high, normal, or low) of an e-mail message.
	Digitally signs an e-mail message, allowing the recipient to verify the sender's authenticity.
	Encrypts, or scrambles, an e-mail message, preventing someone other than the recipient from reading the message.
	Allows you to work offline.

To Delete an E-Mail Message

After reading and replying to an e-mail message, you may want to delete the original e-mail message from the Message list. Deleting a message moves it from the Inbox folder to the Deleted Items folder. If you do not delete unwanted messages, large numbers of messages in the Inbox folder make it difficult to find and read new messages; this also wastes disk space. The following step deletes the e-mail message from Andrew Eisler.

1

- If necessary, click the message from Andrew Eisler in the Message list to select it.

- Click the Delete button on the toolbar to delete the message from Andrew Eisler (Figure 3–14).

Q&A

What should I do if I accidentally delete an e-mail message?

If you accidentally delete an e-mail message, the message remains on your computer until you delete it from the Deleted Items folder. To retrieve a message from the Deleted Items folder, click the folder, and drag the message to the Inbox folder.

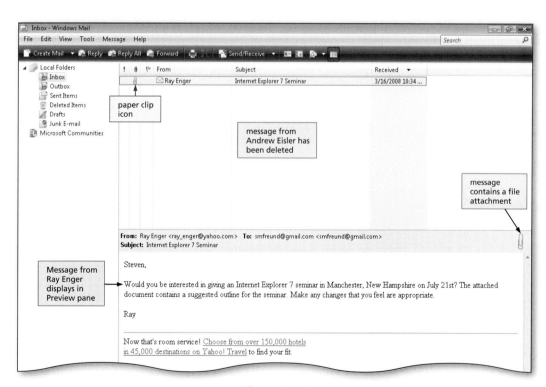

Figure 3–14

Other Ways

1. Drag e-mail message to Deleted Items folder in Folder list
2. On Edit menu click Delete
3. Right-click e-mail message, click Delete on shortcut menu
4. Press ALT+E, press D
5. Press CTRL+D

Mail Folders
If Windows Mail becomes slow or sluggish, you may be able to improve performance by removing old messages from the Inbox. You can either delete the messages or create a new folder and move messages from the Inbox into your new folder.

As you delete messages from the Inbox, the number of messages in the Deleted Items folder increases. To delete an e-mail message permanently, you should select the Deleted Items folder in the Folders list and then delete the message from that folder. Similarly, as you send and reply to messages, the number of messages in the Sent Items folder increases. To delete an e-mail message from the Sent Items folder, click the Sent Items folder icon in the Folders list, highlight the message in the message list, and then click the Delete button on the toolbar in the Sent Items - Windows Mail window.

To Open a File Attachment

The remaining message in the message list, from Ray Enger, contains a file attachment, as indicated by the paper clip icon displayed in the column below the second header. The following steps open the file attachment.

1
- Double-click the row containing the paper clip icon to the left of the Ray Enger name in the Message list.
- Maximize the Internet Explorer 7 Seminar window (Figure 3–15).

Q&A
Is it okay to open a file attachment if I do not know who has sent it to me?

You should never open a file attachment sent from an unknown source. It is usually best to only open file attachments when you are expecting them from a trusted source.

Figure 3–15

2
- Double-click the Internet Explorer 7 Outline.txt icon in the Attach box (Figure 3–16).

Q&A
What types of files can be attached to an e-mail?

File attachments can be anything from spreadsheets to pictures. If the Windows Mail dialog box appears when you attempt to open an attachment, you can open the attachment by clicking the Open button.

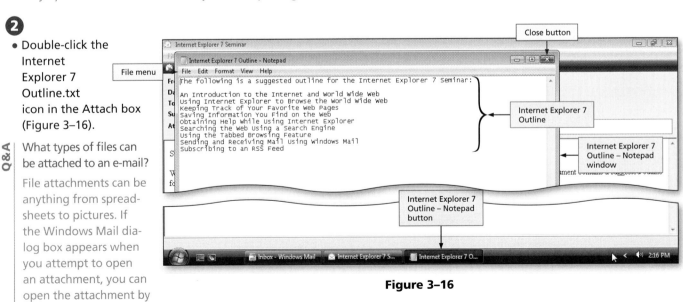

Figure 3–16

To Save and Close a File Attachment

After scanning the attachment in Notepad, you decide to save it to your computer to read at a later time. The following steps save and close the file attachment.

1 To display the Save As dialog box, click File on the menu bar and then click Save As.

2 If necessary, click the Browse Folders button and then click the Documents link to save the file to the Documents folder.

3 Click the Save button.

Q&A If I make changes to a file attachment before saving it, will the file attached to the original e-mail also change?

No. If you open the e-mail containing the attachment again, you will not see any of your changes. However, if you open the file that was saved to your computer, your changes will display.

4 Click the Close button in the Internet Explorer 7 Outline - Notepad window.

5 Click the Close button in the Internet Explorer 7 Seminar window.

Composing a New Mail Message

In addition to opening and reading, replying to, and deleting e-mail messages, you also need to compose and send new e-mail messages. When composing an e-mail message, you enter a brief one-line subject that identifies the purpose or contents of the message in the subject line, and type your text in the message area. You must know the e-mail address of the message recipient before you can send it.

You also can format e-mail messages to enhance their appearance. **Formatting** is the process of altering how a document looks by modifying the style, size, or color of its text, or by changing its background. One method of formatting an e-mail message is to select stationery. **Stationery** allows you to add a colorful background image, unique text sizes and colors, and custom margins to an e-mail message. For example, the Shades of Blue stationery causes a decorative blue background and the text of the e-mail message to appear using the Arial 10-point font and black text. The **Arial font** is one of many fonts, or typefaces, available to format an e-mail message. In addition, any links within the e-mail message will be underlined and displayed in blue text. It is important to note that in a business environment, it may be inappropriate to apply stationery to e-mail messages. In most cases, work-related e-mail uses the default background and text colors (black text on a white background). If you are sending a personal or informal e-mail message, selecting a stationery may be more appropriate.

To Compose an E-Mail Message Using Stationery

The next steps compose an e-mail message to one of the authors (Steven Freund) of this book using the Shades of Blue stationery.

1

- Click the Create Mail button arrow on the toolbar to display the Create Mail menu (Figure 3–17).

Q&A

What are the three commands at the bottom of the Create Mail menu?

The three commands at the bottom of the menu allow you to select from a larger list of stationeries, choose not to use stationery, or send a Web page as an e-mail message.

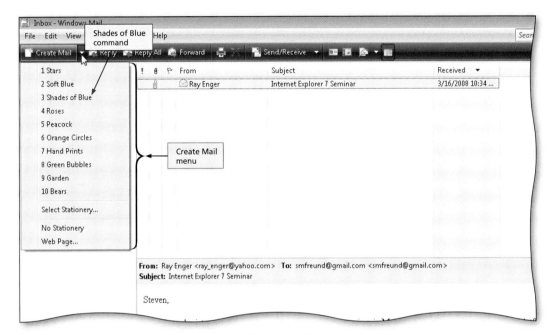

Figure 3–17

2

- Click Shades of Blue on the Create Mail menu to display the New Message window and apply the Shades of Blue stationery to the new message.

- Maximize the New Message window (Figure 3–18).

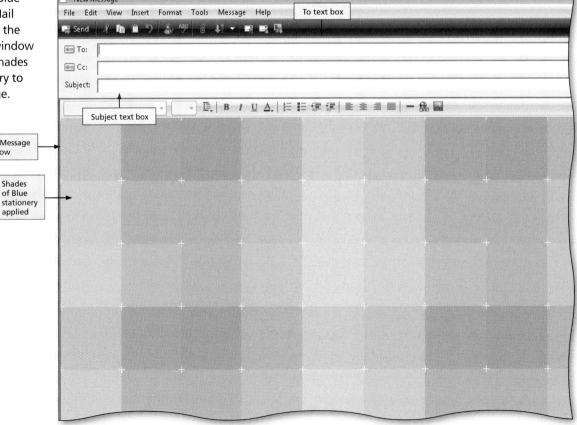

Figure 3–18

- Type
  smfreund@gmail.com
  in the To text box.

- Click the Subject
  text box.

- Type Internet
  Explorer 7
  Seminar in
  the Subject
  text box
  (Figure 3–19).

Q&A

What should I use as
a subject for e-mails
that I send?

You should choose
an e-mail subject that
briefly describes the
contents of the e-mail
message. It is not good
practice to leave the
Subject blank, as some
spam filters will mark
your e-mail message
as spam and it will not
reach the intended
recipient.

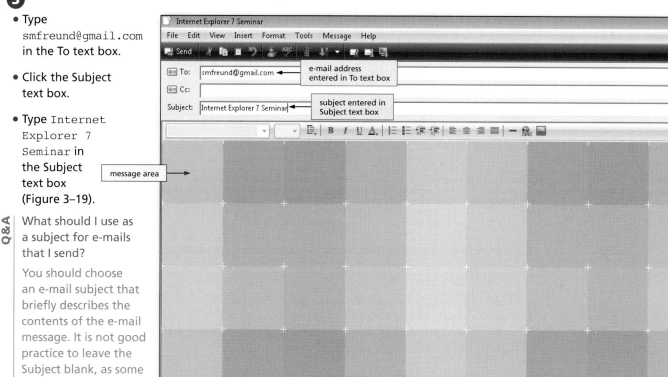

Figure 3–19

- Press the TAB key
  on the keyboard to
  move the insertion
  point into the message
  area of the Internet
  Explorer 7 Seminar
  window.

- Type Internet
  Explorer 7
  Seminar and
  then press
  the ENTER
  key twice.

- Type There will
  be an Internet
  Explorer 7
  Seminar in
  Manchester, NH on
  July 21st. Would you
  like to attend? Please see the attached file for more details. in the
  message area and then press the ENTER key twice.

- Type your name and then press the ENTER key (Figure 3–20).

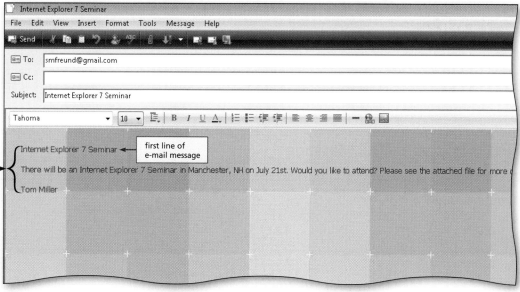

Figure 3–20

Formatting an E-Mail Message

The Internet Explorer 7 Seminar message window contains two toolbars. The toolbar containing buttons specific to replying to an e-mail or composing a new e-mail message is displayed below the menu bar. The Formatting toolbar is displayed below the Subject text box. The buttons on the toolbar below the menu bar are explained in Table 3–3 on page IE 154.

The **Formatting toolbar** (Figure 3–21) contains options for changing the appearance of your e-mail message. Table 3–4 shows the buttons and boxes on the Formatting toolbar and their functions.

Table 3–3 on page IE 154.

Figure 3–21

Table 3–4 Formatting Toolbar Buttons / Boxes and Functions

Button/Box	Function	Button/Box	Function
Tahoma	Changes the font of text in the message.		Decreases the indentation of a paragraph.
10	Changes the font size of text in the message.		Increases the indentation of a paragraph.
	Changes the paragraph style in the message.		Aligns text with the left margin.
B	Bolds text in the message.		Centers text between the left and right margins.
I	Italicizes text in the message.		Aligns text with the right margin.
U	Underlines text in the message.		Aligns text with the left and right margins.
A	Changes the color of text in the message.	—	Adds a horizontal line to the message.
	Creates a numbered list in the message.		Inserts a link in the message.
	Creates a bulleted list in the message.		Inserts a picture in the message.

To Format an E-Mail Message

The following steps use the Formatting toolbar to center the text, Internet Explorer 7 Seminar, and format it using the 36-point font size.

• Select the phrase
Internet Explorer 7
Seminar in the first
line of the e-mail
message by pointing
to any word and then
triple-click to select
the entire phrase
(Figure 3–22).

Q&A
I have never
heard of triple-
clicking. What does it
mean to triple-click?

Similar to how
double-clicking refers
to clicking the mouse twice
in rapid succession, triple-clicking refers to clicking the mouse three times in rapid succession.

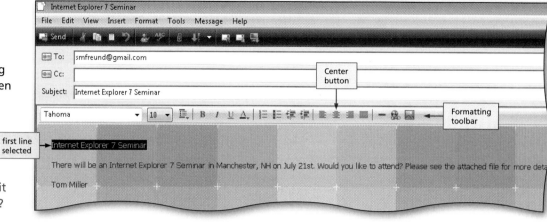

Figure 3–22

• Click the Center
button on the
Formatting toolbar
to center the selected
words, Internet
Explorer 7 Seminar
(Figure 3–23).

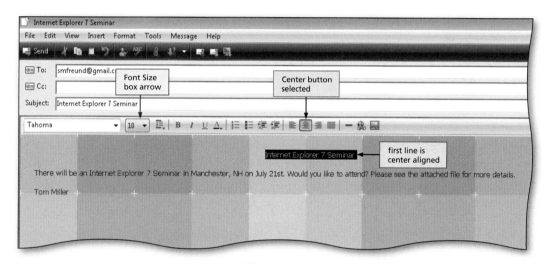

Figure 3–23

• Click the Font Size
box arrow to display
a list of available font
sizes (Figure 3–24).

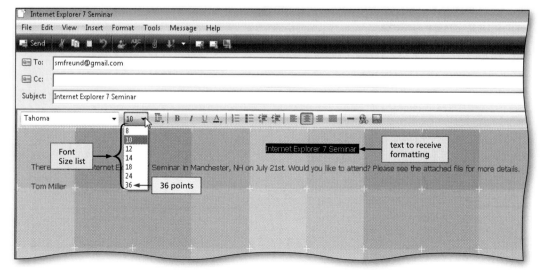

Figure 3–24

4

- Click 36 in the Font Size list to change the font size of the words, Internet Explorer 7 Seminar, to 36 points.

- Click the highlighted text to remove the highlight (Figure 3–25).

Q&A

Will the recipient of this e-mail message be able to view the formatting?

Many e-mail programs are capable of displaying e-mails formatted with various fonts, styles, and backgrounds. If this e-mail message is read with an e-mail program that does not support this formatting, the text of the e-mail message will be formatted as plain text.

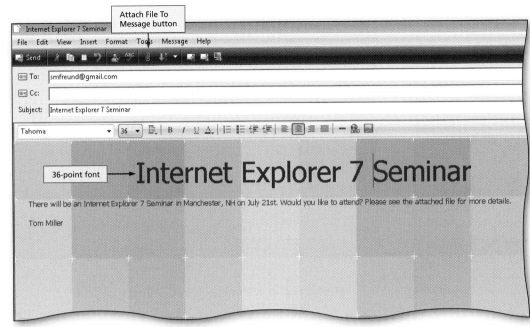

Figure 3–25

To Attach a File to an E-Mail Message

It sometimes may be necessary to supplement your e-mail by attaching a file. Individuals attach files to e-mails for different reasons: friends and family share pictures, students submit assignments to their instructors, and professionals send important documents to colleagues. The following steps attach a file to an e-mail message.

1

- Click the Attach File To Message button on the toolbar to display the Open dialog box (Figure 3–26).

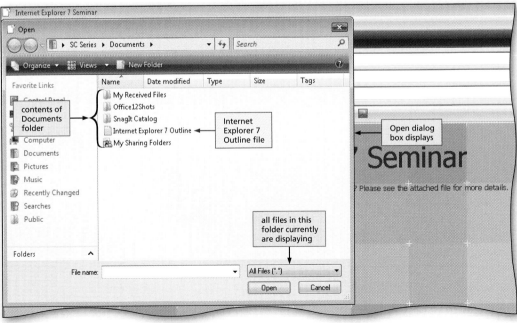

Figure 3–26

2

- Click the Internet Explorer 7 Outline file in the Open dialog box to select it (Figure 3–27). If the Internet Explorer 7 Outline file does not display, navigate to the folder containing the file.

What types of files should I attach to my e-mail messages?

You can attach just about any type of file to an e-mail message, but you should make sure that the files are not too large in size. If you attach a large file, it may take the recipient a long time to download the attachment, or the recipient's e-mail program may reject the message.

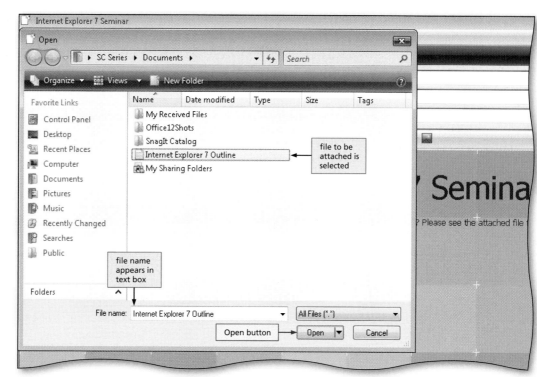

Figure 3–27

3

- Click the Open button to attach the Internet Explorer 7 Outline file to the e-mail message (Figure 3–28).

How do I know that my file has been attached?

After you click the Open button, the name and size of the file should display in the Attach box. If the file does not display, repeat the previous steps to try again.

Figure 3–28

To Send an E-Mail Message

After composing and formatting an e-mail message, send the message. The following step illustrates how to send an e-mail message.

 Click the Send button on the toolbar below the menu bar to send the e-mail message to Steven Freund. Sending the e-mail closes the Internet Explorer 7 Seminar window, stores the e-mail message in the Outbox folder temporarily while it sends the message, and then moves the message to the Sent Items folder (Figure 3–29).

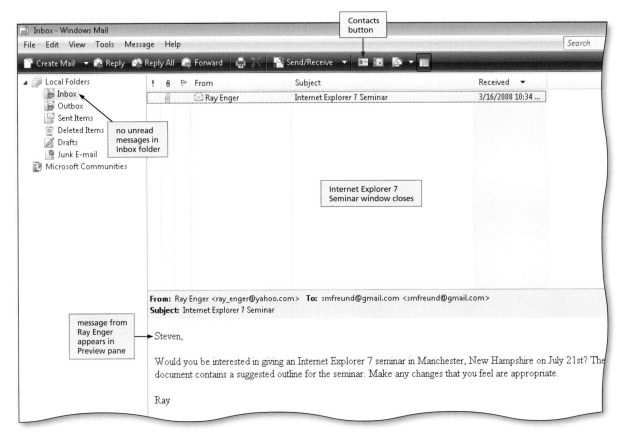

Figure 3–29

Windows Contacts

The **Contacts** feature included with Windows Vista allows you to store information about your family, friends, colleagues, and others. Contact information includes e-mail addresses, home and work addresses, telephone and fax numbers, digital IDs, notes, Web site addresses, and personal information such as birthdays or anniversaries. The information stored in the Contacts folder about an individual is referred to as a **contact**.

Although most contact information is stored in the **Contacts folder**, Windows Vista also allows you to create additional folders in which to store groups of contacts, making it easy to send an e-mail message to a group of contacts, such as business associates, relatives, or friends, because you do not have to remember or type each person's e-mail address.

Now you will add a contact to the Contacts folder, edit and print the information, send an e-mail to her, and finally delete her information.

To Add a Contact to the Contacts Folder

Before you can use the Contacts folder to send an e-mail to an individual, you need to add the contact information to the Contacts folder. The following steps add the contact information (first name, last name, e-mail address, home telephone, and business telephone) for Miriam Winick.

1

- Click the Contacts button on the toolbar in the Inbox - Windows Mail window to open the Contacts window.

- If necessary, maximize the Contacts window (Figure 3–30).

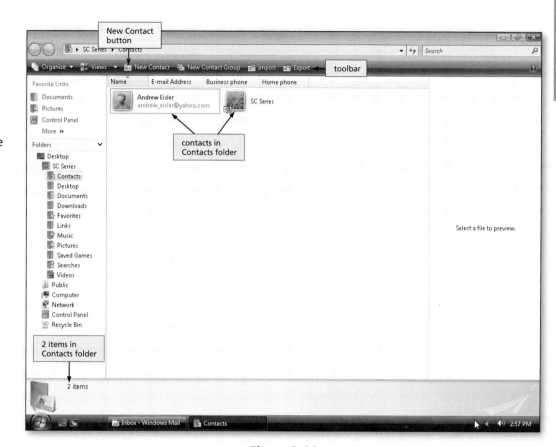

Figure 3–30

- Click the New Contact button on the toolbar to display the Properties window (Figure 3–31).

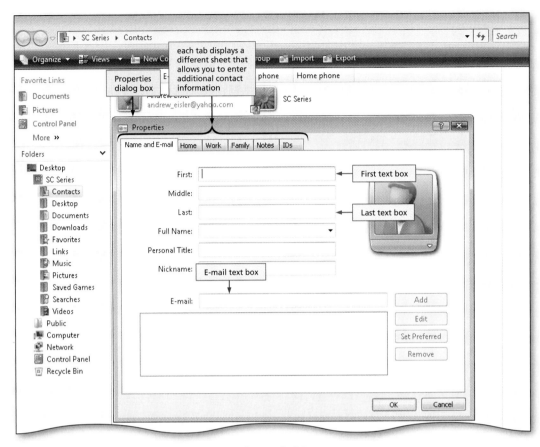

Figure 3–31

- Type `Miriam` in the First text box.
- Click the Last text box and then type `Winick` in the text box.
- Click the E-mail text box and then type `miriam_winick@hotmail.com` in the text box (Figure 3–32).

Figure 3–32

4

- Click the Add button in the Name and E-mail sheet to display the E-mail address in the E-mail list box (Figure 3–33).

Why do I have to click the Add button instead of just leaving the e-mail address in the E-mail text box?

Windows Vista can store multiple e-mail addresses for a single contact. The Add button allows you to add the e-mail address in the E-mail text box to the E-mail list box, and clear the E-mail text box so you can add another e-mail address.

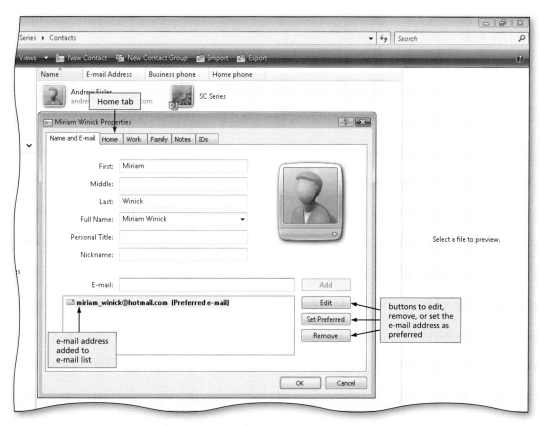

Figure 3–33

5

- Click the Home tab in the Properties dialog box.

- Type 17325 Winding Lane in the Street text box.

- Click the City text box and then type Brea as the name of the city.

- Click the State/Province text box and then type CA as the name of the state.

- Click the Postal Code text box and then type 92821 as the postal code.

- Click the Phone text box and then type (714) 555-3292 as the telephone number (Figure 3–34).

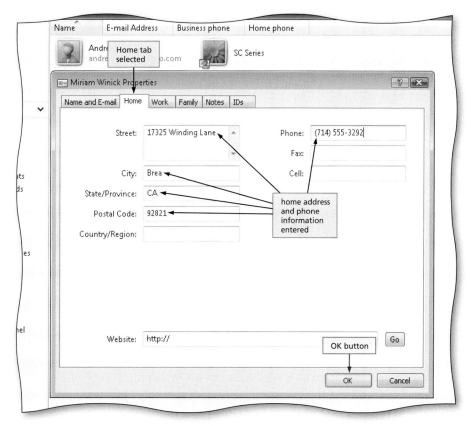

Figure 3–34

6

- Click the OK button in the Properties dialog box to close the Properties dialog box and add the contact to the Contacts folder (Figure 3–35).

- Close the Contacts window.

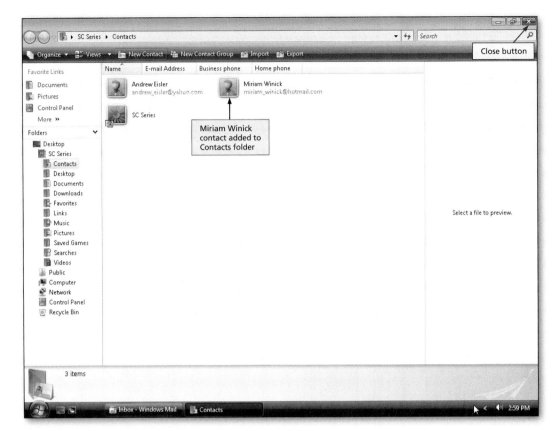

Figure 3–35

When you add a contact in Windows Vista, the Properties dialog box contains a series of tabs. Each tab allows you to store different types of information about the contact. If you are entering information for a business contact, you can enter business-related information on the Work tab. Clicking the Work tab shown in Figure 3–34 on the previous page allows you to not only enter the company's name and business address (street address, city, state/province, postal code, and country/region), but also business information (such as job title, department, and office), telephone numbers (telephone, fax, and pager), and the URL of the company's Web page. By using the Family tab, you can enter personal information about your contact, such as spouse or partner's name, children's names and gender, and birthday and anniversary dates. Clicking the Notes tab allows you to enter notes about the contact. Clicking the IDs tab allows you to view the Digital IDs of a selected e-mail address. A **Digital ID** allows you to encrypt messages sent over the Internet and to prove your identity in an electronic transaction on the Internet in a manner similar to showing your driver's license when you cash a check.

To Compose an E-Mail Message Using the Contacts Folder

When you compose an e-mail message, you must know the e-mail address of the recipient of the message. Previously, you addressed an e-mail message by typing the e-mail address in the To text box in the New Message window. Now you use the Contacts folder to enter an e-mail address. The following steps compose an e-mail message to Miriam Winick using her e-mail address in the Contacts folder.

- Click the Create Mail button to display the New Message window.

- Maximize the New Message window (Figure 3–36).

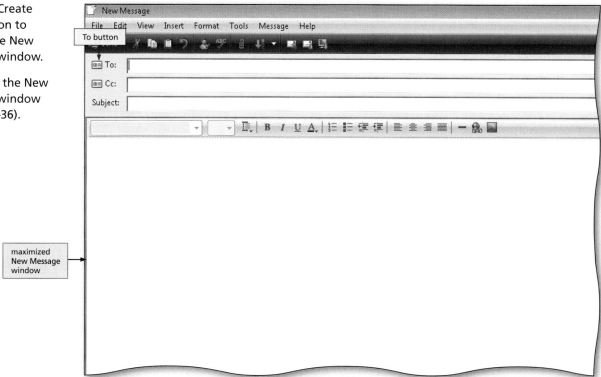

Figure 3–36

2

- Click the To button in the New Message window to display the Select Recipients dialog box.

- Click the Miriam Winick entry in the list box to select it (Figure 3–37).

Q&A Should I add additional recipients to the Cc: field or to the Bcc: field?

The names and e-mail addresses of recipients listed in the Cc: field will be visible to all recipients. However, the names and e-mail addresses of recipients listed in the Bcc: field will be hidden from all recipients.

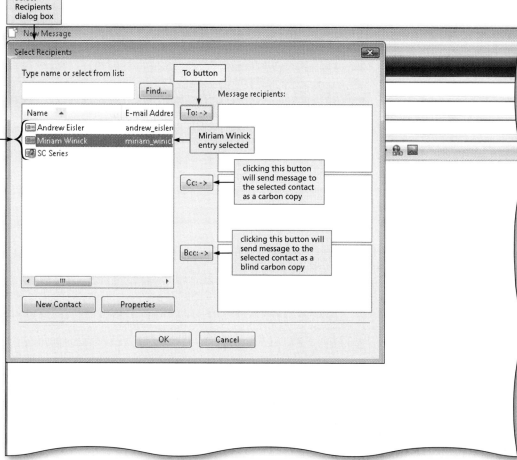

Figure 3–37

3

- Click the To button in the Select Recipients dialog box to add Miriam Winick to the Message recipients list (Figure 3–38).

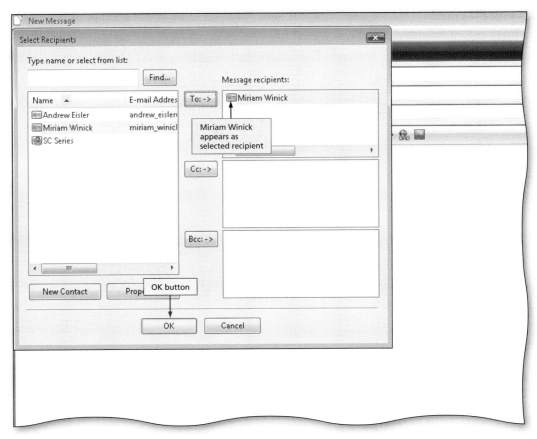

Figure 3–38

4

- Click the OK button in the Select Recipients dialog box to close the Select Recipients dialog box and add Miriam Winick's name and e-mail address to the To text box in the New Message window.

- Click the Subject text box and then type `Contacts Folder` in the text box (Figure 3–39).

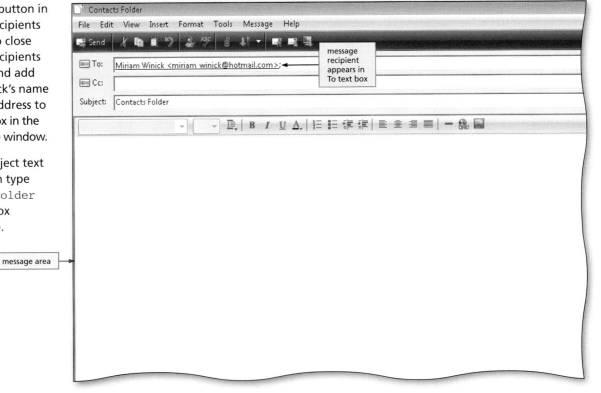

Figure 3–39

5

- Press the TAB key to move the insertion point to the message area.

- Type Great News! and then press the ENTER key twice.

- Type I have learned to enter an e-mail address using the Contacts folder. and then press the ENTER key twice.

- Type your name and then press the ENTER key.

- Select the words, Great News!, in the message area, click the Center button on the Formatting toolbar to center the text, click the Font size box arrow, and then click 36 in the Font Size list to increase the font size to 36 points.

- Click the highlighted text to remove the highlight (Figure 3–40).

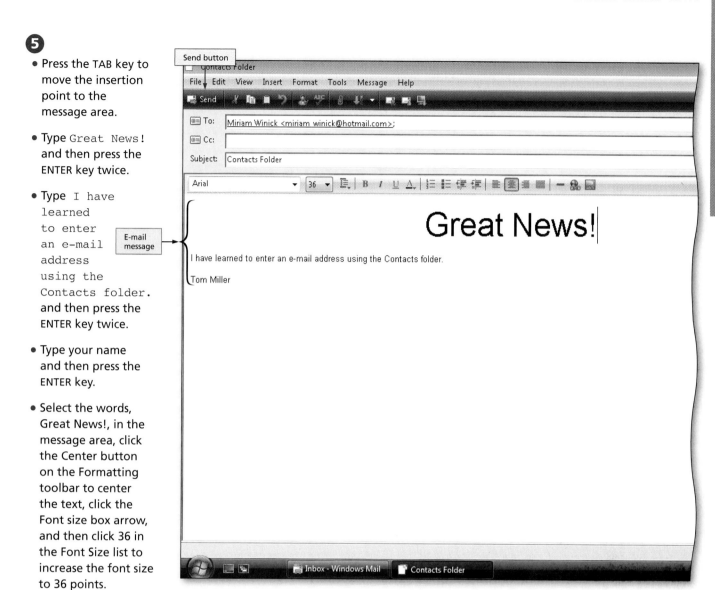

Figure 3–40

To Send an E-Mail Message

The following step sends the e-mail message.

1 Click the Send button on the toolbar to send the message (Figure 3–41).

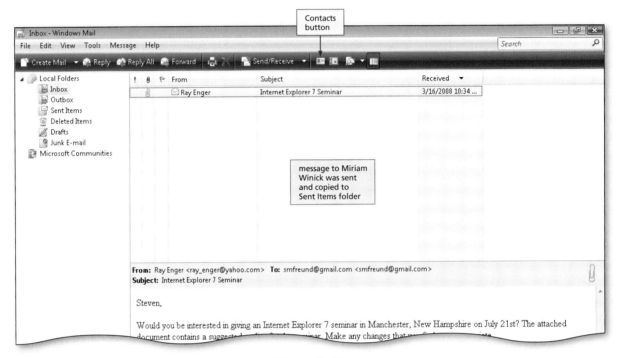

Figure 3–41

To Delete a Contact from the Contacts Folder

Occasionally, you will want to remove a contact from the Contacts Folder. The following steps remove the Miriam Winick contact from the Contacts folder.

- Click the Contacts button on the toolbar to display the Contacts window.

- If necessary, maximize the Contacts window.

- Click the Miriam Winick entry in the Contacts folder (Figure 3–42).

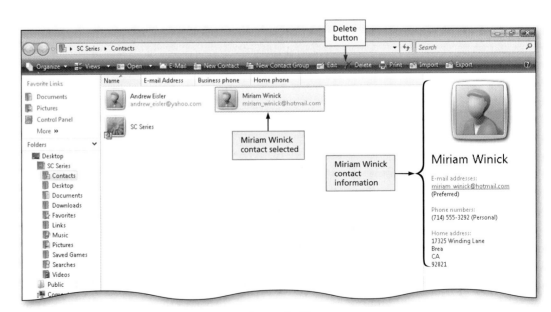

Figure 3–42

2

- Click the Delete button on the toolbar to display the Delete File dialog box (Figure 3–43).

Q&A

Why is the dialog box called the Delete File dialog box when I am deleting a contact?

Each contact in Windows Vista is stored as a file. When you delete a contact, you are moving the associated file to the Recycle Bin.

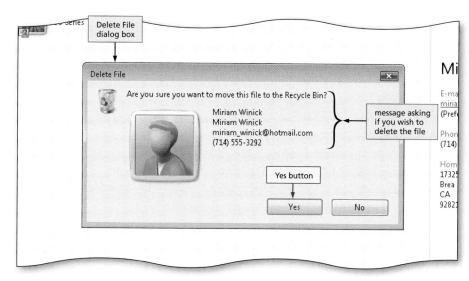

Figure 3–43

3

- Click the Yes button in the Delete File dialog box to delete the Miriam Winick contact (Figure 3–44).

Figure 3–44

To Close the Contacts Window

The following step closes the Contacts window.

1 Click the Close button on the Contacts window.

Other Ways

1. Click contact entry, on File menu click Delete, click Yes button

2. Right-click contact entry, click Delete on shortcut menu, click Yes button

Internet Newsgroups

Besides exchanging e-mail messages, another method of communicating over the Internet is to read and place messages on a **newsgroup**. A newsgroup is a collection of messages posted by many people on a topic of mutual interest that you can access via the Internet. Each newsgroup is devoted to a particular topic. A special computer, called a **news server**, contains related groups of newsgroups.

To participate in a newsgroup, you must use a program called a **newsreader**. The newsreader enables you to access a newsgroup to read a previously entered message, or **article**, and to add a new message, called **posting**. A newsreader also keeps track of which articles you have and have not read. In this chapter, Windows Mail, which includes a newsreader, will be used to read newsgroup articles.

Newsgroup members often post articles in reply to previous postings - either to answer questions or to comment on material in the original. These replies often prompt the author of the original article, or other interested members, to post additional articles. This process resembles a conversation, one which can be short-lived or go on indefinitely, depending on the nature of the topic and the interest of the participants. The original article and all subsequent related replies are called a **thread**, or **threaded discussion**. Figure 3–45 shows some articles and threads from a newsgroup called microsoft.public. access.internet.

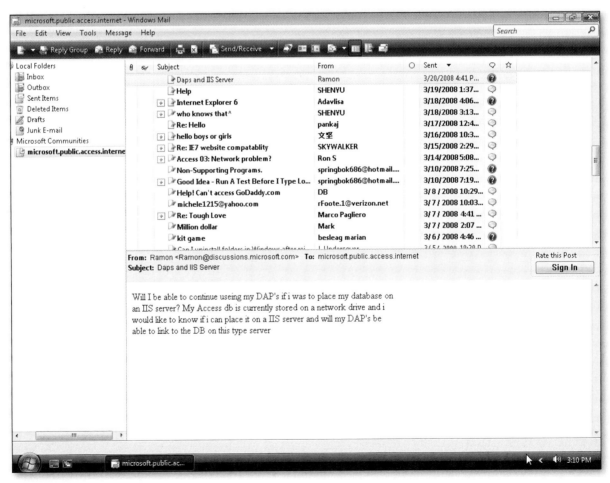

Figure 3–45

Newsgroups exist to discuss products, such as those from Microsoft and IBM; subjects such as recipes, gardening, and music; and just about any other topic you can imagine. A **newsgroup name** consists of a **prefix** and one or more subgroup names. For example, the comp.software newsgroup name consists of a prefix (comp), which indicates that the subject of the newsgroup is computers, a period (.), and a **subgroup name** (software), which indicates that the subject is further narrowed down to a discussion of software. A list of some prefix names and their descriptions is shown in Table 3–5.

Table 3–5 Prefix Names and Descriptions	
Prefix	**Description**
alt	Groups on alternative topics
biz	Business topics
comp	Computer topics
gnu	GNU Software Foundation topics
ieee	Electrical engineering topics
info	Information about various topics
misc	Miscellaneous topics
news	Groups pertaining to newsgroups
rec	Recreational topics
sci	Science topics
talk	Various conversation groups

The newsgroup prefixes found in Table 3–5 are not the only ones used. Innovative newsgroups are being created every day. Some colleges and universities have their own newsgroups on topics such as administrative information, tutoring, campus organizations, and distance learning. A large corporation like Microsoft warrants its own prefix, microsoft.

In addition, some newsgroups are supervised by a **moderator**, who reads each article before it is posted to the newsgroup. If the moderator thinks an article is appropriate for the newsgroup, then the moderator posts the article for all members to read. If the moderator thinks an article is inappropriate, he or she may decide to delete the article without posting it.

Subscribing to a Newsgroup

Before you can access the articles in a newsgroup or post to a newsgroup, you must first establish a news account on your computer. A **news account** allows access to the news server.

Several hundred newsgroups are listed in the Newsgroup Subscriptions dialog box. If you find a newsgroup that you particularly like and want to visit on a frequent basis, you should subscribe to it. **Subscribing to a newsgroup** permanently adds the newsgroup name to the Folders list and allows you to return to the newsgroup quickly by clicking the newsgroup name in the Folders list instead of searching or scrolling to find the newsgroup name each time you wish to visit it.

To Display and Subscribe to a Newsgroup on the Microsoft News Server

The following steps use Windows Mail to view the articles in the microsoft.public.windows.vista.mail newsgroup.

1

• Click the Microsoft Communities link in the Inbox - Windows Mail window to display the Windows Mail dialog box (Figure 3–46).

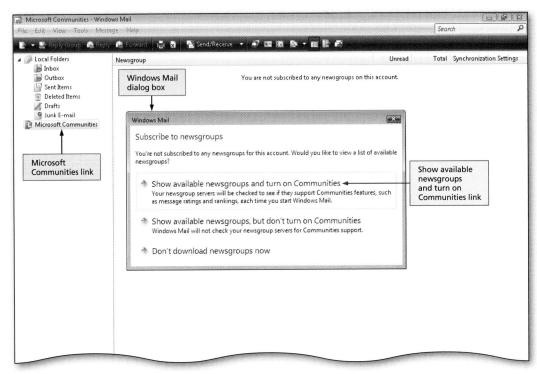

Figure 3–46

2

• Click the Show available newsgroups and turn on Communities link to download a list of available newsgroups on the Microsoft news server and display the list in the Newsgroup Subscriptions dialog box (Figure 3–47).

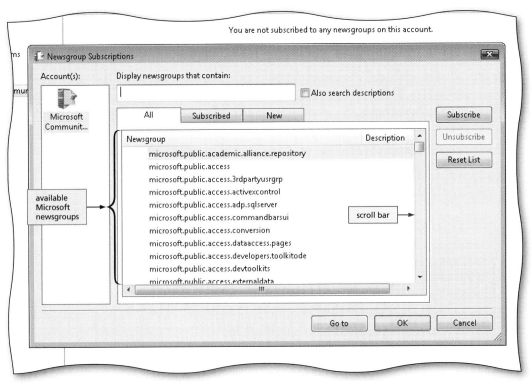

Figure 3–47

• Scroll to display the microsoft.public. windows.vista. mail entry in the Newsgroup list (Figure 3–48).

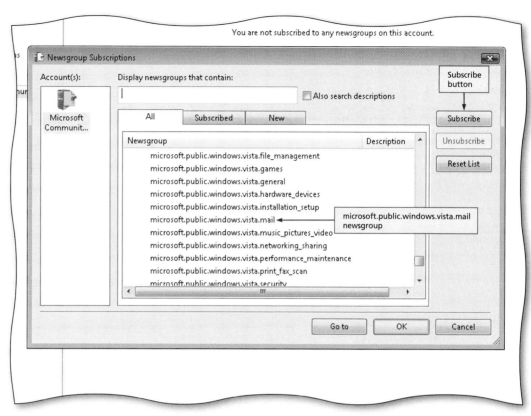

Figure 3–48

❹

• Click the microsoft. public.windows. vista.mail entry in the Newsgroup list to select it, and then click the Subscribe button to subscribe to the newsgroup (Figure 3–49).

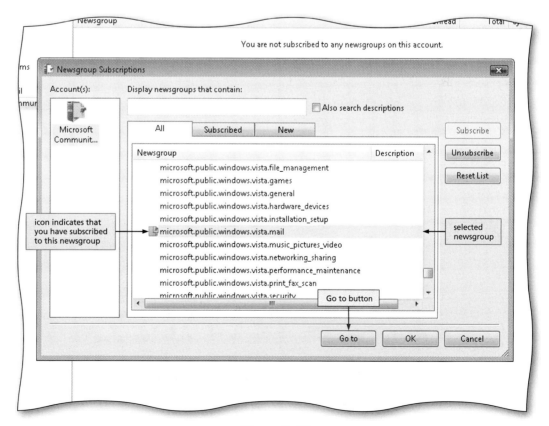

Figure 3–49

5

- Click the Go to button in the Newsgroup Subscriptions dialog box to close the dialog box and display the articles in the microsoft.public. windows.vista.mail newsgroup.

- If a horizontal scroll bar displays at the bottom of the Folder list, if necessary, drag the scroll bar to the left (Figure 3–50).

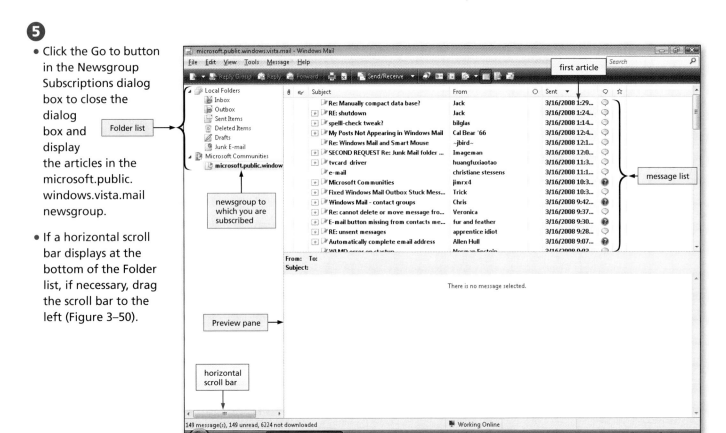

Figure 3–50

Newsgroup Functions

The toolbar below the menu bar shown in Figure 3–50 contains buttons specific to working with news messages (Write Message, Reply Group, Reply, and so on). Table 3–6 provides a brief explanation of the function of each button.

Button	Function
	Displays a window used to post an article to the newsgroup.
Reply Group	Displays a window that allows you to reply to all authors of articles in a newsgroup by e-mail.
	Displays a window that allows you to reply to the author of an article in a newsgroup by e-mail.
	Displays a window that allows you to forward an article in a newsgroup by e-mail.
	Prints the highlighted article in the message area.
	Stops the transfer of articles from a news server to the message area.
	Displays the Windows Mail dialog box, contacts the news server, and displays new news messages in the message area.
	Displays the Sign in to Microsoft Communities login screen.

Table 3–6 Toolbar Buttons and Functions

Button	Function
Table 3–6 Toolbar Buttons and Functions (continued)	
Button	**Function**
	Displays the Contacts folder containing a list of frequently used contacts.
	Displays the Windows Calendar.
	Displays the Find Message window that allows you to search for an article in the message area based on sender name, recipient name, subject, message, and date.
	Hides/shows the Folder list.
	Displays a dialog box that allows you to select a newsgroup on the current news server.
	Downloads more message headers from the news server.

BTW

Newsgroups
Instructors sometimes use newsgroups in courses taught over the Internet by posting a question and allowing students to respond by posting an article. Students can read the articles in the thread to be aware of all responses and subscribe to the newsgroup to quickly return to it.

Internet Explorer Chapter 3

To Read a Newsgroup Article

The entries in the Subject column in the message list allow you to review the subjects of a list of articles before deciding which one to read. The following step selects a newsgroup article to read.

1

- Click the first article in the message list to display the article in the Preview pane (Figure 3–51).

Experiment

- Click some of the other articles in the message list to display the contents in the Preview pane. Once you are done, click the first article in the message list.

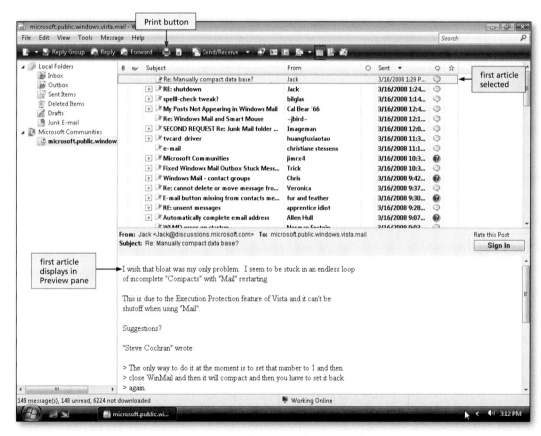

Figure 3–51

Other Ways

1. Press CTRL+< to read previous article

2. Press CTRL+> to read next article

Expanding and Collapsing a Thread

When a plus sign appears to the left of an article in the message list, the article is part of a thread and can be expanded. **Expanding the thread** displays the replies to the original article indented below the original article and changes the plus sign to a minus sign. Figure 3–45 on page IE 174 shows multiple threads that can be expanded.

After reading the replies within a thread, you may want to collapse the expanded thread. **Collapsing the thread** removes any replies from the thread, displays the original article in the Preview pane, and changes the minus sign to the left of the original article to a plus sign.

To Print a Newsgroup Article

After reading an article, you may want to print it. The method of printing a newsgroup article is identical to how you print an e-mail message, with similar results (see Figure 3–8 on page IE 151). The following steps print the contents of the first article in the newsgroup.

1 Click the Print button on the toolbar.

2 Click the Print button in the Print dialog box to print the newsgroup article (Figure 3–52).

Page 1 of 1

Steven Freund

From:	"Jack"
Newsgroups:	microsoft.public.windows.vista.mail
Sent:	Friday, March 16, 2008 1:29 PM
Subject:	Re: Manually compact data base?

I wish that bloat was my only problem. I seem to be stuck in an endless loop of incomplete "Compacts" with "Mail" restarting.

This is due to the Execution Protection feature of Vista and it can't be shutoff when using "Mail".

Suggestions?

"Steve Cochran" wrote:

> The only way to do it at the moment is to set that number to 1 and then
> close WinMail and then it will compact and then you have to set it back
> again.
>
> I don't think compaction is as big an issue as it was in OE, as the messages
> are not in the database files any longer, so there is less bloat.
>
> steve
>
> "Bob" wrote in message
> news:utuI7RURHHA.1200@TK2MSFTNGP04.phx.gbl...
> > Is there a way to manually compact the data base in Mail? All I see is the
> > option to change the number of "runs" before it compacts automatically.
> > You could manually do it in OE.
> > Thanks,
> > Bob
>

Figure 3–52

Posting a Newsgroup Article

Once you become familiar with a newsgroup, you may want to post a reply to a newsgroup article. In order to be able to post to a newsgroup, you first need to be subscribed to it. After subscribing to the newsgroup and displaying the list of articles in the message list, click the Write Message button to display the New Message window to compose your newsgroup posting. The New Message window (Figure 3–53) contains menus, buttons, and text boxes that are specific to newsgroup postings. Once you type a subject and text for the posting, click the Send button to post the newsgroup article. Because many people will be able to read your posting, make sure that the posting is free from grammatical and spelling errors. If the newsgroup is moderated, postings may not appear immediately after sending them.

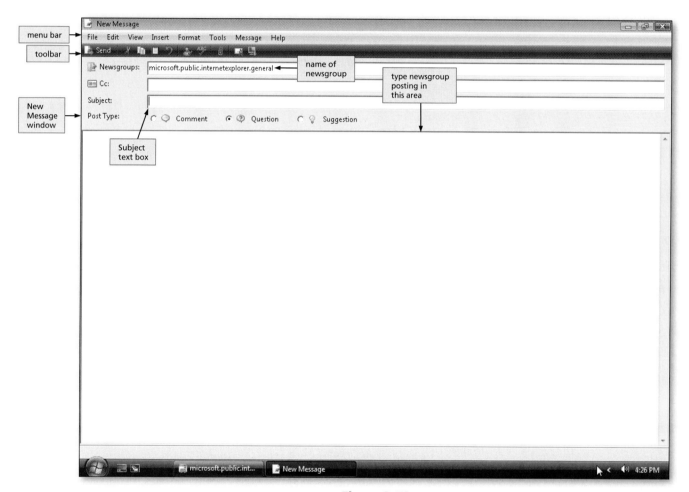

Figure 3–53

The buttons on the toolbar illustrated in Figure 3–53 on the previous page (Send, Cut, Copy, Paste, and so on) are useful when posting a new article. Table 3–7 shows the buttons on the toolbar and their functions.

Table 3–7 Toolbar Buttons and Functions	
Button	**Function**
	Sends the article in the New Message window to a news server.
	Moves a selected item in an article to the Clipboard and removes the item from the article.
	Copies a selected item in an article to the Clipboard.
	Copies an item from the Clipboard to an article.
	Undoes the previous operation.
	Checks the recipient's name against the Contacts folder.
	Spell checks the article.
	Attaches a file to the article.
	Digitally signs an article, allowing the recipient to verify the sender's identity.
	Allows you to work without being connected to a news server (offline).

To Unsubscribe from a Newsgroup

When you no longer need quick access to a newsgroup, you can cancel the subscription to the newsgroup, or **unsubscribe**, and then remove the newsgroup name from the Folder list. The next steps unsubscribe from the microsoft.public.windows.vista.mail newsgroup.

- Right-click the microsoft.public. windows.vista.mail newsgroup name in the Folder list to display the shortcut menu (Figure 3–54).

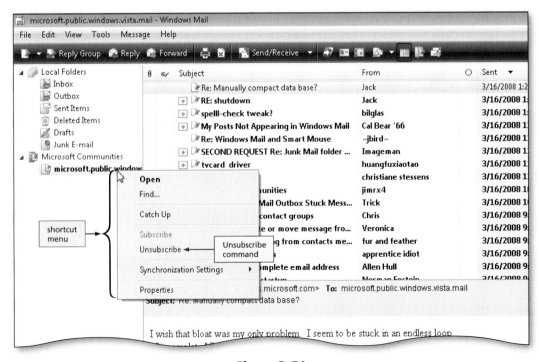

Figure 3–54

❷

- Click Unsubscribe on the shortcut menu.

- If the Windows Mail dialog box appears, click the OK button in the dialog box to unsubscribe from the microsoft.public. windows.vista.mail newsgroup.

- If a second Windows Mail dialog box appears asking if you would like to view a list of available newsgroups, click the No button in the dialog box (Figure 3–55).

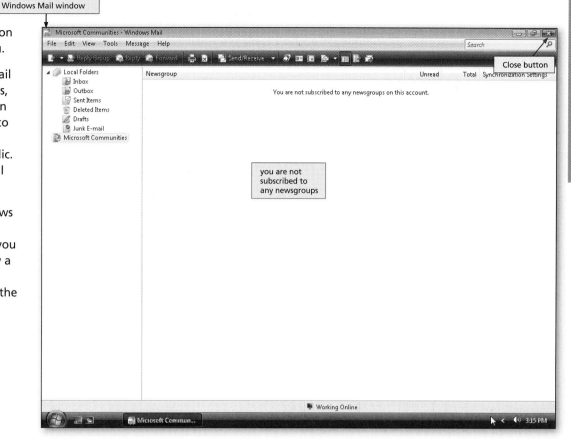

Figure 3–55

To Quit Windows Mail

Now that you have finished working with e-mails and newsgroups, the following step quits Windows Mail.

 Click the Close button in the Microsoft Communities - Windows Mail window to quit Windows Mail.

Other Ways

1. Select newsgroup name in Newsgroup Subscriptions dialog box, click Unsubscribe button

2. Double-click newsgroup name in Newsgroup Subscriptions dialog box

RSS

One of the newer technologies on the Internet is **RSS**, which stands for Really Simple Syndication. RSS allows Web page authors to easily distribute, or syndicate, Web content. For example, the CNN Web site contains two RSS feeds that allows people to view top stories and recent stories in one convenient location by clicking the Feeds button in the Favorites Center. If you frequently visit multiple Web sites that offer RSS feeds, by subscribing to their RSS feeds, you can quickly review the feed content of all the Web sites in a simple list in your browser, without having to first navigate to each individual site. If you subscribe to an RSS feed using Internet Explorer, you will be able to access the feed in the Favorites Center. RSS feeds are typically found on news Web sites, discussion boards, blogs, and other Web sites that frequently update their content.

To Subscribe to an RSS Feed

Before you can view the contents of an RSS feed, you must subscribe to it. The following steps subscribe to an RSS feed on the CNET.com Web site.

1

• Start Internet Explorer.

• Type www.cnet.com in the Address bar and then press the ENTER key to display the CNET.com Web page (Figure 3–56).

Figure 3–56

2

• Click the View feeds on this page button arrow to display a menu containing the available RSS feeds (Figure 3–57).

Figure 3–57

3

- Click the Buzz weekly (new) command on the menu to display the Buzz weekly RSS feed (Figure 3–58).

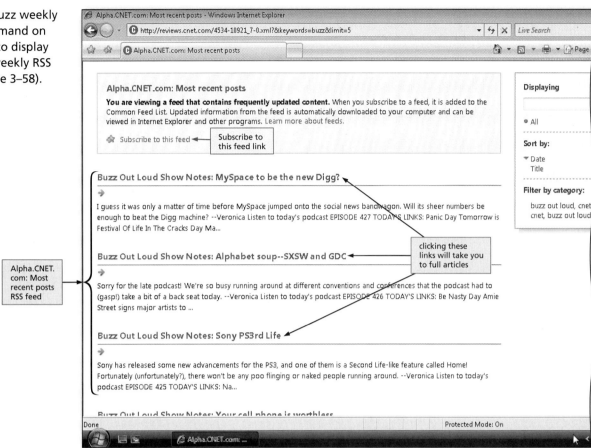

Figure 3–58

4

- Click the Subscribe to this feed link in the Alpha.CNET.com: Most recent posts - Windows Internet Explorer window to display the Internet Explorer dialog box (Figure 3–59).

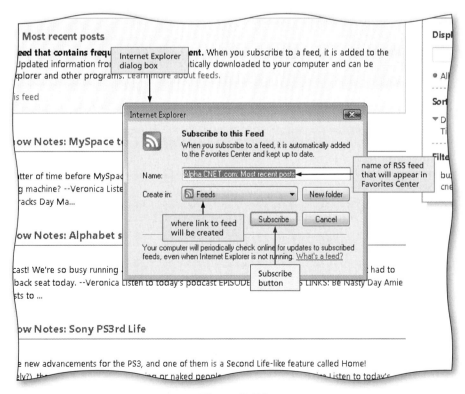

Figure 3–59

5

- Click the Subscribe button in the Internet Explorer dialog box to subscribe to the RSS feed (Figure 3–60).

Figure 3–60

To View Your RSS Feeds in the Favorites Center

After you subscribe to an RSS feed, you are able to view the RSS feeds in the Favorites Center. The following steps display the RSS feeds to which you have subscribed in the Favorites Center.

1

- Click the Home button on the Command Bar to display your home page.

- Click the Favorites Center button to display the Favorites Center (Figure 3–61).

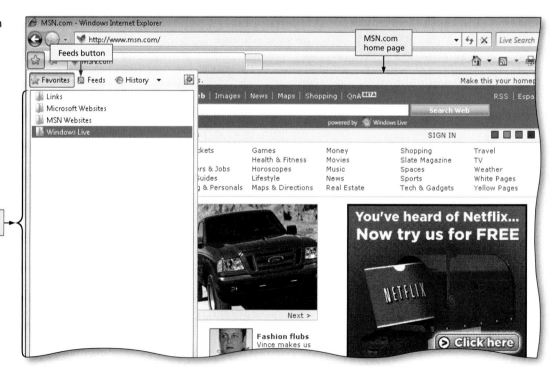

Figure 3–61

• Click the Feeds
button in the
Favorites Center to
display the list of
RSS feeds to which
you have subscribed
(Figure 3–62).

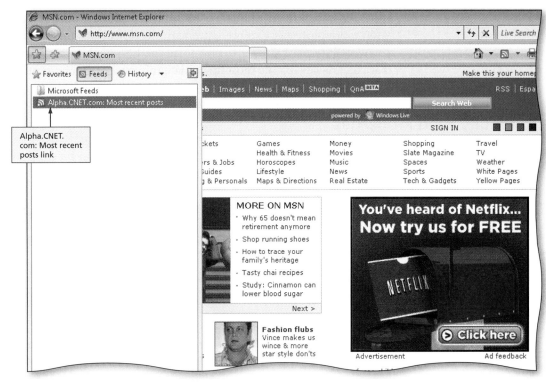

Alpha.CNET.
com: Most recent
posts link

Figure 3–62

❸

• Click the Alpha.CNET.
com: Most recent
posts link to display
the RSS feed. If neces-
sary, click the Close
the Favorites Center
button to close the
Favorites Center
(Figure 3–63).

news articles
on CNET.com

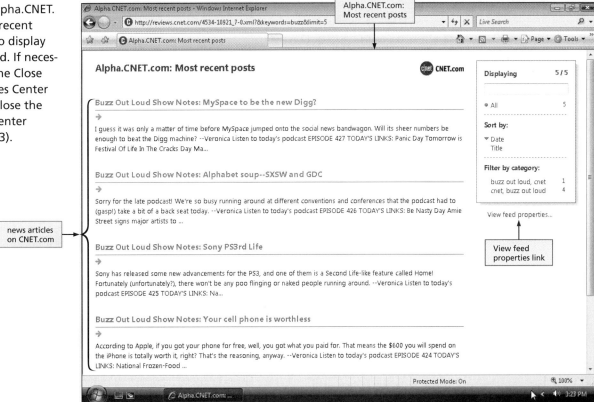

View feed
properties link

Figure 3–63

Feed Properties

As previously mentioned, because RSS feeds disseminate frequently updated information, Internet Explorer automatically downloads updated RSS content every day. If you want Internet Explorer to download the RSS feeds more frequently so that you are sure that you are viewing the most up-to-date information, you can modify the feed properties.

To Modify Feed Properties

The following steps modify the properties for the Alpha.CNET.com: Most recent posts RSS feed so that the feed will update every four hours.

1

• Click the View feed properties link in the Alpha.CNET.com: Most recent posts - Windows Internet Explorer window to display the Feed Properties dialog box (Figure 3–64).

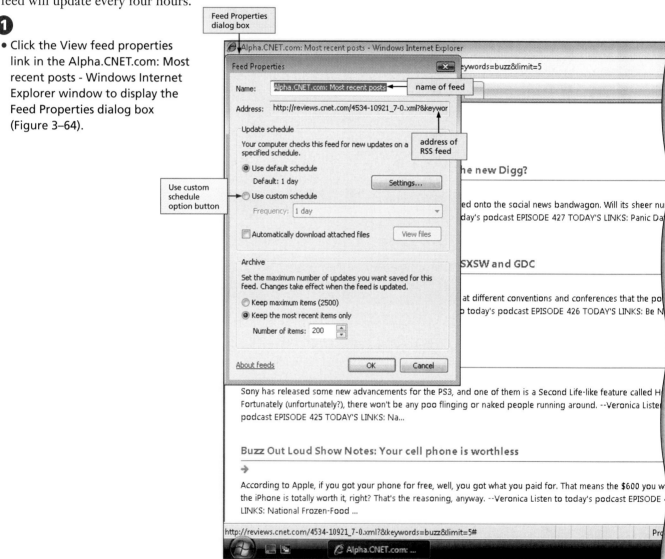

Figure 3–64

• Click the Use custom schedule
option button in the Update schedule area of the Feed Properties
dialog box (Figure 3–65).

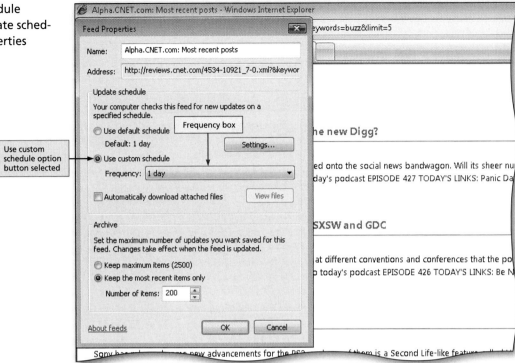

Figure 3–65

❸

• Click the Frequency box arrow
to display the Frequency list
(Figure 3–66).

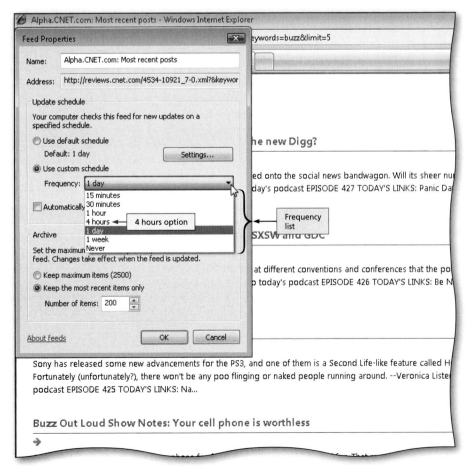

Figure 3–66

- Click 4 hours in the Frequency list (Figure 3–67).

- Click the OK button in the Feed Properties dialog box to save your changes and to close the Feed Properties dialog box.

- Close Internet Explorer.

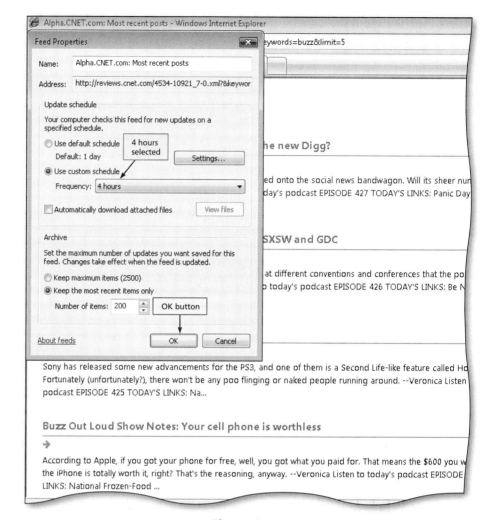

Figure 3–67

Other Communication Methods

This chapter has so far discussed how to communicate over the Internet by using e-mail, newsgroups, and RSS feeds. In addition to these methods, several other Web applications facilitate communication between individuals over the Internet, including wikis, blogs, online social networks, groups, chat rooms, and instant messaging.

As you may recall from Chapter 2, blogs, wikis, and online social networks are types of Web sites that allow one or more people to directly communicate with each other. Some Web sites, such as Google and Yahoo, allow their visitors to communicate with others via groups. A **group** is a Web application that enables people to form an online community for discussion around specific topics, such as ballooning, Internet Explorer 7, or your favorite video game. You also can create Web pages inside your group. If you are unable to find a group that matches your interests, you can create a new group. Figure 3–68 shows the Google Groups Web site (http://groups.google.com).

Figure 3–68

Similar to a group, a **chat room** application allows people to communicate with each other. However, unlike a group, the communication that takes place in a chat room happens in real time. **Real-time communication** means that users participating in the communication must be online at the same time. For example, a phone conversation is one type of communication that takes place in real time. If one person was not on the phone, it would be impossible for the phone conversation to take place. On the other hand, an e-mail conversation does not take place in real time because you are able to send someone an e-mail regardless of whether or not they are online. When you enter a chat room, messages that you send are viewable by everyone else who is in the same chat room. Some chat rooms are available via Web sites, and others are accessible only by first downloading a special program to your computer that allows you to enter and participate in chat rooms. Figure 3–69 on the next page shows a Web site that allows you to download a popular chat program called mIRC.

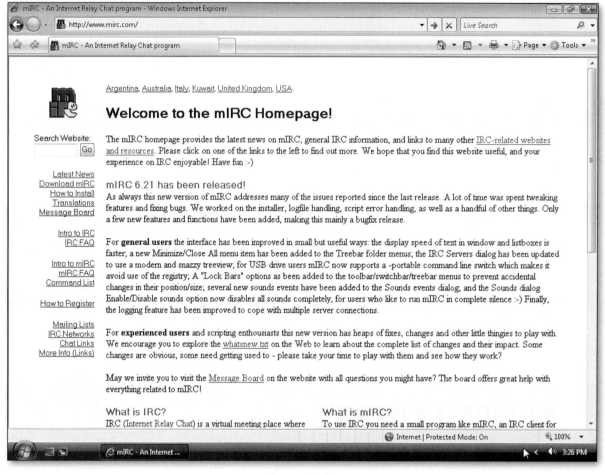

Figure 3–69

Another way by which people on the Internet can communicate is via a mailing list. A **mailing list** allows an individual to send the same e-mail to multiple recipients at the same time. For example, many colleges and universities allow instructors to communicate with their students outside of class by using a mailing list. At the beginning of the semester, students manually subscribe to the mailing list with their e-mail address or the instructor automatically subscribes them. When the instructor needs to disseminate information to the students, he or she sends a message to the mailing list, which is forwarded to everyone who has subscribed. In addition to schools using mailing lists, many companies also offer mailing lists to periodically update their customers about their products or services. If you have subscribed to a mailing list and no longer wish to receive e-mail from the list, you have to unsubscribe from it. Mailing lists offer different methods of unsubscribing, the instructions for which are usually located at the bottom of each e-mail sent to the list. If you are unable to find instructions for unsubscribing, contact the mailing list administrator. Figure 3–70 shows a Web page that contains a subscription form for a mailing list that distributes the DivX newsletter.

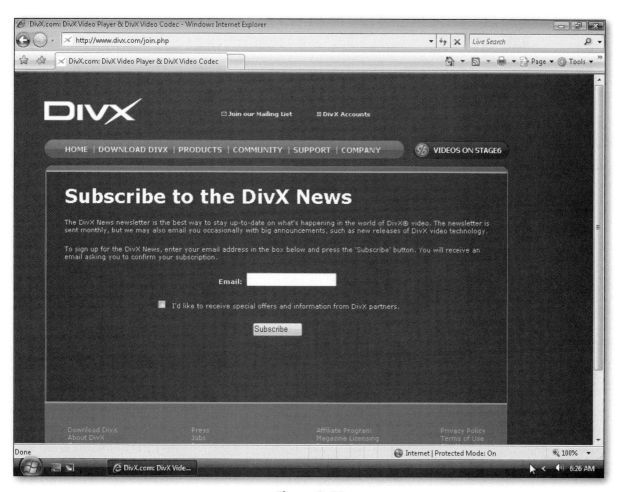

Figure 3–70

Windows Live Messenger and Instant Messaging

Another communication tool is instant messaging (IM). An instant messaging application allows two people who are online at the same time to exchange messages in real time. **Windows Live Messenger**, an instant messaging application, is available for free from the MSN.com Web site. The advantage of using Windows Live Messenger over e-mail is that once sent, your instant message appears immediately on the recipient's computer, and they can reply immediately, provided they also have signed in to Windows Live Messenger.

Windows Live Messenger users can perform a variety of functions, including adding a contact to the contact list; viewing a list of online and offline contacts; performing real-time communication with a single contact or a group of contacts; placing a telephone call from the computer and talking using the microphone and headset; sending files to another computer; sending instant messages to a mobile device; and inviting someone to an online meeting or to play an Internet game.

You sign into Windows Live Messenger using your Windows Live ID. This section assumes that you already have Windows Live Messenger installed, and a Windows Live ID created. If you need a Windows Live ID, see your instructor for assistance.

Before using Windows Live Messenger, your contact also must have a Windows Live ID and have the Windows Live Messenger software installed on their computer. If you have a Windows Live Hotmail account, you already have a Windows Live ID, because your Windows Live Hotmail sign-in name and password are your Windows Live username and password. Your **Windows Live ID** is a secure way for you to sign in to multiple Microsoft Web sites.

To Start Windows Live Messenger and Sign In

Before using Windows Live Messenger, you must start Windows Live Messenger and sign in using your Windows Live ID and password. The following steps start and sign in to Windows Live Messenger.

- Display the Start menu.

- Display the All Programs list.

- Click Windows Live Messenger on the All Programs list to start Windows Live Messenger (Figure 3–71).

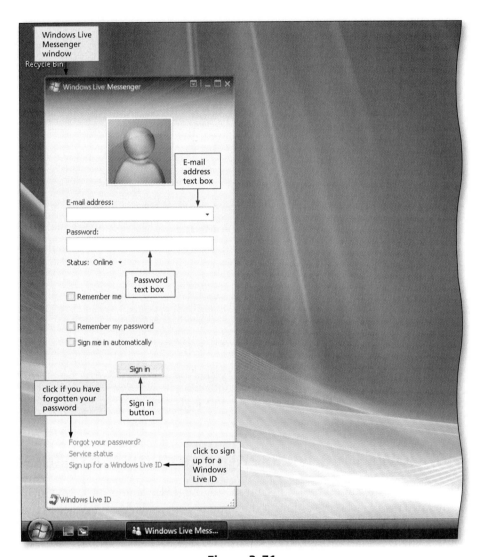

Figure 3–71

2

- Type your Windows Live ID into the E-mail address text box in the Windows Live Messenger window.

- Type your Windows Live password into the Password text box in the Windows Live Messenger window.

- Click the Sign in button to sign in to Windows Live Messenger and to display your Contact list (Figure 3–72).

- If the Welcome to Windows Live Messenger window displays, click the Close button to close the window.

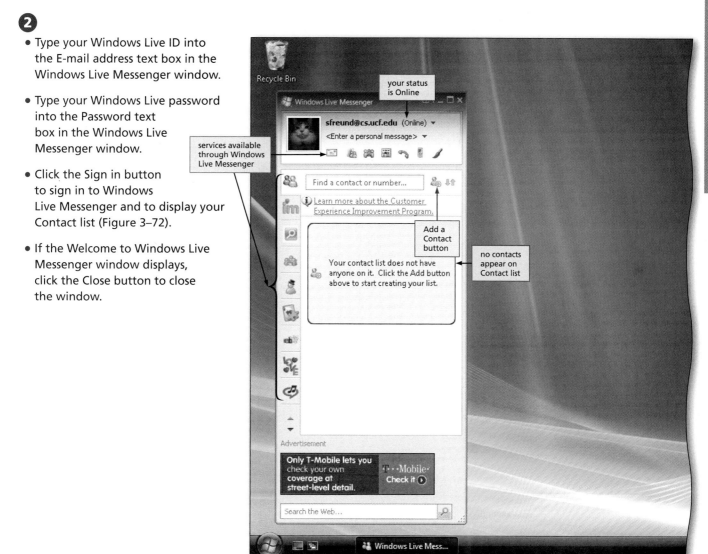

Figure 3–72

Adding a Contact to the Contact List

After starting Windows Live Messenger, you can add a contact to the contact list if you know their instant messaging address. A contact must have a Windows Live Hotmail account or a Windows Live ID and have the Windows Live Messenger software installed on his or her computer. If you want to add a contact that does not meet these requirements, you can send the contact an e-mail invitation or text message on their mobile device that explains how to get a Windows Live ID and download the Windows Live Messenger software.

To Add a Contact to the Contact List

The following steps add a contact to the contact list using the e-mail address of someone you know who has signed in to Windows Live Messenger.

- Click the Add a Contact button in the Windows Live Messenger window to display the Windows Live Contacts - Add a Contact dialog box (Figure 3–73).

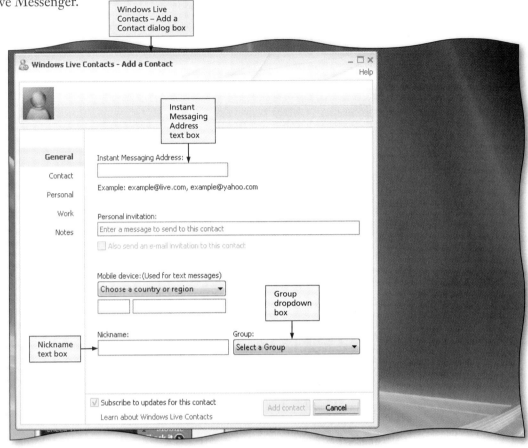

Figure 3–73

2

- Type Shelly_ Cashman@hotmail. com in the Instant Messaging Address text box.

- Type Shelly Cashman Series in the Nickname text box.

- Click the Group drop-down box to display a list of available groups (Figure 3–74).

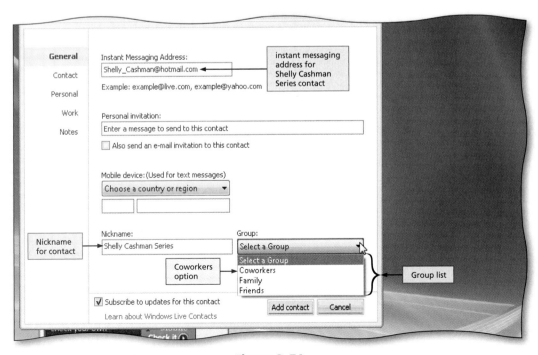

Figure 3–74

3

- Click the Coworkers option in the Group list (Figure 3–75). You may have different options than those listed in the Group list.

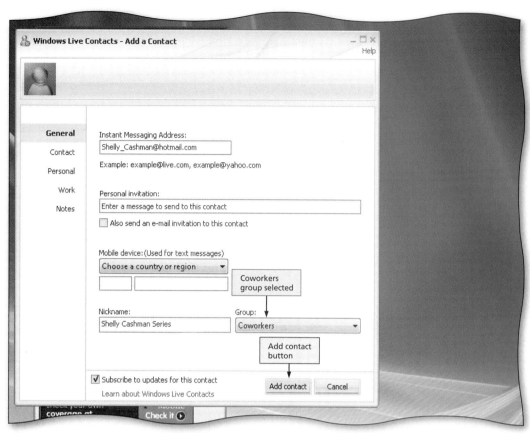

Figure 3–75

4

- Click the Add contact button to close the Windows Live Contacts - Add a Contact dialog box and add the Shelly Cashman Series contact to your contact list (Figure 3–76).

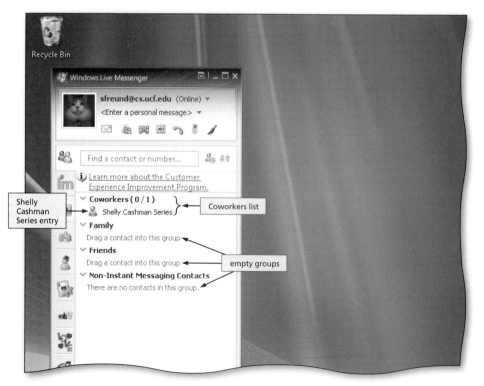

Figure 3–76

To Send an Instant Message

To use Windows Live Messenger, the person with whom you want to communicate must be online. The Online list shown in Figure 3–76 on the previous page displays the Shelly Cashman contact. The following steps send an instant message to someone who you know is online.

1

• Double-click the Shelly Cashman entry in the Coworkers group to display the Shelly Cashman Series window (Figure 3–77). If the Shelly Cashman contact is not online, double-click the name of another online contact.

• **Type** I have learned how to use Windows Live Messenger! Do you have some time to chat? in the Send text box.

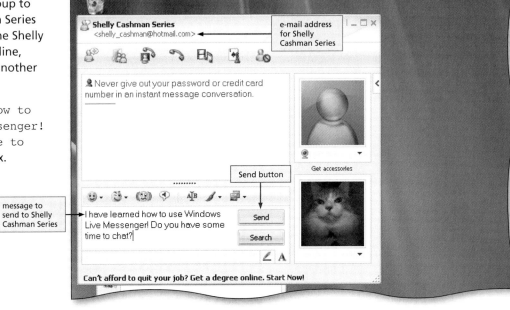

Figure 3–77

2

• Click the Send button in the Shelly Cashman Series window to send the instant message (Figure 3–78).

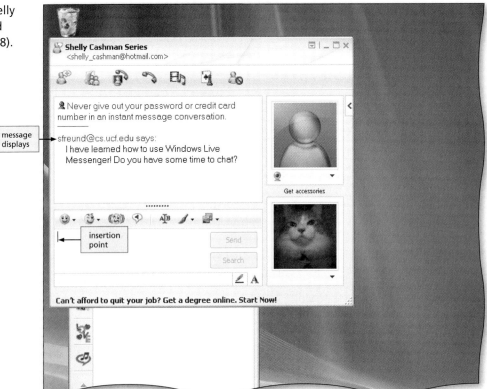

Figure 3–78

3

- The receiver of the message types and then sends a response (Figure 3–79).

 Experiment

- Feel free to send additional messages to the Shelly Cashman contact or the contact you are communicating with in Windows Live Messenger.

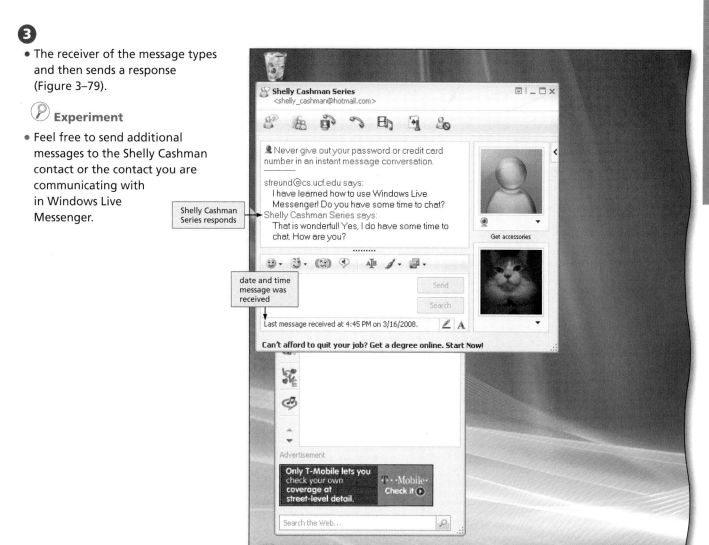

Figure 3–79

Other Ways

1. Right-click contact name, click Send an instant message on shortcut menu

To Close the Shelly Cashman Series Window

When you have finished with your conversation, you should close the instant messaging window to end the conversation. The next step closes the Shelly Cashman Series window.

1 Click the Close button in the Shelly Cashman Series window to close the Shelly Cashman Series window.

To Delete a Contact on the Contact List

The Shelly Cashman Series contact remains on the contact list and the Shelly Cashman Series icon appears below the Coworkers heading in the Windows Live Messenger window. If you lose touch with a contact, you may want to delete them from your contact list. The following steps delete the Shelly Cashman Series contact and remove the entry from the Online list.

1

• Right-click the Shelly Cashman Series entry under the Coworkers heading to display the shortcut menu (Figure 3–80).

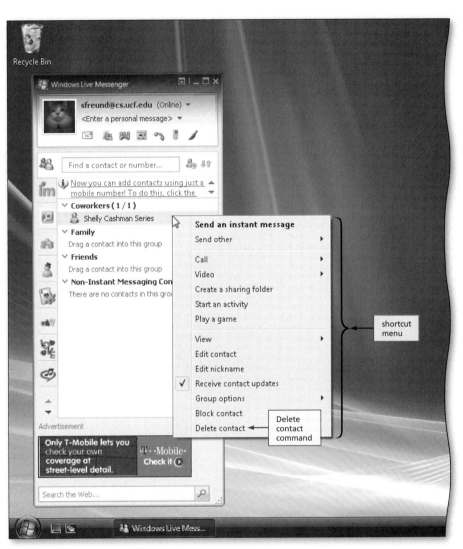

Figure 3–80

2

- Click Delete contact on the shortcut menu (Figure 3–81).

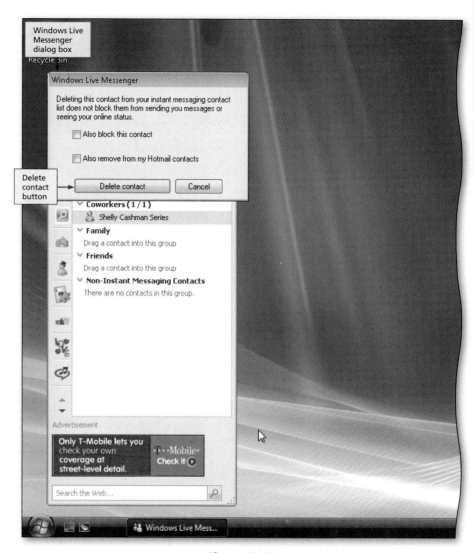

Figure 3–81

3

- Click the Delete contact button in the Windows Live Messenger dialog box to delete the Shelly Cashman Series contact and remove the Shelly Cashman Series entry from the contact list (Figure 3–82).

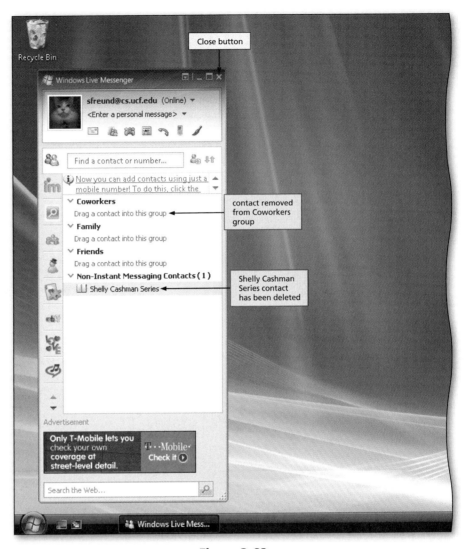

Figure 3–82

To Close and Sign Out from Windows Live Messenger

When you have finished using Windows Live Messenger, close the Windows Live Messenger window. The following step closes the Windows Live Messenger window and signs out from the Windows Live Messenger service.

1 Click the Close button in the Windows Live Messenger window to close Windows Live Messenger (Figure 3–83).

2 Click the Windows Live Messenger - Signed In icon in the notification area on the Windows taskbar.

3 Click the Sign Out command on the shortcut menu to sign out from Windows Live Messenger.

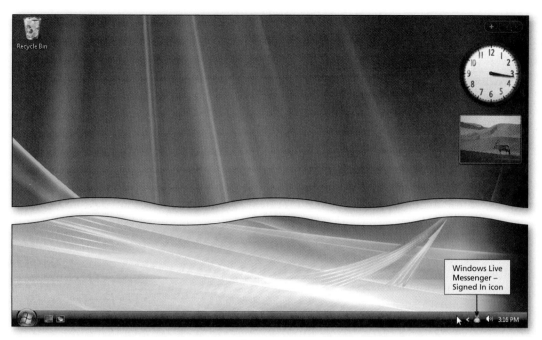

Figure 3–83

Chapter Summary

In this chapter, you have learned to use Windows Mail to read, write, format, and send e-mail messages, and to attach and view file attachments. You added and deleted contacts in the Windows Vista Contacts folder. You also used Windows Mail to work with newsgroups and RSS feeds. You learned about other Web applications including groups, mailing lists, and chat rooms. Finally, you used Windows Live Messenger to send an instant message. The items listed below include all the new skills you have learned in this chapter.

1. Start Windows Mail (IE 145)
2. Open (Read) an E-Mail Message (IE 149)
3. Print an Opened E-Mail Message (IE 150)
4. Close an E-Mail Message (IE 152)
5. Reply to an E-Mail Message (IE 152)
6. Delete an E-Mail Message (IE 155)
7. Open a File Attachment (IE 156)
8. Save and Close a File Attachment (IE 157)
9. Compose an E-Mail Message Using Stationery (IE 158)
10. Format an E-Mail Message (IE 160)
11. Attach a File to an E-Mail Message (IE 162)
12. Send an E-Mail Message (IE 164)
13. Add a Contact to the Contacts Folder (IE 165)
14. Compose an E-Mail Message Using the Contacts Folder (IE 168)
15. Send an E-Mail Message (IE 172)
16. Delete a Contact from the Contacts Folder (IE 172)
17. Close the Contacts Window (IE 173)
18. Display and Subscribe to a Newsgroup on the Microsoft News Server (IE 176)
19. Read a Newsgroup Article (IE 179)
20. Print a Newsgroup Article (IE 180)
21. Unsubscribe from a Newsgroup (IE 182)
22. Quit Windows Mail (IE 183)
23. Subscribe to an RSS Feed (IE 184)
24. View Your RSS Feeds in the Favorites Center (IE 186)
25. Modify Feed Properties (IE 188)
26. Start Windows Live Messenger and Sign In (IE 194)
27. Add a Contact to the Contact List (IE 196)
28. Send an Instant Message (IE 198)
29. Close the Shelly Cashman Series Window (IE 199)
30. Delete a Contact on the Contact List (IE 200)
31. Close and Sign Out from Windows Live Messenger (IE 202)

Learn It Online

Test your knowledge of chapter content and key terms.

Instructions: To complete the Learn It Online exercises, start your browser, click the Address bar, and then enter the Web address scsite.com/ie7/learn. When the Internet Explorer 7 Learn It Online page is displayed, click the link for the exercise you want to complete and then read the instructions.

Chapter Reinforcement TF, MC, and SA
A series of true/false, multiple-choice, and short answer questions that test your knowledge of the chapter content.

Flash Cards
An interactive learning environment where you identify chapter key terms associated with displayed definitions.

Practice Test
A series of multiple-choice questions that test your knowledge of chapter content and key terms.

Who Wants To Be a Computer Genius?
An interactive game that challenges your knowledge of chapter content in the style of the television quiz show.

Wheel of Terms
An interactive game that challenges your knowledge of chapter key terms in the style of the television show *Wheel of Fortune*.

Crossword Puzzle Challenge
A crossword puzzle that challenges your knowledge of key terms presented in the chapter.

Apply Your Knowledge

Reinforce the skills and apply the concepts you learned in this chapter.

Sending an E-Mail Message to Your Instructor
Instructions: Start Internet Explorer and Windows Mail. You want to send an e-mail to the instructor of your course stating what you like best about his or her class. Use Windows Mail to send the e-mail.

Perform the following tasks.
1. Search for the home page for your college or university. Figure 3–84 shows the home page for Valencia Community College.
2. Find and write down the e-mail address of your instructor.
3. Start Windows Mail.
4. Click the Create Mail button on the Mail toolbar.
5. Using the e-mail address of the instructor you obtained in Step 2, compose a mail message to this instructor stating what you like best about his or her class.
6. Send the e-mail message to your instructor.

Valencia
Community
College
home page

Figure 3–84

Extend Your Knowledge

Extend the skills you learned in this chapter and experiment with new skills. You may need to use Help to complete the assignment.

Posting a Newsgroup Article

Instructions: Start Windows Mail. Locate a newsgroup on Windows Internet Explorer 7, and compose and post a message about a new feature to the newsgroup. After posting the article, find your message in the message pane, and then print the article.

Perform the following tasks.

1. Search for and subscribe to a newsgroup that contains articles about Windows Internet Explorer 7.

2. Locate and click the newsgroup name in the Folder list.

Continued >

STUDENT ASSIGNMENTS

Extend Your Knowledge *continued*

3. Click the Write Message button to display the New Message window (Figure 3–85).

New Message window

Figure 3–85

4. Compose and then post a message to the newsgroup that explains your favorite feature of Internet Explorer 7.

5. Find your message in the Message list. Print the message, write your name on the printed message, and submit it to your instructor.

In the Lab

Use Internet Explorer and Windows Mail by employing the guidelines, concepts, and skills presented in this chapter. Labs are listed in order of increasing difficulty.

Lab 1: Adding Your Friends to the Contacts Folder

Instructions: Start Windows Mail. You want to use the Contacts folder in Windows Vista to keep track of the names, e-mail addresses, home addresses, and home telephone numbers of your favorite school friends.

Perform the following tasks:

1. Click the Contacts button on the toolbar to open the Contacts folder. If necessary, maximize the window (Figure 3–86).

2. Use the New Contact button on the toolbar to add the contacts listed in Table 3–8 to the Contacts folder.

Figure 3–86

Table 3–8 Contact List for Contacts Folder

Name	E-mail Address	Address	Home Phone
Theresa Collins	tcollins@isp.com	8451 Colony Dr., Brea, CA 92821	(714) 555-2831
Sean Geftic	sgeftic@isp.com	3544 Clayton Rd., Placentia, CA 92871	(714) 555-1484
Jessica McEwen	jmcewen@isp.com	5689 State St., Fullerton, CA 92834	(714) 555-2318
Tami Newell	tnewell@isp.com	7812 Bennington Dr., Atwood, CA 92811	(714) 555-8622
Amanda Silva	asilva@isp.com	257 W. Wilson St., Yorba Linda, CA 92885	(714) 555-2782
Cherry Tran	ctran@isp.com	648 Flower Rd., Brea, CA 92821	(714) 555-6495

3. Print the information for each contact by right-clicking a contact name, clicking the Print command on the shortcut menu, and then clicking the Print button in the Print dialog box. Write your name on each printed contact.

4. Delete each contact by selecting the contact name and then clicking the Delete button on the toolbar.

In the Lab

Lab 2: E-mailing Your Class Schedule as an Attachment

Instructions: Start Notepad and Windows Mail. Type your class schedule into a new Notepad document and save the file. Switch to Windows Mail, type an e-mail message to your instructor and attach the Notepad file containing your class schedule.

Perform the following tasks:
1. Type your class schedule into the Notepad document, organizing your classes using a method of your choosing. A sample Notepad document containing a class schedule is illustrated in Figure 3–87.

Untitled - Notepad			
File Edit Format View Help			
Course	Name	Day(s)	Time
CS101	Computer Literacy	Tues/Thurs	12:30 p.m. – 1:45 p.m.
CS127	Internet Explorer	Tues/Thurs	2:00 p.m. – 3:15 p.m.
AC101	Intro to Accounting	Mon/Wed/Fri	1:00 p.m. – 1:50 p.m.
PS211	Physical Science	Mon/Wed/Fri	2:00 p.m. – 2:50 p.m.

Figure 3–87

2. Using your first and last name as the file name (put a space between your first and last names), save the Notepad document to your Documents folder.
3. In Windows Mail, compose a new e-mail message to your instructor. Type your instructor's e-mail address into the To text box. Type My Class Schedule for the Subject. For the body of the e-mail message, type I have created a document with Notepad that contains my class schedule. The file is attached to this e-mail message.
4. Press the ENTER key twice.
5. Type your name and then press the ENTER key.
6. Click the Attach File To Message button, navigate to the Documents folder, and then attach the Notepad file you created to the e-mail message.
7. Send the e-mail message.
8. Display the contents of the Sent Items folder to verify that your message was sent.

In the Lab

Lab 3: Subscribing to the microsoft.public.access.gettingstarted Newsgroup

Instructions: Start Windows Mail. Locate and subscribe to the microsoft.public.access.gettingstarted newsgroup, select a thread that contains at least three replies, and then print each article in the thread.

Perform the following tasks:
1. Right-click the Microsoft Communities link in the Folder list and click Newsgroups on the shortcut menu to display the Newsgroup Subscriptions dialog box.
2. Locate and click the microsoft.public.access.gettingstarted entry in the Newsgroup list (Figure 3–88) to select it.

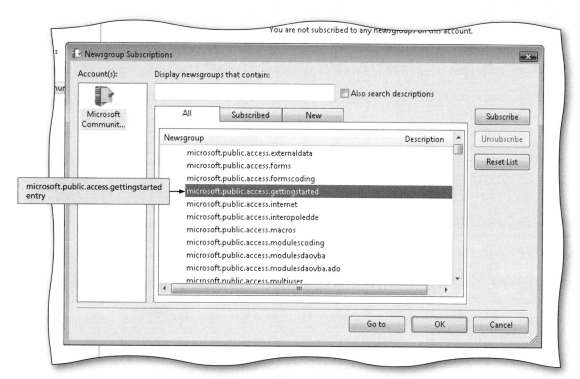

Figure 3–88

3 Click the Subscribe button.

4. Click the Go to button.

5. Find a thread that contains the original article and at least three replies.

6. Read and then print each article in the thread. Write your name on each printed article and then submit them to your instructor.

In the Lab

Lab 4: Subscribing to RSS Feeds on Various News Web Sites

Instructions: Start Internet Explorer. Subscribe to an RSS feed that contains the local news for Boston, MA, as well as two additional RSS feeds that contain national news. After subscribing to these feeds, display the feeds in Internet Explorer and print the first story for each feed.

Perform the following tasks:

Part 1: Subscribe to an RSS Feed on CNN.com

1. Navigate to the CNN.com Web site (www.cnn.com).

2. Subscribe to and display RSS feed on the an CNN.com Web site that contains recent national news.

Continued >

In the Lab *continued*

3. Click the link for the first news story (Figure 3–89). The news story that displays on your computer will be different than the one in Figure 3–89.

story on CNN.com

Figure 3–89

4. Print the Web page and write your name on it.

Part 2: Subscribe to the FOX News U.S. RSS Feed

1. Navigate to the FOXNews.com Web site (www.foxnews.com).

2. Subscribe to and display the FOX News RSS feed.

3. Click the link for the first news story.

4. Print the Web page and write your name on it.

Part 3: Subscribe to the Boston.com / News RSS Feed

1. Navigate to the Boston.com News Web site (www.boston.com/news).

2. Subscribe to and display the Boston.com / News RSS feed.

3. Click the link for the first news story.

4. Print the Web page and write your name on it.

5. Submit the printed Web pages to your instructor.

In the Lab

Lab 5: Using Windows Live Messenger

Instructions: Start and sign in to Windows Live Messenger. Add a new person to your Windows Live Messenger contact list. After adding the contact, send instant messages to each other, and then save and print the entire conversation.

Perform the following tasks:

Part 1: Add a Contact to the Contact List

1. Click the Add a contact button in the Windows Live Messenger window.

2. Type the Windows Live ID or Windows Live Hotmail e-mail address of a friend in the Instant Messaging Address text box, choose an appropriate nickname, and then click the Add contact button.

Part 2: Send an Instant Message

1. Double-click the icon of the contact you added in the contact list.

2. Type a message in the Message area, click the Send button, wait for the response, and type your response.

3. Continue conversing in this manner until you have typed at least four messages. Figure 3–90 shows a sample conversation.

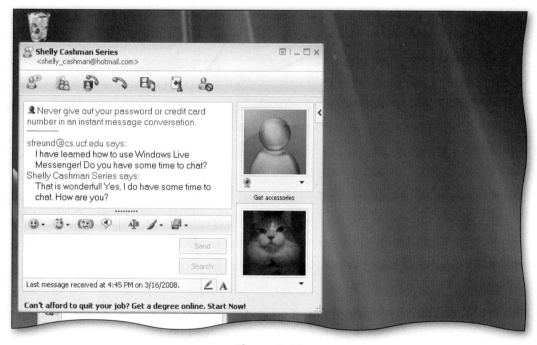

Figure 3–90

Part 3: Save the Conversation

1. Press ALT to display the menu bar.

2. Click File on the menu bar to display the file menu.

3. Click Save as on the File menu. If the Windows Live Messenger dialog box displays click the OK button.

4. Save the file with the filename Conversation, to the Documents folder on your computer.

Continued >

In the Lab *continued*

Part 4: Delete a Contact on the Contact List

1. In the Windows Live Messenger window, right-click the contact you want to delete.

2. Click Delete contact on the shortcut menu.

3. Click the OK button in the Windows Live Messenger dialog box.

Part 5: Close Windows Live Messenger Window and Sign Out from the Windows Live Messenger Service

1. Click the Close button in the Windows Live Messenger window.

2. Right-click the Windows Live Messenger - Signed In icon in the notification area on the Windows taskbar.

3. Click Exit on the shortcut menu.

4. E-mail the Conversation file to your instructor as an e-mail attachment.

In the Lab

Lab 6: Sending an E-Mail Message Containing Stationery to a Contact in your Contacts Folder

Instructions: Add a contact to the Contacts folder, and send the contact an e-mail message containing Stationery.

Perform the following tasks:

1. Start Windows Mail.

2. Click the Create Mail button arrow to compose a new e-mail message, and select the Garden stationery.

3. Click the To button to display the Select Recipients dialog box.

4. Click the New Contact button.

5. Type your instructor's first name, last name, and e-mail address in the appropriate text boxes and then click the OK button. Be sure to click the Add button after entering the e-mail address. (Figure 3–91).

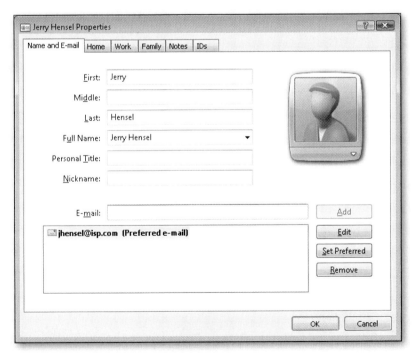

Figure 3–91

6. Click the OK button, add the contact as a message recipient, and then click the OK button.

7. Type `Chapter 3 Exercise 6` as the subject of the e-mail message.

8. Type a short message to your instructor explaining that you have learned how to send an e-mail message to a contact in the Contacts folder. Do not forget to include your full name in the e-mail message.

9. Send the e-mail message to your instructor.

10. Display the contents of the Sent Items folder to verify that your message was sent.

Cases and Places

Apply your creative thinking and problem solving skills to use the Internet to find the information you need.

• Easier   •• More Difficult

• 1: Compare Windows Mail and Microsoft Office Outlook 2007

Using computer magazines, advertising brochures, the Internet, or other resources, compile information about Windows Mail and Microsoft Office Outlook 2007. In a brief report, compare the two programs. Include the differences and similarities, how to obtain the software, the function and features of each program, and so forth. If possible, test Microsoft Office Outlook 2007 and add your personal comments.

• 2: Discuss Digital IDs

A digital ID allows you to encrypt e-mail and to prove your identity in electronic transactions. In a brief report, discuss how to obtain a digital ID, who might benefit by having a digital ID, and what types of electronic transactions might require a digital ID.

• 3: Discuss the Use of False Online Identities

Some individuals have expressed concerns that some users try to disguise their identities by displaying false information when signing up for a free e-mail account. In a brief report, summarize the reasons why you should correctly identify yourself on the Internet, what kinds of problems result when users disguise their identities, and offer some suggestions as to how to prevent this problem.

•• 4: Research E-mail Programs

Using computer magazines, advertising brochures, the Internet, or other resources, compile information about two e-mail programs other than Windows Mail and Microsoft Office Outlook. In a brief report, compare the two programs and the Windows Mail e-mail program. Include the differences and similarities, how to obtain the software, the functions and features of each program, and so forth. Submit the report to your instructor.

•• 5: Locate an RSS Feed

Many news Web sites provide their content via an RSS feed. Locate at least two news Web sites (other than CNN, Fox News, or Boston.com) and at least two other Web sites that allow you to subscribe to an RSS feed. What are the advantages of subscribing to an RSS feed? Would you rather subscribe to an RSS feed or navigate directly to the Web site to view its content? Why or why not? Submit your answers to your instructor.

Continued >

Cases and Places *continued*

• • 6: Create a Google Group

Working Together

Groups are a popular way for people to communicate with each other about a certain topic via the Internet. Create a Google Group about a topic of your choice (http://groups.google.com) and have each team member post a message to the group to initiate a conversation. Wait two days to see if anyone outside of your team has signed up for your group. Find one other group that discusses a similar topic. How many people have joined that group? Discuss how you could attract more people to your group. Submit your answers to your instructor.

Appendix A
Internet Options

Internet Options Dialog Box

When you use Internet Explorer to browse the World Wide Web, learn about Web research techniques, and communicate using the Internet, default Internet Explorer settings control your interaction with the application. You can view and modify many of these settings by using the **Internet Options dialog box** shown in Figure A–1.

The Internet Options dialog box contains seven tabs (General, Security, Privacy, Content, Connections, Programs, and Advanced) that allow you to view and modify Internet Explorer's default settings. Using these settings, you can change the home page that is displayed when you start Internet Explorer; delete cookies and temporary Internet files; specify a privacy setting when using the Internet; select tabbed browsing options; assign a Web site to a security zone; control the Internet content a user can access; set up an Internet connection; and choose which programs will send and receive e-mail.

To display the Internet Options dialog box, click Tools on the Command Bar and then click Internet Options. The remainder of this appendix explains the contents of the seven sheets in the Internet Options dialog box.

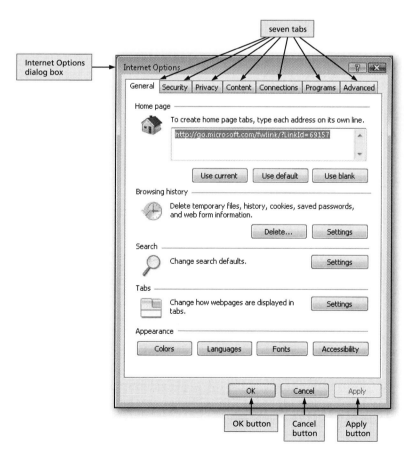

Figure A–1

The General Sheet

The **General sheet** (Figure A–2) contains the Home page area, Browsing history area, Search area, Tabs area, and Appearance area. The **Home page area** allows you to change the URL of the **home page**, which is the Web page that is displayed when you launch Internet Explorer. Consider making your home page the Web page that you visit most frequently. You can designate multiple home pages by typing the URL for each home page on a separate line in the text box. When you have multiple home pages, each page will open in its own tab when you start Internet Explorer. The text box in the Home page area contains the URL for the current home page. The three buttons below the text box allow you to use the Web page or Web pages currently displayed in the Internet Explorer window as the home page (Use current), use the default home page (Use default), or not display a home page (Use blank).

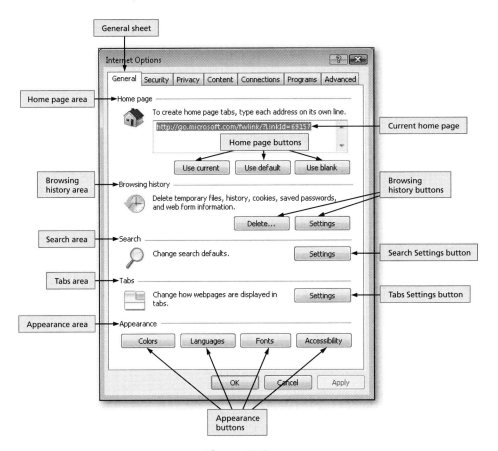

Figure A–2

The **Browsing history area** permits you to delete temporary files, your browsing history, cookies, saved passwords, and any information you may have entered on a Web page. A cookie is a file created by a Web site that captures information about your visit to that site, such as your preferences or shopping cart items. The Delete button in the Browsing history area allows you to delete some or all of the files that are associated with your browsing history.

When you display a Web page in the Internet Explorer window, one or more files called temporary Internet files are stored in the Temporary Internet Files folder. **Temporary Internet files** store information about and components of the Web page you are viewing. The next time you display that Web page, the page appears quickly because Internet Explorer retrieves the page from the Temporary Internet Files folder instead of from the Internet. You can delete all files in the Temporary Internet Files folder by using the Delete files button in the **Temporary Internet Files area**. By using the Settings button, you can view a list of the temporary Internet files, set how long Internet Explorer checks for new versions of pages that you visit, change the amount of disk space reserved to store the files, and move the Temporary Internet Files folder to another location on the hard drive. The Settings button also lets you control the number of days the Web pages in the History list are kept before being automatically deleted.

The **Search area** on the General sheet allows you to add, modify, and remove search providers that appear in the Instant Search box.

You can view and modify the tabbed browsing settings through the Settings button in the **Tabs area**. You can enable and disable tabbed browsing, modify other tab browsing settings, and decide how Internet Explorer treats pop-ups and links from other programs.

You can use the four buttons in the **Appearance area** of the General sheet to change the default text, background, and link colors; specify the language to use when displaying Web pages; change the default fonts used to display a Web page; and set whether the color and font settings you select should override the settings specified by a Web page.

The Security Sheet

The **Security sheet** shown in Figure A–3 allows you to specify how Internet Explorer handles content from various Web pages. If you visit a Web site for the first time, you might not completely trust the site's content. Because some Web sites may contain malicious code that can automatically download to your computer, you may want to prevent them from having the ability to download anything to your computer without your intervention. On the other hand, you may frequently visit a Web site that you trust. You can use the Security sheet to configure Internet Explorer so that you are not prompted before a Web site you trust attempts to download anything to or install anything on your computer.

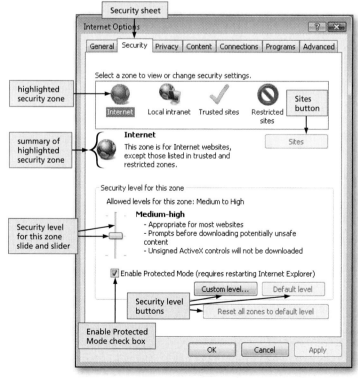

Figure A–3

Internet Explorer divides the Internet into four zones of content to which you can assign a security setting. These zones are called **security zones** (Internet, Local intranet, Trusted sites, and Restricted sites), and Internet Explorer allows you to assign a Web site to a zone with a suitable security level. The four security zones are described below:

- **Internet**: This zone contains all Web pages that you have not placed in other zones. The default security level for this zone is Medium-high.

- **Local intranet**: This zone contains all Web sites that are on an organization's intranet, including sites specified on the Connections sheet in the Internet Options dialog box, network paths, and local intranet sites. The default security level for this zone is Medium-low.

- **Trusted sites**: This zone contains Web sites that are trusted not to damage the computer or the data on the computer. The default security level for this zone is Medium. You must manually add a Web site to this zone by clicking the Trusted sites zone and then clicking the Sites button.

- **Restricted sites**: This zone contains Web sites that you do not trust because they could possibly damage the computer or the files on the computer. The default security level for this zone is High. You might put a site in this zone if you feel that the content on the site is malicious.

To assign a Web site to a security zone, click the appropriate icon in the security zone box, click the Sites button, and then follow the instructions to assign a security zone. After assigning a Web page to a security zone, the icon of the zone to which the Web site is assigned appears at the right side of the status bar in the Internet Explorer window. Each time you attempt to open or download content from a Web site, Internet Explorer checks the security settings and responds appropriately.

The three buttons at the bottom of the Security sheet allow you to customize the settings for a security zone (Custom level) and set the security level or reset the security level to the default level for the security zone (Default level). You also can reset all zones to their default security zone.

To change the security level of the highlighted security zone, click the Default level button in the Security level for this zone area and then move the slider along the slide to display the different security levels.

The Privacy Sheet

The **Privacy sheet** shown in Figure A–4 contains the Settings area and Pop-up Blocker area. The **Settings area** displays the privacy setting (Medium) and allows you to change the privacy setting for the four security zones (Internet, Local intranet, Trusted sites, and Restricted sites) by moving the slider along the slide. When you select a privacy setting, a description appears on the Privacy sheet in the Internet Options dialog box.

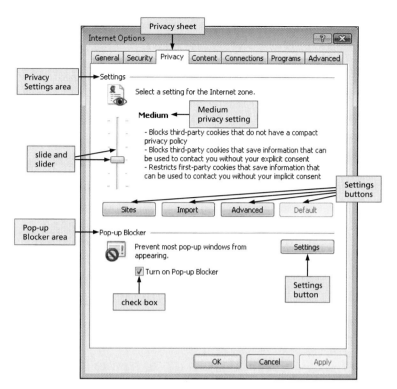

Figure A–4

The four buttons at the bottom of the Settings area allow you to customize privacy settings and override the default setting for cookies. Two types of cookies that may be downloaded to your computer are first-party cookies and third-party cookies. A **first-party cookie** is a cookie that either originates on or is sent to a Web site you currently are viewing. A **third-party cookie** is a cookie that either originates on or is sent to a Web site other than the one you are viewing.

The **Pop-up Blocker area** allows you to enable and disable the pop-up blocker, which prevents Web sites you visit from opening unwanted tabs or browser windows. The Settings button allows you to specify which Web sites are allowed to open the pop-up windows. You also can set whether you hear a sound or see the Information Bar when a pop-up is blocked.

The Content Sheet

The **Content sheet** illustrated in Figure A–5 contains five areas: Parental Controls area, Content Advisor area, Certificates area, AutoComplete area, and Feeds area. The **Parental Controls area** allows you to access the Windows Vista parental controls, where you can select which Web sites can be accessed by each user account on your computer. You also can collect information about computer usage and restrict computer usage.

The **Content Advisor area** permits you to control the types of content (violent content, sexual content, and so on) that a user can access on the Internet. After turning on Content Advisor, content that does not meet or exceed the chosen criteria will not be displayed. Initially, Content Advisor is set to the most conservative (least likely to offend) setting. The two buttons in the Content Advisor area allow you to turn on Content Advisor (Enable) and modify the Content Advisor ratings for Internet sites (Settings).

The **Certificates area** allows you to positively authenticate identity and provide security for browser communication. A **certificate** is a statement guaranteeing the identity of a person or the security of a Web site. The **Personal certificate** guarantees your identity to Web sites that require certification. The **Web site certificate** guarantees that a Web site is secure and no other Web site has falsely assumed the identity of the Web site. The Clear SSL state button allows you to remove all client authentication certificates from the SSL cache. The **SSL cache** is a memory location that stores all certificates until you restart your computer. The Certificates button in the Certificates area allows you to require a Web site to send a security certificate to you before sending them information, and the Publishers button displays a list of trusted software publishers whose software can safely be placed on the computer.

In the **AutoComplete area,** you can set whether Internet Explorer uses the AutoComplete feature to store personal information that you enter on forms or Web

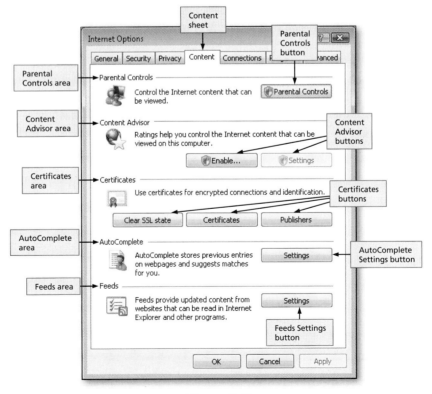

Figure A–5

addresses you enter in the Address bar. For example, if you begin to enter the URL for
a Web site you previously have visited, Internet Explorer will display matching URLs so
that you do not have to type it entirely. You also can clear the AutoComplete history.

The **Feeds area** allows you to set RSS feed properties, including how often to
check RSS feeds for updates, as well as other actions to perform when a feed is discovered
on a Web page or when a feed is read.

The Connections Sheet

The **Connections sheet** shown in Figure A–6 allows you to set up a new connection
to the Internet, control dial-up and virtual private networking connections, and modify local
area network (LAN) settings. The Setup button at the top of the sheet lets you create a new
Internet connection. The **Dial-up and Virtual Private Network settings area** displays the
current dial-up settings and allows you to add, remove, and modify connections. The **Local
Area Network (LAN) settings area** permits you to edit the LAN settings if the computer
is connected to a local area network.

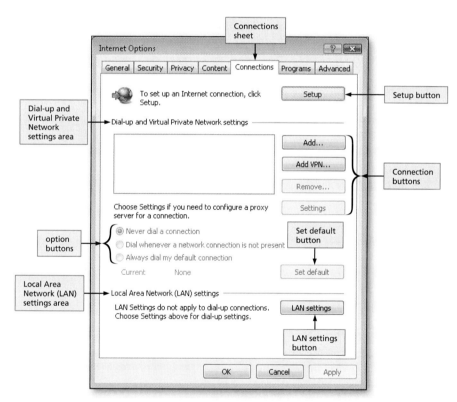

Figure A–6

The Programs Sheet

The **Programs sheet** shown in Figure A–7 allows you to select the default Web browser, manage browser add-ons, choose the default program that Internet Explorer uses to edit Web pages, and set the programs that Internet Explorer uses for other services. If Internet Explorer is not the default Web browser, click the Make default button to make it the default Web browser. The Manage add-ons button allows you to enable and disable Internet Explorer add-ons that have been installed in addition to the Web browser. Internet Explorer add-ons may come with Internet Explorer, they may be installed when you are installing another program on your computer, or you can install them manually. The **HTML editing area** allows you to select the program you would like to use to edit Web pages. The **Internet programs area** allows you to set the programs that Windows uses for various other Internet services such as e-mail or newsgroup readers.

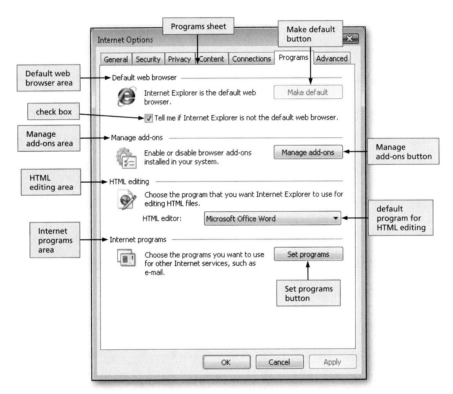

Figure A–7

The Advanced Sheet

The **Advanced sheet** (Figure A–8) contains a list of settings, organized into the following categories: Accessibility, Browsing, HTTP 1.1 settings, International, Multimedia, Printing, Search from the Address bar, and Security. A check mark indicates that the setting is selected. The Restore advanced settings button returns all settings in the Settings list box to their original (default) settings, and the Reset button returns the browser to its original state.

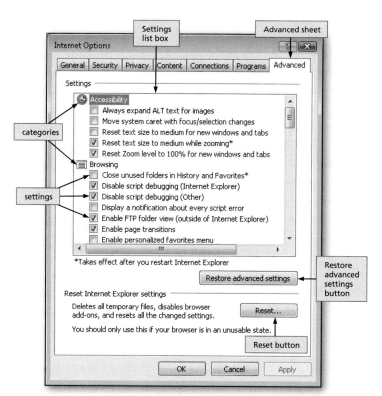

Figure A–8

Appendix B

Signing up for a Free Web-Based E-Mail Account

Windows Live Hotmail

Chapter 3 assumes that you have an e-mail account set up in Windows Mail as you work through the steps. If you cannot set up an e-mail account in Windows Mail, you might consider signing up for a free Web-based e-mail account. Many free Web-based e-mail providers exist on the Internet, including Windows Live Hotmail, Yahoo Mail, and Gmail from Google. The following steps sign you up for a free Windows Live Hotmail account.

1. Start Internet Explorer.
2. Navigate to the Windows Live Hotmail home page (www.hotmail.com) (Figure B–1).

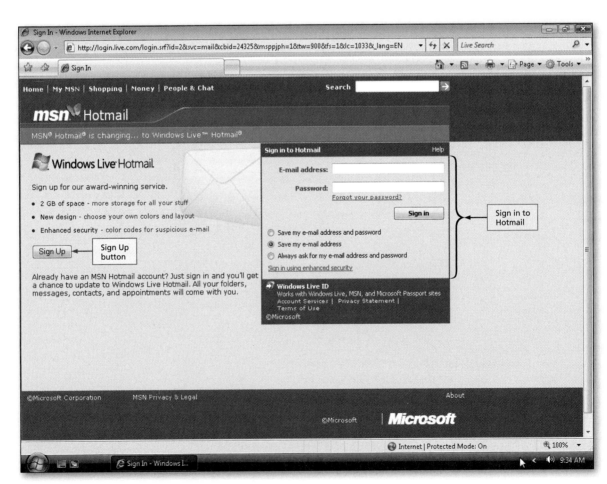

Figure B–1

3. Click the Sign Up button to begin the process of creating a new Windows Live Hotmail e-mail account.

4. Click the Get it button in the Windows Live Hotmail window to sign up for the free e-mail service and display the Sign up for Windows Live Web page (Figure B–2).

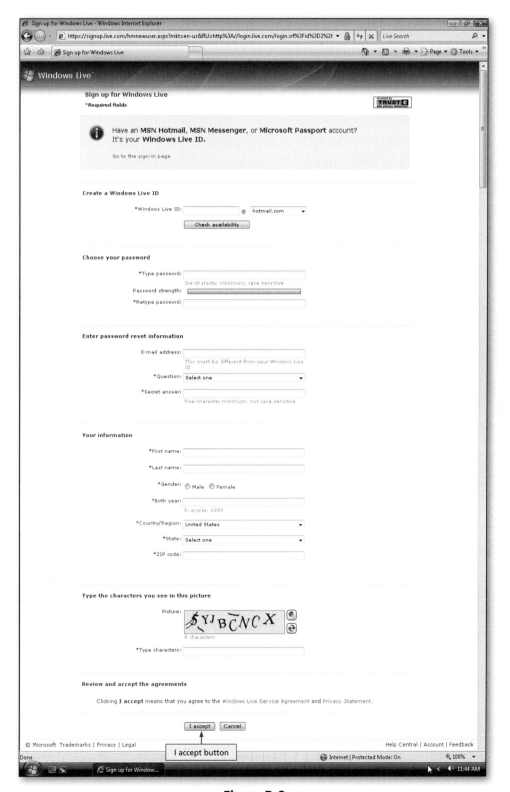

Figure B–2

5. Create your Windows Live account by entering your information into the appropriate fields. As you create your Windows Live account, keep the following in mind:

   • Your Windows Live ID must be different from all other registered Windows Live IDs. After choosing a Windows Live ID, you can click the Check availability button to determine whether the ID you chose is available.

   • Choose a password that is easy for you to remember, but difficult for others to guess. A password that is difficult for others to guess might include uppercase and lowercase letters, numbers, special characters, and be at least 8 characters in length.

   • Note that in order to sign up for a Windows Live account, you should have another e-mail address to use as a backup, in case you forget your password and must have it e-mailed to you.

6. Read the Windows Live Service Agreement and Privacy Statement.

7. Click the I accept button.

8. You can sign into your Windows Live Hotmail account at any time by navigating to the Windows Live Hotmail home page (www.hotmail.com), typing your Windows Live Hotmail e-mail address in the E-mail address text box and your password in the Password text box, and then clicking the Sign in button.

Index

Quick Reference Summary

In Windows Internet Explorer 7, you can accomplish a task in a number of ways. The following table provides a quick reference to each task presented in this textbook. The first column identifies the task. The subsequent columns list the different ways the task in the first column can be carried out.

Windows Internet Explorer 7 Quick Reference Summary

Basic Navigation

Task	Mouse	Keyboard Shortcut
Go back one page	Back button	ALT+LEFT ARROW
Go forward one page	Forward button	ALT+RIGHT ARROW
Stop transfer of current page	Stop button	ESC
Refresh current page	Refresh button	F5 OR CTRL+F5
Go to your home page	Home button	ALT+M, PRESS ENTER
Print current page	Print button	CTRL+P
Move insertion point to Address bar	Click Address bar	ALT+D
Scroll down	Down scroll arrow	SPACEBAR
Scroll up	Up scroll arrow	SHIFT+SPACEBAR
Find a word or phrase on a page	Edit menu | Find on this Page	CTRL+F
Zoom in	Hold CTRL and move mouse wheel up	CTRL + +
Zoom out	Hold CTRL and move mouse wheel down	CTRL + -
100% zoom	Click Change Zoom Level button arrow and select 100%	CTRL+0
Close Internet Explorer	Close button	ALT+F4

Address Bar Shortcuts

Task	Mouse	Keyboard Shortcut
Select the Address bar	Click Address bar	ALT+D
Add "http://www." and ".com" to Address bar entry		CTRL+ENTER
Open address in Address bar in new tab		ALT+ENTER
View previously typed addresses	Click Address bar arrow	F4

Windows Internet Explorer 7 Quick Reference Summary *(continued)*

Window and Tab Shortcuts

Task	Mouse	Keyboard Shortcut
Open link in new window	SHIFT+click	
Open current Web page in a new window	Page menu | New Window	CTRL+N
Open a new tab	New tab button	CTRL+T
Close a tab	Click middle mouse button on tab or close button on tab	CTRL+W
Open link in new foreground tab		CTRL+SHIFT+LEFT MOUSE BUTTON
Open link in new background tab	Middle mouse button	CTRL+LEFT MOUSE BUTTON
Open Quick Tabs view	Quick Tabs button	CTRL+Q
Open Tab List	Tab List button	CTRL+SHIFT+Q
Switch to next tab	Next tab	CTRL+TAB
Switch to previous tab	Previous tab	CTRL+SHIFT+TAB

Instant Search Box Shortcuts

Task	Mouse	Keyboard Shortcut
Select the Instant Search box	Click Instant Search box	CTRL+E
Display Instant Search box menu	Click Instant Search box arrow	CTRL+DOWN ARROW
Open search query in new tab		ALT+ENTER

Favorites Center Shortcuts

Task	Mouse	Keyboard Shortcut
Open Favorites	Favorites Center button | Favorites button	CTRL+I
Open Favorites in pinned mode	Favorites Center button | Favorites button | Pin the Favorites Center button	CTRL+SHIFT+I
Organize Favorites	Favorites menu | Organize Favorites	CTRL+B
Add current page to Favorites	Add to Favorites button	CTRL+D
Open RSS Feeds	Favorites Center button | Feeds	CTRL+J
Open RSS Feeds in pinned mode	Favorites Center button | Feeds button | Pin the Favorites Center button	CTRL+SHIFT+J
Open History	Favorites Center button | History button	CTRL+H
Open History in pinned mode	Favorites Center button | History button | Pin the Favorites Center button	CTRL+SHIFT+H